THE COMPLEAT
MOTION PICTURE QUIZ BOOK

THE COMPLEAT MOTION PICTURE QUIZ BOOK

Or
60,000 Points About Motion Pictures*

by HARRY D. TRIGG
& YOLANDA L. TRIGG

*30,000 Points for Buffs, and
30,000 Points for the Duffers!

DOUBLEDAY & COMPANY, INC.

GARDEN CITY, NEW YORK

1975

Library of Congress Cataloging in Publication Data

Trigg, Harry D
  The compleat motion picture quiz book

  1. Moving-pictures—Miscellanea. I. Trigg,
Yolanda L., joint author. II. Title.
PN1993.85.T7   791.43'076
ISBN 0-385-05185-9
Library of Congress Catalog Card Number 74–27590

THIS BOOK IS LOVINGLY DEDICATED TO . . .

Roger Adams, Arthur Alexander, Bill Andrews, Alan Ash, George Back, Ben Barry, Charlie Britt, Hal Brown, Alec Campbell, Lee Cannon, Howard Christensen, Bill Clark, Bernice Coe, Gerry Corwin, Dick Colbert, Dalton Danon, Dick Dinsmore, Bud Donnelly, Stan Dudelson, Erwin Ezzes, Dick Feiner, Len Firestone, Ray Fox, Lou Friedland, Jack Garrison, Hank Gillespie, Sully Ginsler, Alan Gleitsman, Keith Godfrey, Ira Gottlieb, Mike Gould, Jonny Graff, Marv Gray, Art Greenfield, Art Gross, George Harper, Bill Hart, Jack Heim, Paul Hoffman, Bob Horen, Joe Indelli, Andy Jaeger, Ken Joseph, Dick Lawrence, Stan Levy, Marvin Lowe, Charlie McGregor, Abe Mandell, Ed Montanus, Bob Morin, Red Moscato, Wynn Nathan, Bob Neece, Bob Newgard, Murray Oken, Al Ordover, Kevin O'Sullivan, Art Pickens, Harvey Rheinstein, Bill Rhodes, Jack Rhodes, Bob Rich, Marty Robinson, Pete Rodgers, Johnny Rohrs, Carl Russell, Tommy Seehof, Sig Shore, Arnold Stern, Jimmy Stern, Al Sussman, Warren Tomassene, Al Unger, Jimmy Victory, Karl von Schallern, Pierre Weis, Jerry Weisfeldt, Paul Weiss, Ken Weldon, Charlie Whipple, Henry White, Pete Yeager, and Joe Zaleski . . .

. . . all of whom are good friends, but all of whom must have wondered at one time or another if anyone in the Trigg family knew anything at all about feature films!

HOW THE COMPLEAT MOTION PICTURE QUIZ
BOOK WORKS

We are movie-quiz buffs, and there is nothing we like more than sitting around with others of our kind and shooting questions at each other to really test our movie knowledge. But we've noticed that occasionally someone hovers *around* the group, though they're reluctant to really join *in*. We can only surmise that when they were watching Deanna Durbin, or Bobby Breen, or Henry Armetta—back there in the thirties and forties—their investment was for entertainment value only, and not the storing-up of trivial data to spring on another movie fan thirty-five years later.

We have seen other books which offer quizzes about motion picture lore, and while they are basically well done, their appeal seems a bit narrow. To survive with one such publication, you would have had to be sitting at the foot of every movie-maker from Griffith to Friedkin. Great for the real movie buff, but it is doubtful that the casual movie-goer could've answered anything beyond the title. Another publication was the opposite: interesting for the casual movie-goer, but really a piece of cake for the expert who can toss off the title of every film Toby Wing ever made, or who can tell you in a flash the middle name of Samuel S. Hinds.

In THE COMPLEAT MOTION PICTURE QUIZ BOOK, we've attempted to take this into account. For the most part, each quiz is presented in *two* versions. The first version is for the real movie fan, and some of the quizzes are—admittedly—terribly difficult. But we have also presented a second version of each quiz, and we refer to these easier versions as "The Duffers' Tee." These were written for the movie fan whose movie-going is limited to the Midnight Movie, now and then.

Each quiz offers a number of points, and the name of the game is to garner as many points as possible to determine your rating of Motion Picture Expertise. Get all of the Movie Buff Quizzes correct, and you'll amass an impressive total; or, if you play the Duffers' Tees, you may get fewer points, but you'll have just as much fun. Or, if you find one of the Movie Buff Quizzes a little too tough, then skip it, and go on to the Duffers' Tee. And for those who play the Duffers' Tee from the outset, take a look at one of the Movie Buff Quizzes now and then. Maybe you'll find one that will be right up your alley, after all.

But whatever you feel your Motion Picture Expertise is—Movie Buff or Duffer—we think you'll enjoy THE COMPLEAT MOTION PICTURE QUIZ BOOK. We had a lot of fun—and a few arguments—putting this quiz together. If nothing else, you may be sure that this book is thoroughly "home-tested."

So, go to it. If you have fun, we're pleased. If a factual error has crept in, we're sorry. If we exasperate you, we apologize. But nobody's life depends on whether you get an answer right or wrong . . . you should enjoy!

So, as Charles Coburn once said: "Damn the torpedoes—full speed ahead!"

The Authors

SCORE CARD

POSSIBLE SCORE

	BUFFS	DUFFERS	YOUR SCORE
1. ANIMALS	100	100	_____
2. NUMERICAL ORDER	55	50	_____
3. NAMES	240	240	_____
4. THE GREATEST!	150	150	_____
5. WHAT ARE THEY TRYING TO SAY? PART I	100	100	_____
6. CHARACTER SCRAMBLE	150	150	_____
7. WHO KILLED . . . ?	150	75	_____
8. THE GORY DETAILS	150	100	_____
9. TELL US WHEN	100	100	_____
10. FIRST, THE WORD	150	100	_____
11. THE BETTER HALF	250	150	_____
12. LINK-UPS—BUFFS AND DUFFERS	50	50	_____
13. SPOT THE BIO: MALES	350	300	_____
14. ODD MAN OUT	100	100	_____
15. NAME THE PLACE, BABY	100	100	_____
16. WHO IS IT?	50	25	_____
17. TELL US WHO	250	250	_____
18. RE-DOS	200	150	_____
19. TYPE-CASTING	375	375	_____
20. QUOTABLES	225	150	_____
21. CAREERS IN COMMON	200	100	_____
22. MORE RE-DOS	200	150	_____
23. THE TEENY-TINY MARQUEE	60	60	_____
24. STRUCTURES	120	120	_____
25. MENTION MY NAME	225	225	_____
26. THE LAST REEL (WILD CARD—BUFFS AND DUFFERS)	100	100	_____

	BUFFS	DUFFERS	YOUR SCORE
119. SOME DIRECTION, PLEASE	100	100	_____
120. MORE OF "THE VIOLENT END"	225	150	_____
121. AND YET STILL MORE "NAME THE STAR"	100	50	_____
122. OSCAR SHUFFLE #4— WILD CARD	25	25	_____
123. THE ETERNAL TRIANGLE	400	400	_____
124. OH, JOHNNY!	100	100	_____
125. OUT OF THE LIMELIGHT	100	100	_____
126. PROTOCOL	75	75	_____
127. HISTORY IS MADE IN THE MOVIES PART III	800	600	_____
128. HISTORY IS MADE IN THE MOVIES PART IV	1,000	750	_____
129. THE FINAL FADE-OUT	500	500	_____
130. HOMESTRETCH—BUFFS AND DUFFERS	3,855	7,765	_____
grand total:	30,000	30,000	!!!

WHAT YOUR SCORE MEANS

Buffs

30,000 points!	So you should have written the book!
27,500–29,999	Close, but no cigar!
25,000–27,499	Hang onto your Scotty Beckett button—you show promise.
20,000–24,999	Unless the TV station clips them, start reading the credits.
12,750–19,999	Let's just say you went out for popcorn a lot, maybe.
5,000–12,749	Maybe the flesh was willing, but the mind was weak?
1,000– 4,999	Answer one question: Why did you play the Buffs' version?
Under 1,000 pts.	Next time, buy a book of crossword puzzles.

Duffers

30,000 points!	If you got this score as a Duffer—then sorry about your complex.
27,500–29,999	Scoring this high is very good. Puff up your chest!
25,000–27,499	Above average, but don't bet heavily in a trivia match.
20,000–24,999	Probably about average—sorry about that.
12,750–19,999	Refunding your money is in our hearts, but out of our hands.
5,000–12,749	It's okay with us if you combine scores with a friend.
1,000– 4,999	Checkers would be a much better leisure-time pursuit . . .
Under 1,000 pts.	Kindly refer to a dictionary—look up "motion pictures" . . .

THE COMPLEAT
MOTION PICTURE QUIZ BOOK

ANIMALS

Many films have titles which include the name of animals. Insert the correct animal, and complete the following film titles. You will earn 4 points for each correct answer. But with twenty-five questions, you can knock off a fast 100 points on your first time out!

1. "The _ _ _ _ _ man of Alcatraz"
2. "The Cat and the _ _ _ _ _ _"
3. "_ _ _ and the Pussycat"
4. "_ _ _ _ _ Soldier"
5. "A Man Called _ _ _ _ _ _"
6. "_ _ _ _ _ _ Squadron"
7. "_ _ _ _ _ Soup"
8. "Track of the _ _ _"
9. "Lad, a _ _ _"
10. "Return of the _ _ _ People"
11. "The Sea _ _ _ _ _"
12. "The Under _ _ _"
13. "The _ _ _"
14. "The _ _ _ _ _ men"
15. "_ _ _ _ _ _ _ _ Walk"
16. "_ _ _ _ _ _ _ with a Whip"
17. "Cult of the _ _ _ _ _"
18. "20 _ _ _ _ _ Team"
19. "_ _ _ _ _ _ _ _ Mail"
20. "The _ _ _ _ _ _ man"
21. "The _ _ _ _ _ _"
22. "The _ _ _ _ _ _ That Roared"
23. "King _ _ _"
24. "To Kill a _ _ _ _ _ _ _ _ _ _ _ _"
25. "Night of the _ _ _ _ _ _ _"

_____points

(*Answers on page 251*)

ANIMALS—DUFFERS' TEE

Below we list twenty-five incomplete film titles. Each of these may be completed by selecting the appropriate animal name from Column Two. You may have 4 points for each title you complete correctly—so here's your chance to start off with a fast 100 points!

1. "The _____man of Alcatraz"
2. "The Cat and the _____"
3. "_____ and the Pussycat"

a. Jackass
b. Pup
c. Elephant

1

4. "_____ Soldier"	d. Birds
5. "A Man Called _____"	e. Duck
6. "_____ Squadron"	f. Cobra
7. "_____ Soup"	g. Cat
8. "Track of the _____"	h. Pony
9. "Lad, a _____"	i. Horse
10. "Return of the _____ People"	j. Frog
11. "The Sea _____"	k. Dog
12. "The Under_____"	l. Mule
13. "The _____"	m. Rat
14. "The _____men"	n. Eagle
15. "_____ Walk"	o. Cat
16. "_____ with a Whip"	p. Canary
17. "Cult of the _____"	q. Iguana
18. "20 _____ Team"	r. Mockingbird
19. "_____ Mail"	s. Wolf
20. "The _____man"	t. Owl
21. "The _____"	u. Bird
22. "The _____ That Roared"	v. Fly
23. "King _____"	w. Kitten
24. "To Kill a _____"	x. Mouse
25. "Night of the _____"	y. Sheep

_____points

(*Answers on page 251*)

NUMERICAL ORDER

On this quickie, you will knock off a fast 55 points, provided you can put the titles listed below in their proper numerical order. Merely complete each title and each such completed title will suggest a number enabling you to arrive at the correct order. One hitch, though—you receive no score at all unless you complete *all* titles.

"_____ Pennies"

"_____ Girls and a Sailor"

"_____ Little Foys"

"Ceiling _____"

"_____, Two, Three"

"_____ on the Lam"

"_____ Bridges to Cross"

"_____ in a Jeep"

"_____ Days a Queen"

"_____ Godfathers"

"_____ North Frederick"

_____points

(*Answers on page 251*)

NUMERICAL ORDER—DUFFERS' TEE

All you have to do on this quiz is to select the correct word from Column Two and use it to appropriately complete the titles in Column One. Once you have done this, it should be a simple matter for you to rearrange the titles into the proper numerical order. When you have this done—*completely*—you may add 50 points to your score. But you must complete *all* of the titles. No partial scores may be taken!

"_____ Pennies"	a. Three
"_____ Girls and a Sailor"	b. Seven
"_____ Little Foys"	c. Nine
"Ceiling _____"	d. Five
"_____, Two, Three"	e. One
"_____ on the Lam"	f. Two
"_____ Bridges to Cross"	g. Eight
"_____ in a Jeep"	h. Zero
"_____ Days a Queen"	i. Ten
"_____ Godfathers"	j. Four
"_____ North Frederick"	k. Six

_____points

(*Answers on page 251*)

3

NAMES

Below we have listed a dozen casting combinations which use the *real* names of the stars, rather than the marquee names with which all fans have become familiar. If you know the real names, you should be able to determine the film title we are seeking. You may take 20 points for each correct answer.

1. Frank Cooper and Audrey Hepburn-Ruston

   "_ _ _ _ _ _ _ _ _
   _ _ _ _ _ _ _ _"

2. Bernie Schwartz and Rosetta Jacobs

   "_ _ _ _ _ _ _ _ _ _ _ _
   _ _ _ _ _ _ _ _ _"

3. Issur D. Demsky, Betty Jane Perske, and Doris von Kappelhoff

   "_ _ _ _ _ _ _ _ _ _ _ _
   _ _ _ _ _"

4. Sophia Sciccolone and Archibald Leach

   "_ _ _ _ _ _ _ _ _"

5. Judy Tuvim and Dino Croccetti

   "_ _ _ _ _ _ _ _ _ _ _
   _ _ _ _ _ _"

6. Reginald Truscott-Jones and Sarah Jane Fulks

   "_ _ _ _ _ _ _ _ _ _ _ _ _ _"

7. Marion M. Morrison, Maureen Fitzsimmons, and William J. Shields

   "_ _ _ _ _ _ _ _ _ _ _"

8. Bill Gable, Lucille Langhanke, and Harlean Carpenter

   "_ _ _ _ _ _ _"

9. Frederick Austerlitz and Susan Burce

   "_ _ _ _ _ _ _ _ _ _ _ _"

10. Zelma Hedrick and Alfred Arnold Cocozza

    "_ _ _ _ _ _ _ _ _ _ ' _ _
    _ _ _ _"

11. Spangler Arlington Brugh and Vivien Mary Hartleigh

    "_ _ _ _ _ _ _ _ _ _ _ _ _ _"

12. Issur D. Demsky, Judy Turner, Patrick Barry, and Luis Antonio Damasco de Alonso

    "_ _ _ _ _ _ _ _ _ _
    _ _ _ _ _ _ _ _"

_____points

(*Answers on page 252*)

NAMES—DUFFERS' TEE

Below we have listed a dozen casting combinations which use the *real* names of the stars, rather than the marquee names with which all fans have become familiar. In Column Two, we have listed—out of order—the titles which the star combinations in Column One represent. If you can correctly match the film title in Column Two with the appropriate star combinations in Column One, you may have 20 points for each correct pairing.

1. Frank Cooper and Audrey Hepburn-Ruston

   a. "The Lost Weekend"

2. Bernie Schwartz and Rosetta Jacobs

   b. "Royal Wedding"

3. Issur D. Demsky, Betty Jane Perske, and Doris von Kappelhoff

   c. "The Bad and the Beautiful"

4. Sophia Sciccolone and Archibald Leach

   d. "The Prince Who Was a Thief"

5. Judy Tuvim and Dino Croccetti

   e. "Waterloo Bridge"

6. Reginald Truscott-Jones and Sarah Jane Fulks

   f. "Red Dust"

7. Marion M. Morrison, Maureen Fitzsimmons, and William J. Shields

   g. "Love in the Afternoon"

8. Bill Gable, Lucille Langhanke, and Harlean Carpenter

   h. "Houseboat"

9. Frederick Austerlitz and Susan Burce

   i. "The Quiet Man"

10. Zelma Hedrick and Alfred Arnold Cocozza

    j. "Young Man with a Horn"

11. Spangler Arlington Brugh and Vivien Mary Hartleigh

    k. "The Bells Are Ringing"

12. Issur D. Demsky, Judy Turner, Patrick Barry, and Luis Antonio Damasco de Alonso

    l. "Because You're Mine"

_____points

(Answers on page 252)

THE GREATEST!

Below are a number of titles, all with the word GREAT in the title. All you have to do in this exercise is to tell us who played the title role in these GREAT films. You may add 10 points to your score for each correct GREAT answer. GREAT Scott? GREAT guns!

1. "The Great Impostor"   ____ _____
2. "The Great John L."   ____ _____
3. "The Great McGinty"   _____ _____
4. "Catherine the Great"   _____ _____
5. "Alexander the Great"   _____ _____
6. "Patrick the Great"   _____ _____
7. "The Great Dictator"   _____ _____
8. "The Great Ziegfeld"   _____ _____
9. "The Great Gildersleeve"   ___ _____
10. "The Great Gatsby"   ____ ____
11. "The Great Caruso"   _____ _____
12. "The Great Gatsby"   _____ _____
13. "The Great Profile"   ____ _____
14. "The Great Garrick"   _____ _____
15. "The Great Man Votes"   ____ _____

_____points

(*Answers on page 253*)

THE GREATEST!—DUFFERS' TEE

Below are a number of films, all with the word GREAT in their title. Your task is to select the player from Column Two who portrayed the title role of the films in Column One, and pair them accordingly. You get a GREAT 10-point addition to your score for each GREAT answer—which is correct.

1. "The Great Impostor"   a. Richard Burton
2. "The Great John L."   b. Elisabeth Bergner
3. "The Great McGinty"   c. Robert Redford
4. "Catherine the Great"   d. Brian Aherne

5. "Alexander the Great"   e. John Barrymore
6. "Patrick the Great"   f. Tony Curtis
7. "The Great Dictator"   g. Greg McClure
8. "The Great Ziegfeld"   h. Donald O'Connor
9. "The Great Gildersleeve"   i. Mario Lanza
10. "The Great Gatsby"   j. William Powell
11. "The Great Caruso"   k. Charlie Chaplin
12. "The Great Gatsby"   l. Brian Donlevy
13. "The Great Profile"   m. John Barrymore
14. "The Great Garrick"   n. Alan Ladd
15. "The Great Man Votes"   o. Hal Peary

————points

(*Answers on page 253*)

WHAT ARE THEY TRYING TO SAY? PART I

Often the most painstakingly researched and best-organized books about motion pictures slip up, and an innocuous error which creeps in takes on the proportions of a *glaring* error to the dyed-in-the-wool movie buff. Here are a few slip-ups we've detected over the years, so let's see how well you do. Take 20 points for each boo-boo you pin down.

1. From *The Garden of Allah*, by Sheilah Graham:
   "(Paul) Muni, whose real name was Paul Weisenfreund, had an unusual contract with Warner's."

2. From *The Gangster Film*, by John Baxter:
   "Despite the tangled psychological web and visual bravura of 'Vertigo,' his (James Stewart's) best film is 'Call Northside 777,' where he relentlessly tracks down a killer in the seedier parts of New York."

3. From *The Movies*, by Richard Griffith and Arthur Mayer, concerning "I Am a Fugitive from a Chain Gang":
   "A jobless veteran (Paul Muni) tries to pawn the Congressional Medal of Honor he won in the A.E.F."

4. From *Immortals of the Screen*, by Ray Stuart, concerning "Treasure Island":
   "Jackie Cooper played the part of the cabin boy and Lionel Barrymore enacted the role of Long John Silver."

7

5. From *The Name Above the Title*, by Frank Capra:

"One day in July, 1939, a letter came from Washington. It came while film editor Gene Havlick and I were comparing the last two preview tapes of 'Mr. Smith.' What's a preview tape? . . . But previews were trial runs to expose the 'bugs,' to collect reliable data for further film editing. But how to collect objective, recallable data? Selah! A tape recorder. Tape the preview . . . let Cohn take a hundred wise guys to the preview. I sent one man with a tape recorder."

———————points

(*Answers on page 254*)

WHAT ARE THEY TRYING TO SAY? PART I—
DUFFERS' TEE

In the Movie Buff version of WHAT ARE THEY TRYING TO SAY? which immediately precedes this Duffers' version, we present some statements which, *we* believe, contain errors of fact. The surprising thing is that these statements come from well-researched and well-organized books about the motion picture. If you've read through the Movie Buff version, you may have already detected the errors. But if you haven't found them, in this Duffers' version we provide you with a multiple choice for each answer. Take 20 points for each one you get correct:

1. From *The Garden of Allah*, by Sheilah Graham:
(a) Paul Muni's real name was Muni Weisenfreund, (b) Paul Muni's real name was Paul Muniweisen, or (c) Paul Muni had an unusual contract at RKO.

2. From *The Gangster Film*, by John Baxter:
(a) The correct title of the film was "Call Northside 737," (b) he was tracking an embezzler, not a killer, or (c) the city in question was Chicago, not New York.

3. From *The Movies*, by Richard Griffith and Arthur Mayer, concerning "I Am a Fugitive from a Chain Gang":
(a) He did not win the medal, but found it on the street, (b) he won the medal, but in the R.A.F., not the A.E.F., or (c) it was not the Congressional Medal of Honor, but the Belgian Croix de Guerre.

4. From *Immortals of the Screen,* by Ray Stuart, concerning "Treasure Island":

(a) The film being described is not "Treasure Island," but "Kidnapped," (b) Jackie Cooper actually played the part of a midshipman, not a cabin boy, or (c) Lionel Barrymore played Captain Billy Bones, while the role of Long John Silver was played by Wallace Beery.

5. From *The Name Above the Title,* by Frank Capra:

(a) Tape recorders had not yet been invented in 1939, (b) "Mr. Smith (Goes to Washington)" was not made until 1942, or (c) the film editor Capra refers to was actually Douglas Shearer.

_____points

(*Answers on page 254*)

CHARACTER SCRAMBLE

Below we have scrambled the names of fifteen of Hollywood's great character players. Unscramble their names, and receive 10 points for each correct answer.

1. G R A M E L R U K A   A_____ _____
2. T A G R E L S Y A R   L_____ _____
3. M A R I N E C U L A V E R   M_____ _____
4. C Y P H E R L O N T E   P_____ _____
5. S W E L L S H I B I T   W_____ _____
6. J I R C V H M E N G O   J_____ _____
7. A L A T E R Y   R_____ _____
8. P R A N G F I K U L A   F_____ _____
9. G E E T S R E V A N Y   S_____ _____
10. O D R O N G A M Y R   M_____ _____
11. C E B R U G N I E L   N_____ _____
12. L O M I A D C L E A R   M_____ _____
13. W A J S E O R E Y   J_____ _____
14. J A W N L R A D E L E   J_____ _____
15. G A N T E V O L O M U   M_____ _____

_____points

(*Answers on page 254*)

CHARACTER SCRAMBLE—DUFFERS' TEE

Below we have scrambled the names of fifteen of Hollywood's great character players. Unscramble their names, and take 10 points for each answer you get correct. And because this is the Duffers' Tee, we've provided some assistance we did not give to the Movie Buff in his version. Good luck!

1.	G R A M E L R U K A	A _ _ _ K _ _ _ _ _ _
2.	T A G R E L S Y A R	L _ _ _ _ _ G _ _ _ _
3.	M A R I N E C U L A V E R	M _ _ _ _ _ _ _
		U _ _ _ _ _ _
4.	C Y P H E R L O N T E	P _ _ _ _ _ H _ _ _ _ _ _
5.	S W E L L S H I B I T	W _ _ _ B _ _ _ _ _ _
6.	J I R C V H M E N G O	J _ _ _ M _ _ _ _ _ _ _
7.	A L A T E R Y	R _ _ T _ _ _
8.	P R A N G F I K U L A	F _ _ _ _ _ P _ _ _ _ _ _
9.	G E E T S R E V A N Y	S _ _ _ _ _ _ G _ _ _ _
10.	O D R O N G A M Y R	M _ _ _ G _ _ _ _ _ _
11.	C E B R U G N I E L	N _ _ _ _ _ B _ _ _ _ _
12.	L O M I A D C L E A R	M _ _ _ _ _ _ D _ _ _ _ _
13.	W A J S E O R E Y	J _ _ S _ _ _ _ _ _
14.	J A W N L R A D E L E	J _ _ _ D _ _ _ _ _ _ _
15.	G A N T E V O L O M U	M _ _ _ _ _ _ _ L _ _ _

_____points

(Answers on page 254)

WHO KILLED . . . ?

Important staples of exciting cinema are violence and murder. Below, we list fifteen cinematic victims of foul play. Your task is to tell us the actor or actress who committed the killing. You may have 10 points for each correctly pointed finger of accusation!

1. Janet Leigh, in "Psycho"?
2. Chuck Connors, in "The Big Country"?
3. Tyrone Power, in "Jesse James"?

4. Gregory Peck, in "The Gunfighter"?

5. Basil Rathbone, in "The Mark of Zorro"?

6. Steve Cochran, in "White Heat"?

7. Anne Francis, in "Bad Day at Black Rock"?

8. Zachary Scott, in "Mildred Pierce"?

9. Broderick Crawford, in "All the King's Men"?

10. Joseph Henabery, in "The Birth of a Nation"?

11. Bruce Cabot, in "The Last of the Mohicans"?

12. Edward G. Robinson, in "Little Caesar"?

13. Shelley Winters, in "A Double Life"?

14. Paul Hurst, in "Gone with the Wind"?

15. Leslie Howard, in "The Petrified Forest"?

_____points

(*Answers on page 255*)

WHO KILLED . . . ?—DUFFERS' TEE

The preceding exercise lists fifteen victims—and asks the Movie Buff to name the killer. On the assumption that you're not Charlie Chan, or even Number One Son, we've provided a list of suspects for you to use in matching the slayer to the slayee, as they say. Take 5 points for each correct matching of the "killer" names from Column Two with the "victims" and titles of Column One.

1. Janet Leigh, in "Psycho"?

2. Chuck Connors, in "The Big Country"?

3. Tyrone Power, in "Jesse James"?

4. Gregory Peck, in "The Gunfighter"?

5. Basil Rathbone, in "The Mark of Zorro"?

6. Steve Cochran, in "White Heat"?

7. Anne Francis, in "Bad Day at Black Rock"?

8. Zachary Scott, in "Mildred Pierce"?

9. Broderick Crawford, in "All the King's Men"?

a. Raoul Walsh

b. Robert Barrat

c. Robert Ryan

d. Tony Perkins

e. Shepperd Strudwick

f. Ronald Colman

g. Vivien Leigh

h. Burl Ives

i. Skip Homeier

10. Joseph Henabery, in "The Birth of a Nation"?

    j. Humphrey Bogart

11. Bruce Cabot, in "The Last of the Mohicans"?

    k. Ann Blyth

12. Edward G. Robinson, in "Little Caesar"?

    l. Tyrone Power

13. Shelley Winters, in "A Double Life"?

    m. Thomas Jackson

14. Paul Hurst, in "Gone with the Wind"?

    n. James Cagney

15. Leslie Howard, in "The Petrified Forest"?

    o. John Carradine

————points

(*Answers on page 255*)

THE GORY DETAILS

In the WHO KILLED . . . ? exercise just preceding, you unerringly (we assume) put your finger on the actor or actress who committed the foul deed. Now we want you to answer some questions about the gory details . . . that's why we've called you together here! All of the following questions refer to WHO KILLED . . . ? if you *must* look back, and you get 15 points for each correct answer.

1. Of the list of fifteen fatalities, how many of the victims did *not* meet death by gunfire?

2. One of the victims was standing on a chair at the time he met his death. Name the actor, the character he portrayed, and the title of the film.

3. Three of the slayings were supposed re-enactments of historical events or were fictionalized parallels of alleged historical events. Which were they?

4. Of the three slayings in the preceding question, one of the victims was identified by a fictitious character name. Provide that character name, as well as the real-life victim the picture was said to have portrayed.

5. One of the slayings in the list was by drowning. Which one?

6. Contrary to the Production Code of the day, one of the murderers on the list finally got away with very little retribution following his crime. He was ultimately punished, however, by being slain for revenge in a sequel to the original film. Name the actor and the film in the preceding list whose killer got off lightly; name the assassin (the character name as well as the actor who portrayed

12

him); and tell us the name of the sequel in which he finally paid the price.

7. Which of those slain in the preceding list died of stabbing, or "by the blade"?

8. Name the victim(s) in the preceding list who were rewarded with an Oscar for the films in which they met these particular deaths.

9. Which of the *murderers* of the victims on the preceding list also received an Oscar for their "misdeeds"?

10. Which of the preceding murders were performed in glorious color?

_____points

(*Answers on page 255*)

THE GORY DETAILS—DUFFERS' TEE

We assume that you Midnight Movie Duffers accurately put the finger on the persons who committed the mortal mayhem in WHO KILLED . . . ?—DUFFERS' TEE. Right? Now, we've called you together here to iron out the gory details. Give us the facts, only the facts—and take 10 points for each question answered correctly. Refer back to WHO KILLED . . . ? if you must.

1. There were three women in the list. One was shot, one was strangled, and one was stabbed. Tell us how the three women met their respective deaths:
    a. Janet Leigh, _____; b. Shelley Winters, _____; c. Anne Francis, _____.

2. How many of the films in the list were Westerns, or included Western elements?
    a. None; b. 3; c. 6; d. 9; e. All.

3. How many of the killings were the result of gunfire?
    a. None; b. 5; c. 9; d. 11; e. All.

4. Going back to the three women in Question One above—one was (a) a waitress, another (b) ran a service station, and the third (c) was a secretary. Below identify which was which:
    Janet Leigh, _____; Shelley Winters, _____; Anne Francis, _____.

5. Of the fifteen films in the list, how many were costume pictures?
    a. None; b. 4; c. 7; d. 13; e. All.

13

6. Of the fifteen films in the list, how many of the slayings occurred—in the framework of the plot—outside the United States?
   a. None; b. 6; c. 9; d. 12; e. All.

7. Back to the three ladies in Question One. In the films in which they met their deaths, the respective plots gave one of the victims (a) a sister, (b) a brother, and (c) no indication of any relatives at all. Identify which was which:
   Janet Leigh, _____; Shelley Winters, _____; Anne Francis, _____.

8. Of the fifteen slayings, how many were committed in glorious color?
   a. None; b. 4; c. 6; d. 10; e. All.

9. One of the ladies in Question One lost her life by the knife. But only one man on the list was run through with a sword. Was it: (a) Tyrone Power, (b) Basil Rathbone, or (c) Paul Hurst?

10. While some of the slayings were indeed justified, only one of the victims met his death at the hands of "an authorized lawman." Was it (a) Leslie Howard, (b) Zachary Scott, or (c) Edward G. Robinson?

_____ points

(Answers on page 256)

TELL US WHEN

The following list of incomplete titles asks you to insert the missing word—which, besides completing the title, *tells us when*. As a clue, we'll let you in on the fact that in a couple of the titles, numbers are needed. Heads up, then, and take 5 points for each correct title that *tells us when!*

1. "Good _____, Miss Dove"
2. "London _____ ____"
3. "_ : ___ to Yuma"
4. "High ____"
5. "Love in the _____"
6. "_____ Boulevard"
7. "Marjorie _____ star"
8. "Dinner at _____"
9. "_____ Lace"

14

10. "Tonight at _ : _ _"
11. "Cheyenne _ _ _ _ _ _ _"
12. "Decision Before _ _ _ _ _"
13. "_ _ _ _ _ _ Carnival"
14. "A _ _ _ _ _ _ _ _ _ _ Night's Dream"
15. "A _ _ _ _ _ _ _ Place"
16. "Suddenly It's _ _ _ _ _ _ _"
17. "Bugles in the _ _ _ _ _ _ _ _ _ _"
18. "History Is Made at _ _ _ _ _ _"
19. "Centennial _ _ _ _ _ _ _"
20. "Dead of _ _ _ _ _ _"

_____points

(*Answers on page 257*)

TELL US WHEN—DUFFERS' TEE

Below we list twenty incomplete film titles. Each of these may be completed by selecting the appropriate word or phrase from the list in Column Two, which *tells us when*. So make your selection, make the proper matching, and take 5 points for each title you complete correctly.

1. "Good _____, Miss Dove"
2. "London _____"
3. "_____ to Yuma"
4. "High _____"
5. "Bugles in the _____"
6. "_____ Boulevard"
7. "Violent _____"
8. "Dinner at _____"
9. "_____ Lace"
10. "Tonight at _____"
11. "Cheyenne _____"
12. "Decision Before _____"
13. "_____ Carnival"
14. "A _____ Night's Dream"

a. Autumn
b. Midsummer
c. Afternoon
d. Eight
e. Spring
f. Christmas
g. Winter
h. Sundown
i. Noon
j. Morning
k. Night
l. After Dark
m. 8:30
n. Daytime

15. "A _____ Place"
16. "Suddenly It's _____"
17. "Hurry _____"
18. "History Is Made at _____"
19. "_____ in Connecticut"
20. "_____ Wife"

o. Summer
p. Dawn
q. Saturday
r. 3:10
s. Sunset
t. Midnight

_____ points

(*Answers on page 257*)

FIRST, THE WORD

Many great films, and some not so great, have sprung from great literary works. Below we list, in Column One, two films which trace their origin to the same author. Here, the question is two-part: (a) You must identify the author—and for each correct identification, you get 10 points; and (b), from the three films listed in Column Two, you are to select the film also attributable to the same author. For this, take 5 points on each correct title. It is required that you get both parts in order to score—isn't that generous of us?

1. "Call of the Wild"
   "The Sea Wolf"

   a. "The Adventures of Martin Eden"
   b. "Why Must I Die?"
   c. "Two Years Before the Mast"

   _____

2. "Mourning Becomes Electra"
   "The Long Voyage Home"

   a. "Two Before Zero"
   b. "Westbound"
   c. "Summer Holiday"

   _____

3. "From Here to Eternity"
   "The Thin Red Line"

   a. "Across the Pacific"
   b. "Air Force"
   c. "Some Came Running"

   _____

4. "Guys and Dolls"
   "The Big Street"

   a. "Carmen Jones"
   b. "Little Miss Marker"
   c. "Bus Stop"

   _____

5. "Captains Courageous"
   "Gunga Din"

   a. "Elephant Boy"
   b. "Kim"
   c. "Four Feathers"

   _____

16

| 6. | "The Glass Menagerie" "Baby Doll" | a. "Boom!" b. "Take Care of My Little Girl" c. "Three Came Home" |

_____

| 7. | "The Old Man and the Sea" "The Killers" | a. "To Have and Have Not" b. "Knock on Any Door" c. "Key Largo" |

_____

| 8. | "The Time Machine" "Things to Come" | a. "The Invisible Man" b. "The Scapegoat" c. "Invisible Stripes" |

_____

| 9. | "All Quiet on the Western Front" "Arch of Triumph" | a. "Thunder in the East" b. "B.F.'s Daughter" c. "The Road Back" |

_____

| 10. | "Giant" "Ice Palace" | a. "So Big" b. "The Fountainhead" c. "The Big Clock" |

_____

_____ points

(Answers on page 258)

FIRST, THE WORD—DUFFERS' TEE

Some great films, and some not so great, have been adaptations of literary or theatrical creations of some stature. Below, in Column One, we list two films which have sprung from the pen of the same author. In Column Two, we list—out of order—the authors in question. And in Column Three, we list (also out of order) another film taken from the same list of authors. Make the proper selections from Columns Two and Three to correspond with the two films of Column One, and take 5 points on each answer—or 10 points per question. If you get only one part of the answer correct, you get point credit for that half answer. Being in a generous mood, we do not require getting both parts correct in order to score.

1. "Call of the Wild" "The Sea Wolf"	A. Rudyard Kipling	a. "Boom!"
2. "Mourning Becomes Electra" "The Long Voyage Home"	B. Edna Ferber	b. "To Have and Have Not"
3. "From Here to Eternity" "The Thin Red Line"	C. Jack London	c. "The Road Back"
4. "Guys and Dolls" "The Big Street"	D. Tennessee Williams	d. "The Adventures of Martin Eden"
5. "Captains Courageous" "Gunga Din"	E. Erich Maria Remarque	e. "So Big"
6. "The Glass Menagerie" "Baby Doll"	F. H. G. Wells	f. "The Invisible Man"
7. "The Old Man and the Sea" "The Killers"	G. Eugene O'Neill	g. "Kim"
8. "The Time Machine" "Things to Come"	H. Damon Runyon	h. "Summer Holiday"
9. "All Quiet on the Western Front" "Arch of Triumph"	I. Ernest Hemingway	i. "Little Miss Marker"
10. "Giant" "Ice Palace"	J. James Jones	j. "Some Came Running"

————points

(*Answers on page 258*)

THE BETTER HALF

Below we list ten triplets of film players. One of the things those in each triplet have in common—and on which we focus in this exercise—is that they all appeared as husbands to the same cinematic wife. In this exercise, which we've chosen to call THE BETTER HALF, we'll give you 10 points for your correct deduction of the actress who played the wife. In addition, because we're such good guys, we'll allow an additional five points for each correct film title you can name in which the marital alliance was included. You can get, then, 25 points on *each* question—or 250 for the pile. Zowie!

1. Bing Crosby, Ray Milland, Donald Sinden.
2. Tom Powers, Humphrey Bogart, Clifton Webb.
3. Gary Merrill, Claude Rains, Herbert Marshall.
4. James Stewart, Alan Ladd, Jose Ferrer.
5. Dirk Bogarde, Gene Kelly, James Mason.
6. Gregory Peck, Robert Stack, Kirk Douglas.
7. Arthur Kennedy, Gary Cooper, James Dunn.
8. Rock Hudson, Don Taylor, Paul Newman.
9. Joel McCrea, Reginald Gardiner, Fred Allen.
10. Steve Cochran, Rex Harrison, James Stewart.

_____points

(*Answers on page 259*)

THE BETTER HALF—DUFFERS' TEE

Below we list triplets of film players and three films in which they appeared. These players, as they appeared in these films, all had one thing in common—they had the same cinematic wife. From these triplets of actors, and the related films, tell us the name of the actress we're seeking who played their BETTER HALF. Take 15 points for each correct answer.

1. Bing Crosby	"The Country Girl"	
Ray Milland	"Dial M for Murder"	
Donald Sinden	"Mogambo"	_____
2. Tom Powers	"Double Indemnity"	
Humphrey Bogart	"The Two Mrs. Carrolls"	
Clifton Webb	"Titanic"	_____
3. Gary Merrill	"All About Eve"	
Claude Rains	"Mr. Skeffington"	
Herbert Marshall	"The Little Foxes"	_____

4. James Stewart   "The Stratton Story"
   Alan Ladd   "The McConnell
                        Story"
   Jose Ferrer   "The Shrike"   _____

5. Dirk Bogarde   "I Could Go On
                        Singing"
   Gene Kelly   "For Me and My Gal"
   James Mason   "A Star Is Born"   _____

6. Gregory Peck   "Designing Woman"
   Robert Stack   "Written on the Wind"
   Kirk Douglas   "Young Man with a
                        Horn"   _____

7. Arthur Kennedy   "A Summer Place"
   Gary Cooper   "Friendly Persuasion"
   James Dunn   "A Tree Grows in
                        Brooklyn"   _____

8. Rock Hudson   "Giant"
   Don Taylor   "Father of the Bride"
   Paul Newman   "Cat on a Hot Tin
                        Roof"   _____

9. Joel McCrea   "Primrose Path"
   Reginald Gardiner "The Black Widow"
   Fred Allen   "We're Not Married" _____

10. Steve Cochran   "Storm Warning"
    Rex Harrison   "Midnight Lace"
    James Stewart   "The Man Who Knew
                        Too Much"   _____

                                      _____points

(Answers on page 260)

LINK-UPS—BUFFS AND DUFFERS

Well, you've been working pretty hard, so here's an exercise for Buffs and Duffers alike. These are not too hard if you'll just concentrate on the screen credits you've seen over the years. Below are two names, in Columns One and Three—first names and surnames respectively. Into Column Two you're asked to insert the one name which will act as a surname for the personality suggested in Column One *and* as a first name for the personality suggested in Column Three.

For example, if this were a quiz concerned with governmental luminaries, we might have listed:

Benjamin _____ Roosevelt

By the simple insertion of "Franklin," you'd have come up with Benjamin Franklin and Franklin Roosevelt—simple? It is—so simple
that we think the Duffers can play right along with the Buffs. And
besides, we're only giving 5 points for each correct answer.

1. Dean _____ Kosleck

2. Vera _____ Mander

3. Jessica _____ Brennan

4. James _____ O'Connor

5. William _____ Nagel

6. Dane _____ Gable

7. James _____ Granger

8. James _____ Stevens

9. Robert _____ Smith

10. Joan _____ Howard

_____ **points**

(*Answers on page 260*)

SPOT THE BIO: MALES

Each of the following actors portrayed well-known entertainers. For
filling in the name of the entertainer portrayed, you receive 5 points;
but if you can also name the film in which the portrayal was
included, you may have an additional 10 points. Get them *all*—15
points for each of the fifteen names, for 225 points—and we'll let
you award yourself a BONUS of an additional 125 points. So for a
possible score of 350 points on this one . . . Godspeed!

	PERFORMER	FILM TITLE
1. Bob Hope	_____ _____	_____
2. Tony Dexter	_____ _____	_____
3. Tony Curtis	_____ _____	_____
4. Donald O'Connor	_____ _____	_____
5. James Cagney	_____ _____	_____

	PERFORMER	FILM TITLE
6. Larry Parks	___ ___	_____
7. Keefe Brasselle	___ ___	_____
8. Errol Flynn	___ ___	_____
9. Mario Lanza	___ ___	_____
10. Frank Sinatra	___ ___	_____
11. James Cagney (again!)	___ ___	_____
12. Will Rogers, Jr.	___ ___	_____
13. Ray Danton	___ ___	_____
14. Fred Astaire	___ ___	_____
15. Richard Burton	___ ___	_____

_____points + _____bonus = _____total points

(*Answers on page 261*)

SPOT THE BIO: MALES—DUFFERS' TEE

Column One below lists fifteen actors. Column Two lists (out of order) fifteen well-known entertainers, all of whom were portrayed by the actors of Column One. Column Three lists (also out of order) the titles of the films which included these portrayals. Your task: Select the entertainer portrayed and the film title, and correctly match these two with the portrayer in Column One. You get 5 points for each correct answer, but for each question for which you select *both* parts correctly, you may have 15 points. Get both parts of all questions correct for 225 points, and add a bonus of 75 points. So for a possible grand total of 300 points, take your time!

Bob Hope	1. Will Rogers	a. "The Eddie Cantor Story"
Tony Dexter	2. Joe E. Lewis	b. "Prince of Players"
Tony Curtis	3. Edwin Booth	c. "The Seven Little Foys"
Donald O'Connor	4. Eddie Foy	d. "The Great Caruso"
James Cagney	5. John Barrymore	e. "The Joker Is Wild"
Larry Parks	6. Enrico Caruso	f. "Houdini"
Keefe Brasselle	7. Lon Chaney	g. "The Story of Vernon and Irene Castle"
Errol Flynn	8. Rudolph Valentino	h. "The George Raft Story"

Mario Lanza	9. George M. Cohan	i.	"The Buster Keaton Story"
Frank Sinatra	10. Vernon Castle	j.	"Man of a Thousand Faces"
James Cagney (again)	11. George Raft	k.	"Valentino"
Will Rogers, Jr.	12. Al Jolson	l.	"Too Much, Too Soon"
Ray Danton	13. Buster Keaton	m.	"Yankee Doodle Dandy"
Fred Astaire	14. Harry Houdini	n.	"The Story of Will Rogers"
Richard Burton	15. Eddie Cantor	o.	"The Jolson Story"

_____points + _____bonus = _____total points

(*Answers on page 261*)

ODD MAN OUT

On each line below, we list four actors. Three of those actors portrayed, at one time or another, the same character from the "Old West." Your task is to provide a two-part answer: (a) the name of the Western character portrayed by three of the actors, and (b) the name of the actor who did *not* play that particular character. Take 10 points for answering each question correctly—*if* you get both parts. So for 100 points . . . wagons ho-oh!

1. Dan Duryea	Howard Duff	Nestor Paiva	William Bishop
2. Jack Buetel	Paul Newman	Audie Murphy	William Campbell
3. Macdonald Carey	Alan Ladd	Richard Widmark	Dewey Robinson
4. Jon Hall	Bill Elliott	Rod Cameron	Johnny Mack Brown
5. Warner Baxter	Cesar Romero	Pedro Armendariz	Gilbert Roland
6. Moroni Olsen	James Ellison	Steve Cochran	Joel McCrea
7. Arthur Hunnicutt	John Wayne	Brod Crawford	Robert Barrat

8.	Anthony Quinn	Victor Mature	John Gavin	Iron Eyes Cody
9.	Robert Shaw	Ronald Reagan	Sheb Wooley	John Dehner
10.	Henry Fonda	Rex Reason	Will Geer	James Garner

————points

(Answers on page 261)

ODD MAN OUT—DUFFERS' TEE

Below we list ten characters out of the "Old West," and follow each character with the names of four actors. Three of those actors portrayed the character listed, but *one* did not. For 10 points each, tell us which actor *doesn't* belong in the grouping by virtue of never having portrayed the character in question:

1. SAM BASS

| Howard Duff | Dan Duryea | Nestor Paiva | William Bishop |

2. BILLY THE KID

| Paul Newman | Jack Buetel | Audie Murphy | William Campbell |

3. JIM BOWIE

| Alan Ladd | Dewey Robinson | Richard Widmark | Macdonald Carey |

4. KIT CARSON

| Jon Hall | Rod Cameron | Bill Elliott | Johnny Mack Brown |

5. THE CISCO KID

| Cesar Romero | Warner Baxter | Gilbert Roland | Pedro Armendariz |

6. BUFFALO BILL

| Joel McCrea | Moroni Olsen | Steve Cochran | James Ellison |

7. DAVY CROCKETT

| John Wayne | Robert Barrat | Brod Crawford | Arthur Hunnicutt |

8. CRAZY HORSE

| John Gavin | Victor Mature | Anthony Quinn | Iron Eyes Cody |

24

9. GENL. CUSTER

Robert	John	Sheb	Ronald
Shaw	Dehner	Wooley	Reagan

10. WYATT EARP

Will	Rex	Henry	James
Geer	Reason	Fonda	Garner

_____points

(*Answers on page 261*)

NAME THE PLACE, BABY

Below we've supplied some incomplete movie titles—and you can complete these titles, merely by NAMING THE PLACE, BABY! Get them right, and you can add 10 points to your score for each correct answer. One clue, which we really shouldn't be giving you: Generally, the name we're seeking is that of a "natural" location and not of a man-made structure. Got that? Go for 100 . . .

1. "Belle of the _ _ _ _ _ "
2. "The Snows of _ _ _ _ _ _ _ _ _ _ _ _ "
3. "_ _ _ _ _ _ _ _ Wedding"
4. "Springtime in the _ _ _ _ _ _ _ "
5. "The White Cliffs of _ _ _ _ _ "
6. "On the _ _ _ _ _ _ _ "
7. "Hell on _ _ _ _ _ _   _ _ _ "
8. "Wind Across the _ _ _ _ _ _ _ _ _ _ "
9. "_ _ _ Hill"
10. "_ _ _ _ _ _ _ _ _ Serenade"

_____points

(*Answers on page 263*)

NAME THE PLACE, BABY—DUFFERS' TEE

Below we've listed ten incomplete movie titles which you can complete merely by NAMING THE PLACE, BABY! In Column Two, we've listed the missing words or phrases, but out of order. Select the appropriate answer and match it correctly with the incomplete title of Column One, and for each correct pairing, add 10 points to your total.

25

1. "Belle of the _____" a. Everglades
2. "The Snows of _____" b. Sun Valley
3. "_____ Wedding" c. Yukon
4. "Springtime in the _____" d. Kilimanjaro
5. "The White Cliffs of _____" e. Riviera
6. "On the _____" f. Nob
7. "Hell on _____" g. Rockies
8. "Wind Across the _____" h. Dover
9. "_____ Hill" i. Waikiki
10. "_____ Serenade" j. Frisco Bay

_____points

(*Answers on page 263*)

WHO IS IT?

Merely fill in the name of the actor or actress who portrayed the character in Column One. All of these characters are from "series" films—or played the part more than once. Get all the names correct, then read downward in the proper vertical column and you'll find the name of another famous character, not from a series. Tell us the name of the star who portrayed this character and add 50 points.

Judge Hardy   _ _ _ _   _ _ _ _
Nora Charles   _ _ _ _   _ _ _
Alfalfa   _ _ _ _   _ _ _ _ _ _
Rochester   _ _ _ _ _   _ _ _ _ _ _ _
Mr. Dithers   _ _ _ _ _ _ _   _ _ _ _
Vera Vague   _ _ _ _ _ _ _   _ _   _ _ _ _
Frog   _ _ _ _ _   _ _ _ _ _ _
Torchy Blane   _ _ _ _ _ _   _ _ _ _ _ _
Dr. Christian   _ _ _ _   _ _ _ _ _ _ _
Pa Kettle   _ _ _ _ _   _ _ _ _ _ _ _ _
Number One Son   _ _ _ _   _ _ _ _
Boy   _ _ _ _ _   _ _ _ _ _ _ _ _ _
Maisie   _ _ _   _ _ _ _ _ _ _

And the star in question is _____!

_____points

(*Answers on page 263*)

WHO IS IT?—DUFFERS' TEE

For this one, merely fill in the name of the actor or actress who portrayed the character in Column One. All of these characters are from various "series" films, or—in any event—the player portrayed the same character more than once. Getting all the names correct will (reading downward) reveal the name of another well-known movie character—not from a series, but from a well-known murder mystery. Your task is to tell us the name of the star who portrayed this character. If you don't get it immediately, use the clues we've supplied. If you're right, add 25 points.

Judge Hardy	_ _ _ _ _ _ (_) _ _ _
Nora Charles	_ _ _ _ _ _ (_) _
Alfalfa	_ _ _ _ _ (_) _ _ _ _ _
Rochester	_ _ _ _ _ _ _ _ _ _ (_) _
Mr. Dithers	_ _ _ _ _ _ _ _ _ _ _ _
Vera Vague	_ _ _ _ _ _ _ _ _ (_) _ _ _ (_) _
Frog	_ _ (_) _ _ _ (_) _ _ _ _ _ _
Torchy Blane	_ _ _ (_) _ _ _ _ _ _ _ _
Dr. Christian	_ _ _ _ _ _ _ _ _ _ (_) _
Pa Kettle	_ _ (_) _ _ _ _ (_) _ _ _ _
Number One Son	_ _ _ (_) _ _ _ _ _
Boy	_ _ _ _ _ _ _ _ _ _ (_) _ _
Maisie	_ _ _ _ _ _ _ (_) _ _

And the name of the star is: _ _ _ _ _ _ _   _ _ _ _!

_____points

(Answers on page 263)

TELL US WHO

Below, in each question, we list two incidents, or plot points, from two films in which the same player—male or female—appeared. From your memory, tell us the name of the performer we're seeking. Take 15 points for each correct identification. But if you can also correctly name the titles of the two films from which the incidents are taken, you may add another 10 points. You must, however, name *both* of the titles to take advantage of the bonus 10 points.

1. He beat Freddie Bartholomew with a cane, and killed John Barrymore unfairly in a duel as Leslie Howard looked on.
2. He refused to help Gary Cooper in his confrontation with "Frank Miller," and was shot in the head by Burgess Meredith.
3. He was a member of Marlon Brando's motorcycle gang, and his advances were spurned by Vivien Leigh.
4. She was Humphrey Bogart's long-suffering mother in a New York tenement, and was later the long-suffering cook for a St. Louis family named Smith.
5. She fought with Una Merkel in a knock-down, drag-out barroom brawl, and later stabbed Tyrone Power in a British courtroom.
6. He made Garbo laugh, and later, Kevin McCarthy tried to buy his New Orleans hotel.
7. He was a neurosurgeon hired by Katharine Hepburn to treat Elizabeth Taylor, and he beat Lee Marvin in a nineteenth-century foot race.
8. He ran crying after the departing Alan Ladd, and later lost his life as his PT boat was destroyed by Japanese shellfire.
9. He was stabbed by Tony Curtis in a duel atop a castle, and was mistakenly shot by a teen-aged sentry in Israel.
10. She was Charles Laughton's unfaithful bride, and was socked on the chin by Fredric March.

————points

(*Answers on page 264*)

TELL US WHO—DUFFERS' TEE

Below we list in each question two incidents—or plot points—from two films in which the same player appeared. From your memory, tell us the name of the player we're seeking. We've provided the names, out of order, in Column Two, so for each star you can match with these incidents from his or her cinematic career, you may have 15 points. If you can *also* tell us *both* film titles represented, you may add another 10 points per question. So good luck for a possible 250-point addition to your score.

1. He beat Freddie Bartholomew with a cane, and killed John Barrymore unfairly in a duel while Leslie Howard looked on.

2. He refused to help Gary Cooper in his confrontation with "Frank Miller," and was shot in the head by Burgess Meredith.

3. He was a member of Marlon Brando's motorcycle gang and his advances were spurned by Vivien Leigh.

4. She was Humphrey Bogart's long-suffering mother in a New York tenement, and was later the long-suffering cook to a St. Louis family named Smith.

5. She fought with Una Merkel in a knock-down, drag-out barroom brawl, and later stabbed Tyrone Power in a British courtroom.

6. He made Garbo laugh, and later, Kevin McCarthy tried to buy his New Orleans hotel.

7. He was a neurosurgeon hired by Katharine Hepburn to treat Elizabeth Taylor, and he beat Lee Marvin in a nineteenth-century foot race.

8. He ran crying after the departing Alan Ladd, and later lost his life as his PT boat was destroyed by Japanese shellfire.

9. He was stabbed in a duel with Tony Curtis atop a castle, and was mistakenly shot by a teen-aged sentry in Israel.

10. She was Charles Laughton's unfaithful bride, and was socked on the chin by Fredric March.

a. Melvyn Douglas

b. Carole Lombard

c. Brandon de Wilde

d. Basil Rathbone

e. Kirk Douglas

f. Marlene Dietrich

g. Montgomery Clift

h. Lee Marvin

i. Marjorie Main

j. Lon Chaney (Jr.)

———points

(*Answers on page 264*)

RE-DOS

We have coined a new word, all our own: "re-dos"—which rhymes with "whee-booze!" In broad terms, when a film is *remade*, there is usually a great deal of alteration, and usually this alteration begins with the title. But when a new version of a film is made, and the title is retained, we submit that the film is merely *redone*, and the result is merely a *re-do!* Below, in Columns One and Two, we list a title followed by two stars who appeared in an early version. In Column Three, we ask you to supply the names of the two performers who played the same part in a later version. The clue to remember is that both versions of the film carried the same title. We've helped a bit by providing the initials of the names sought in Column Three. And you may have 10 points for each correct name you get. That's 20 points a question, or a possible 200-point addition.

1. "The Thirty-nine Steps"	Robert Donat	K_____	M_____
	Madeleine Carroll	T_____	E_____
2. "Magnificent Obsession"	Robert Taylor	R_____	H_____
	Irene Dunne	J_____	W_____
3. "The Ten Commandments"	Theodore Roberts	C_____	H_____
	Estelle Taylor	O_____	D_____
4. "Seventh Heaven"	Charles Farrell	J_____	S_____
	Janet Gaynor	S_____	S_____
5. "The Plainsman"	Gary Cooper	D_____	M_____
	Jean Arthur	A_____	D_____
6. "A Tale of Two Cities"	Ronald Colman	D_____	B_____
	Elizabeth Allen	D_____	T_____
7. "The Swan"	Adolphe Menjou	A_____	G_____
	Frances Howard	G_____	K_____
8. "Cimarron"	Richard Dix	G_____	F_____
	Irene Dunne	M_____	S_____
9. "My Man Godfrey"	William Powell	D_____	N_____
	Carole Lombard	J_____	A_____
10. "My Sister Eileen"	Brian Aherne	J_____	L_____
	Rosalind Russell	B_____	G_____

_____points

(*Answers on page 264*)

RE-DOS—DUFFERS' TEE

We have coined a new phrase all our own: "re-dos"—which rhymes with "whee-booze!" In broad terms, when a feature is *remade,* there is usually a great deal of alteration, and usually this alteration begins with the title. But when a new version of a film is produced, and the title is retained, we submit that the film is merely *redone,* and the result is merely a *re-do.* In Columns One and Two below, we list a title and two of the stars of an early version. In Column Three—out of order—we supply the star combinations who played the same parts in a later version of the film. Your task is to select the proper pair of stars for Column Three to correspond correctly with Columns One and Two. You may take 15 points for each correct matching—or 150 points if you answer all ten correctly.

1. "The Thirty-nine Steps"	Robert Donat Madeleine Carroll	a. Charlton Heston Olive Deering
2. "Magnificent Obsession"	Robert Taylor Irene Dunne	b. Alec Guinness Grace Kelly
3. "The Ten Commandments"	Theodore Roberts Estelle Taylor	c. Jack Lemmon Betty Garrett
4. "Seventh Heaven"	Charles Farrell Janet Gaynor	d. Dirk Bogarde Dorothy Tutin
5. "The Plainsman"	Gary Cooper Jean Arthur	e. David Niven June Allyson
6. "A Tale of Two Cities"	Ronald Colman Elizabeth Allen	f. Don Murray Abby Dalton
7. "The Swan"	Adolphe Menjou Frances Howard	g. James Stewart Simone Simon
8. "Cimarron"	Richard Dix Irene Dunne	h. Rock Hudson Jane Wyman
9. "My Man Godfrey"	William Powell Carole Lombard	i. Kenneth More Taina Elg
10. "My Sister Eileen"	Brian Aherne Rosalind Russell	j. Glenn Ford Maria Schell

_____points

(Answers on page 264)

31

TYPE-CASTING

In this exercise, we list four occupations which a player represented in four of his or her films. Your task is twofold: Name the actor or actress in each question, and also give the titles of the four films. You get 5 points for correctly identifying the player—plus 5 points for each correct title. That's a possible 25 points per question, or a grand potential of 375 points.

1. Roman officer; medieval knight; A-bomb pilot; gambler.
2. Aspiring actress; woman convict; salesgirl; defense plant worker.
3. Secretary of the Interior; gambler; prize-winning physicist; prizefight manager.
4. British general; Pony Express rider; circus foreman; Spanish folk hero.
5. Air Force general; Army psychiatrist; retired sea captain; whaling boat captain.
6. U. S. Navy sailor; prisoner of war; gambler; detective.
7. U.S. diplomat; Nazi officer; Mexican revolutionary; dock worker.
8. Army sergeant; labor racketeer; pawnbroker; ranch hand.
9. Artist; Eskimo-hunter; Pope; Indian brave.
10. U.S. senator, FBI agent; inventor; reporter.
11. Symphony conductor; plantation owner; monarch; Pope.
12. Lawyer's mistress; deranged baby sitter; secretary; band singer.
13. Air Force general; newsreel cameraman; safari guide; city official.
14. U. S. Marine; oil millionaire; circuit-riding preacher; sheep drover.
15. Lady in waiting; general's wife; newspaper editor; heiress.

———points

(*Answers on page 265*)

(*Answers on page 265*)

TYPE-CASTING—DUFFERS' TEE

In this exercise, we group four occupations which a film player limned in his or her career, cinematically. In Column Two, we list the players—out of order—and ask you to match up the player with the groupings in Column One. We'll give you 5 points for each correct matching—and if you can name *at least three* of the films suggested in the grouping, you may add 20 bonus points for that question. So with fifteen questions, and a possible 25 points a question, here's your chance to catch up with a fat 375!

1. Roman officer; medieval knight; A-bomb pilot; gambler.

    a. Rex Harrison

2. Aspiring actress; woman convict; salesgirl; defense plant worker.

    b. Steve McQueen

3. Secretary of the Interior; gambler; prize-winning physicist; prizefight manager.

    c. Anthony Quinn

4. British general; Pony Express rider; circus foreman; Spanish folk hero.

    d. Robert Mitchum

5. Air Force general; Army psychiatrist; retired sea captain; whaling boat captain.

    e. Clark Gable

6. U. S. Navy sailor; prisoner of war; gambler; detective.

    f. Rod Steiger

7. U.S. diplomat; Nazi officer; Mexican revolutionary; dock worker.

    g. Robert Taylor

8. Army sergeant; labor racketeer; pawnbroker; ranch hand.

    h. Ginger Rogers

9. Artist; Eskimo-hunter; Pope; Indian brave.

    i. Marilyn Monroe

10. U.S. senator; FBI agent; inventor; reporter.

    j. James Stewart

11. Symphony conductor; plantation owner; monarch; Pope.

    k. Olivia de Havilland

12. Lawyer's mistress; deranged baby sitter; secretary; band singer.

    l. Edward G. Robinson

13. Air Force general; newsreel cameraman; safari guide; city official.

    m. Marlon Brando

14. U. S. Marine; oil millionaire; circuit-riding preacher; sheep drover.

    n. Gregory Peck

15. Lady in waiting; general's wife; newspaper editor; heiress.

    o. Charlton Heston

    _____**points**

(*Answers on page 265*)

QUOTABLES

Here are some lines of dialogue taken from a number of films. For each question we ask you to tell us the titles of these films. You may have 15 points for each correct film identification.

1. "To think all this began in Brussels, where a little girl with big, staring eyes used to follow you around her father's palace like a beagle."

   " _ _ _ _ _ _ "

2. "I make more money than Calvin Coolidge—put to-gither!"

   " _ _ _ _ _ _ ' _ _
   _ _ _ _ _ _ _ "

3. "I got vision, and the rest of the world wears bifocals."

   " _ _ _ _ _ _ _ _ _ _ _ _ _
   _ _ _ _ _ _ _ _ _ _ _ _ _ _
   _ _ _ "

4. "I am packing my belongings in the little blue cloth my mother used to tie around her hair when she did the house and I am going from the valley—and this time I shall never return."

   " _ _ _ _ _ _ _ _ _ _
   _ _ _ _ _ _ _ _ "

5. "I could'a been somebody, Charlie—I could'a been a contender."

   " _ _ _ _ _
   _ _ _ _ _ _ _ _ _ _ "

6. "Kill! Kill for the love of Kali!"

   " _ _ _ _ _ _ _ _ "

7. "What she needs is a guy that'd take a sock at her every day—whether it's coming to her or not!"

   " _ _ _ _ _ _ _ _ _ _
   _ _ _ _ _ _ _ _ "

8. ". . . et ceterah, et ceterah, et ceterah!"

   " _ _ _ _ _ _ _ _ _ _ "

9. "You can dish it out—but you got so you can't take it no more—"

   " _ _ _ _ _ _ _ _ _ _ _ "

10. "Where do the noses go?"

    " _ _ _ _ _ _ _ _
    _ _ _ _ _ _ _ _ "

11. "Dames are no good—if you wanna have some fun."

    " _ _ _ _ _ _ _ _ _ _ _ _ "

12. "What'sa matter, Howard? Lose the Heinie?"

    " _ _ _ _ _ _ _ _ _
    _ _ _ _ _ _ _ _ "

34

13. "All aboard, folks! Stage for
    Lordsburg—all 'board!"

    "_ _ _ _ _ _ _ _ _ _"

14. "Gort Borada Nikto!"

    "_ _ _ _ _ _ _ _ _ _ _ _ _ _
    _ _ _ _ _ _ _ _ _"

15. "It is a war of the people—of
    all the people—and it must
    be fought not only on the
    battlefields, but in the cities
    and in the villages, in the
    factories and on the farms,
    and in the homes, and in
    the heart of every man,
    woman, and child who loves
    freedom."

    "_ _ _ _ _ _ _ _ _ _ _"

_____points

(*Answers on page 266*)

QUOTABLES—DUFFERS' TEE

Below are some lines of dialogue from a number of films. The motion pictures from which the lines are taken are listed (out of order) in Column Two. If you can select which film included which line of dialogue and match the two correctly, you may add 10 points to your score for each correct answer.

1. "To think all this began in Brussels, where
   a little girl with big, staring eyes used
   to follow you around her father's
   palace like a beagle."

   a. "Stagecoach"

2. "I make more money than Calvin
   Coolidge—put to-gither!"

   b. "The Day the
   Earth Stood
   Still"

3. "I got vision, and the rest of the world
   wears bifocals."

   c. "The Roaring
   Twenties"

4. "I am packing my belongings in the little
   blue cloth my mother used to tie

35

around her hair when she did the house
and I am going from the valley—and
this time I shall never return."

d. "Gunga Din"

5. "I could'a been somebody, Charlie—I
   could'a been a contender."

e. "Juarez"

6. "Kill! Kill for the love of Kali!"

f. "Little Caesar"

7. "What she needs is a guy that'd take a sock
   at her every day—whether it's coming
   to her or not!"

g. "For Whom the
   Bell Tolls"

8. ". . . et ceterah, et ceterah, et ceterah!"

h. "Butch Cassidy
   and the
   Sundance Kid"

9. "You can dish it out—but you got so you
   can't take it no more—"

i. "How Green Was
   My Valley"

10. "Where do the noses go?"

j. "Mrs. Miniver"

11. "Dames are no good—if you wanna have
    some fun."

k. "On the
   Waterfront"

12. "What'sa matter, Howard? Lose the
    Heinie?"

l. "It Happened One
   Night"

13. "All aboard, folks! Stage for Lordsburg
    —all 'board."

m "Singin' in the
   Rain"

14. "Gort Borada Nikto!"

n. "The King and I"

15. "It is a war of the people—of all the
    people—and it must be fought not
    only on the battlefields, but in the cities
    and in the villages, in the factories
    and on the farms, and in the homes,
    and in the heart of every man, woman,
    and child who loves freedom."

o. "Kiss of Death"

————points

(*Answers on page 266*)

CAREERS IN COMMON

In Column One below, we list two stars and films in which they appeared. In the films, the stars pursued the same career. In Column Two, we list another actor who pursued the *same* career in one of *his* roles. Tell us both the career and the film in which the actor in Column Two pursued that career. Answers, then, are in two parts, and you will receive 10 points for each correct part, or a possible 20 points per question.

1. Wallace Beery—"The Champ"   Wayne Morris _____ _____
   Robert Ryan—"The Set-Up"

2. Barry Sullivan—"The Bad and the Beautiful"   Douglas Fowley _____ _____
   Humphrey Bogart—"The Barefoot Contessa"

3. Frank Morgan—"The Wizard of Oz"   Eddie Albert _____ _____
   Fredric March—"Death of a Salesman"

4. Warner Baxter—"The Prisoner of Shark Island"   Jack Kruschen _____ _____
   Cary Grant—"Crisis"

5. Celeste Holm—"High Society"   Fred Astaire _____ _____
   James Stewart—"Rear Window"

6. Charles Bickford—"The Farmer's Daughter"   Ralph Richardson _____ _____
   William Powell—"My Man Godfrey"

7. Warner Baxter—"42nd Street"   Gary Merrill _____ _____
   William Holden—"The Country Girl"

8. Henry Fonda—"The
   Young Mr.
   Lincoln"   Humphrey
   Spencer Tracy—   Bogart   _____ _____
   "Inherit The Wind"

9. Farley Granger—
   "Strangers on a   Ray Milland   _____ _____
   Train"
   Katharine Hepburn
   —"Pat and Mike"

10. Millard Mitchell—
    "Singin' in the
    Rain"   Kirk Douglas _____ _____
    Charles Bickford—
    "A Star Is Born"

                                          _____points

(*Answers on page 267*)

CAREERS IN COMMON—DUFFERS' TEE

In Column One below, we have listed pairs of stars and given the
titles of films in which both had the same occupation. In Columns
Two and Three, we list actors and films in which they appeared. One
of these three had the same occupation as the stars of Column One.
Your task is to select the actor of Column Two who matches the pair
of Column One by virtue of "occupation." Take 10 points for each
correct answer.

1. Wallace Beery—"The Champ"	Ernie Adams	"Pride of the Yankees"
	Tom Tully	"The Caine Mutiny"
Robert Ryan—"The Set-Up"	Wayne Morris	"Kid Galahad"
2. Barry Sullivan—"The Bad and the Beautiful"	Ronald Reagan	"The Winning Team"
	Douglas Fowley	"Singin' in the Rain"
Humphrey Bogart— "The Barefoot Contessa"	Martin Milner	"Sweet Smell of Success"

38

3. Frank Morgan—"The Wizard of Oz"

   Fredric March—"Death of a Salesman"

   Frank Faylen

   Eddie Albert
   Jack Webb

   "The Lost Weekend"

   "Oklahoma!"
   "Sunset Boulevard"

4. Warner Baxter—"The Prisoner of Shark Island"

   Cary Grant—"Crisis"

   Gene Raymond

   Leon Ames

   Jack Kruschen

   "If I Had a Million"

   "Meet Me in St. Louis"

   "The Apartment"

5. Celeste Holm—"High Society"

   James Stewart—"Rear Window"

   Leo G. Carroll

   Fred Astaire
   E. G. Marshall

   "North by Northwest"

   "Funny Face"
   "Broken Lance"

6. Charles Bickford—"The Farmer's Daughter"
   William Powell—"My Man Godfrey"

   Ralph Richardson
   Jack Lemmon
   Richard Quine

   "The Fallen Idol"
   "Phffft!"
   "My Sister Eileen"

7. Warner Baxter—"42nd Street"
   William Holden—"The Country Girl"

   Gary Merrill
   George Segal
   Robert Young

   "All About Eve"
   "California Split"
   "Crossfire"

8. Henry Fonda—"The Young Mr. Lincoln"

   Spencer Tracy—"Inherit the Wind"

   Moroni Olsen

   Humphrey Bogart

   Ben Gazzara

   "Father of the Bride"

   "Knock on Any Door"

   "Anatomy of a Murder"

9. Farley Granger—"Strangers on a Train"
   Katharine Hepburn—"Pat and Mike"

   Gregory Peck
   Otto Hulett
   Ray Milland

   "The Chairman"
   "Saturday's Hero"
   "Dial M for Murder"

10. Millard Mitchell—"Singin' in the Rain"

    Charles Bickford—"A Star Is Born"

    Wallace Beery
    Kirk Douglas

    Clark Gable

    "Grand Hotel"
    "The Bad and the Beautiful"

    "Boom Town"

_____points

(*Answers on page 267*)

MORE RE-DOS

Here again we have features which have had later versions produced, but the title was retained—hence, they have been "redone." While the title did not change in the later version, the stars did. As before, we supply the film title and two stars of the earlier version. In Column Three, you are asked to supply the names of those who played the same parts in the later version. Charitably, we have provided their initials. Take 10 points for each name you get correct. That's a possible 20 points per question, or a potential of 200 points to your score.

1. "Mutiny on the Bounty"	Clark Gable Movita	M_____	B_____ T_____
2. "The Blue Angel"	Emil Jannings Marlene Dietrich	C_____ M_____	J_____ B_____
3. "Imitation of Life"	Warren William Claudette Colbert	J_____ L_____	G_____ T_____
4. "The Farmer Takes a Wife"	Henry Fonda Janet Gaynor	D_____ B_____	R_____ G_____
5. "The Four Horsemen of the Apocalypse"	Rudolph Valentino Alice Terry	G_____ I_____	F_____ T_____
6. "Bird of Paradise"	Joel McCrea Dolores Del Rio	L_____ D_____	J_____ P_____
7. "The Cabinet of Dr. Caligari"	Werner Krauss Lil Dagover	D_____ G_____	O'_____ J_____
8. "Night Must Fall"	Robert Montgomery Dame May Whitty	A_____ M_____	F_____ W_____
9. "The Barretts of Wimpole Street"	Fredric March Norma Shearer	B_____ J_____	T_____ J_____
10. "A Farewell to Arms"	Gary Cooper Helen Hayes	R_____ J_____	H_____ J_____

_____points

(Answers on page 267)

40

MORE RE-DOS—DUFFERS' TEE

Here again are some films which have had later versions produced—hence, they have been "redone." Their titles did not change,
but their stars did. As was the case before, Columns One and Two
have the films' titles and stars of the earlier version. Column Three
lists the star couples (out of order) who played the same parts in the
re-do. The task is to rearrange Column Three in the proper order to
correspond with Columns One and Two. Take 15 points for each
correct answer.

1. "Mutiny on the Bounty"	Clark Gable Movita	a. Curt Jurgens May Britt
2. "The Blue Angel"	Emil Jannings Marlene Dietrich	b. Albert Finney Mona Washbourne
3. "Imitation of Life"	Warren William Claudette Colbert	c. Louis Jourdan Debra Paget
4. "The Farmer Takes a Wife"	Henry Fonda Janet Gaynor	d. Marlon Brando Tarita
5. "The Four Horsemen of the Apocalypse"	Rudolph Valentino Alice Terry	e. John Gavin Lana Turner
6. "Bird of Paradise"	Joel McCrea Dolores Del Rio	f. Dale Robertson Betty Grable
7. "The Cabinet of Dr. Caligari"	Werner Krauss Lil Dagover	g. Rock Hudson Jennifer Jones
8. "Night Must Fall"	Robert Montgomery Dame May Whitty	h. Dan O'Herlihy Glynis Johns
9. "The Barretts of Wimpole Street"	Fredric March Norma Shearer	i. Bill Travers Jennifer Jones
10. "A Farewell to Arms"	Gary Cooper Helen Hayes	j. Glenn Ford Ingrid Thulin

_____points

(*Answers on page 267*)

THE TEENY-TINY MARQUEE

Once upon a time there was a teeny-tiny movie house with a teeny-tiny marquee in front. The marquee was so small that the owner could seldom squeeze on both the title of the film he was playing and its stars. For a while he got along with films like "Pinky," "Heidi," and "Gigi," but that soon got tiresome for his patrons. He implored Hollywood to consider his problem, and suggested casting stars only in films with titles which matched their names. For example, he would've had the producer of "The Power and the Glory" cast Tyrone Power as its star. Then, on his teeny-tiny marquee, he would display the sign: "The Tyrone and the Glory"—thus enabling passers-by to know both the film being shown and who was starring in it.

If you know movie titles and movie stars, the next set of questions should be right up your alley. Just look at the name in the title—it's italicized. If it's a star's first name, merely replace it with the appropriate surname—and vice versa. Do it correctly and you'll deduce the title of the film on the teeny-tiny marquee. Take 5 points for each answer you get right.

1. "The Longest *Laraine*"
2. "Along Came *Jennifer*"
3. "Valiant is the Word for *Snodgress*"
4. "Captain *Bracken*"
5. "My Man *Cambridge*"
6. "*Pearl* Cargo"
7. "*Marc* of Arabia"
8. "Castle on the *Rock*"
9. "The *Michael* Mutiny"
10. "Night of the *Tab*"
11. "The *Bert* Dealers"
12. "*Tommy* of Iwo Jima"

_____points

(*Answers on page 268*)

THE TEENY-TINY MARQUEE—DUFFERS' TEE

Once upon a time there was a teeny-tiny movie house with a teeny-tiny marquee in front. The marquee was so small that the owner could seldom squeeze on both the title of the film he was playing and its stars. For a while he got along with films like "Pinky," "Heidi," and "Gigi," but that soon got tiresome for his patrons. He implored Hollywood to consider his problem, and suggested casting stars only in films with titles which matched their names. For example, he'd have had the producer of "The Power and the Glory" cast Tyrone Power as its star. Then, on his teeny-tiny marquee, he would display: "The Tyrone and the Glory"—thus enabling passers-by to know both the film and who was starring in it.

If you know movie titles and movie stars, the next set of questions should be a snap for you. Just look at the title of Column One, and you'll see that each title has an incorrect word in it which is actually the first name or the surname of a well-known movie player. Whichever name it is, that player's other name is listed in Column Two—out of order. Match the title of Column One with the proper name of Column Two, and you will have corrected the movie owner's *in*correct movie title. Take 5 points for each correct answer.

1. "The Longest *Laraine*"	a. White
2. "Along Came *Jennifer*"	b. Hudson
3. "Valiant Is the Word for *Snodgress*"	c. Godfrey
4. "Captain *Bracken*"	d. Sands
5. "My Man *Cambridge*"	e. Lawrence
6. "*Pearl* Cargo"	f. Wheeler
7. "*Marc* of Arabia"	g. Day
8. "Castle on the *Rock*"	h. Eddie
9. "The *Michael* Mutiny"	i. Hunter
10. "Night of the *Tab*"	j. Jones
11. "The *Bert* Dealers"	k. Carrie
12. "*Tommy* of Iwo Jima"	l. Caine

_____points

(*Answers on page 268*)

STRUCTURES

Below we've listed twelve incomplete movie titles. You can complete them by inserting the correct *structure* in the blank spot. And for each correct structure you come up with, you may add 10 points to your ever increasing score.

1. "The Big _ _ _ _ _ _"
2. "The _ _ _ _ _ of Rothschild"
3. "_ _ _ _ _ _ in the Cotton"
4. "The Little _ _ _"
5. "_ _ _ _ _ _ _ Keep"
6. "_ _ _ _ _ of London"
7. "Jamaica _ _ _"
8. "Hollywood _ _ _ _ _ _"
9. "The Red _ _ _ _ _"
10. "_ _ _ _ _ _ _ _ _ Rock"
11. "Green _ _ _ _ _ _ _ _"
12. "The Old Dark _ _ _ _ _ _"

_____points

(*Answers on page 269*)

STRUCTURES—DUFFERS' TEE

Below we've listed twelve incomplete movie titles. To complete them, select the correct structure from the words we've provided in Column Two. For each correct structure you insert, completing the movie title, you may add 10 points to your ever increasing score!

1. "Willy Wonka and the Chocolate _____"
2. "The Big _____"
3. "_____ in the Cotton"
4. "The Little _____"
5. "_____ Keep"
6. "_____ of London"
7. "Jamaica _____"
8. "Hollywood _____"

a. Mansions
b. Hut
c. House
d. Factory
e. Inn
f. House
g. Cabin
h. Jailhouse

44

9. "The Red _____"

10. "_____ Rock"

11. "Green _____"

12. "The Old Dark _____"

i. Castle

j. Tent

k. Hotel

l. Tower

_____ points

(*Answers on page 269*)

MENTION MY NAME

Below we list the first names of two film players who have the same surname. They are not related, and we ask you to provide the correct surnames they have in common. We warn you that some of these might be relatively obscure, and so with this warning you may wish to go on to the easier Duffers' Tee. But if you really want to sweat this one out, you may have 15 points for each correct answer.

1. Robert and Karen _____

2. Juanita and Porter _____

3. Nigel and Virginia _____

4. Charlie and Barrie _____

5. Glenn and Laurie _____

6. James and Emma _____

7. Marilyn and Edwin _____

8. Rand and Phyllis _____

9. Jon and Thurston _____

10. K. T. and Mark _____

11. Marie and Francis _____

12. Vic and Karen _____

13. Cliff and Dale _____

14. Robert and Charles _____

15. Alice and Scott _____

_____ points

(*Answers on page 269*)

MENTION MY NAME—DUFFERS' TEE

Below we list the first names of two film players who have the same surname. They are not related, and we ask you to peg the common last names. One clue: Usually one of the pair is more prominent than the other. Take 15 points for each correct answer.

1. Paul and Phyllis   _____
2. Loretta and Gig   _____
3. James and Charles   _____
4. James and Peggy Ann   _____
5. Gene and Lawrence   _____
6. James and Elaine   _____
7. Jane and Dick   _____
8. Dana and Julie   _____
9. Joby and Carroll   _____
10. Madeleine and Diahann   _____
11. Debbie and William   _____
12. Milo and Michael   _____
13. Bette and Rufe   _____
14. Robert and Amanda   _____
15. Rock and Rochelle   _____

_____points

(*Answers on page 270*)

WILD CARD—BUFFS AND DUFFERS ALIKE

Here's a little mental exercise for Buffs and Duffers alike. Movie knowledge helps, but logic, orderly thinking, and patience should win out—even when movie memory is faulty. If you analyze, think, and deduce correctly—add 100 points to your score.

The Last Reel

One of the great thrills of the "Thin Man" series was to anticipate the last reel when William Powell would gather all of the possible suspects together, review the clues, apply his unerring logic to the case, and put the finger on the murderer—who would either break down and confess all or make an impossible break for escape. It apparently never occurred to the culprit that he might brazen it out and later try his chances with a jury

46

of his peers—twelve good extras, brave and true. So let's see if you're as good with clues as was Nick Charles. No murder involved here, but if you can work it out, we'd put you up against Dashiell Hammett any time. Here's the story:

A motion picture producer had four young performers under contract. There were three actors and one actress. All were given parts in the producer's super-extravaganza as their cinema debut. As the reviews and audience reaction came in, each looked forward eagerly to the next assignment which might mean one more rung up the ladder to stardom. Three were fortunate, and were given assignments in the producer's future films. The fourth performer was sent on a loan-out to a cheapie producer on Poverty Row. None of the performers ended up working together on the next assignment.

Now—from the clues which follow, give us each performer's *full name,* and the type of feature to which *each* was assigned.

a) COLIN was not loaned out, nor was he assigned to the private eye film.

b) KAY's last name isn't BARTON or COLLINS.

c) MICHAELS is not the last name of either COLIN or MICHAEL; neither of these two was assigned to the horror film.

d) Neither BART nor the actor whose last name is BARTON was loaned out; the performer known as MICHAELS was loaned out, and thus did not end up in the Western, as Michaels' agent had hoped.

e) The actor whose last name is MCKAY did not end up in the private eye film or the horror film.

_____, horror film;   _____, private eye film;
_____, Western film;   _____, loaned out.

_____points

(*Answers on page 271*)

NAME THE STAR

On each line below, we have listed the names of two of the characters played by the same star. Either one should be sufficient for an old movie buff like you to make instant identification. Do so—that is, identify the star correctly—and add 10 points to your score for each star you tab. However, if these are too obscure for you, feel free to move on to the Duffers' Tee.

1. Felicitas Van Kletzingk   Rita Cavallini
2. Spike McManus   Ted Randall
3. Victor Marswell   Big John MacMasters
4. Frank Flannagan   Peter Ibbetson
5. Chuck Tatum   Ned Land
6. Ernst Janning   Doc Delaney
7. Ralph Nickleby   Priam
8. Roger O. Thornhill   Mortimer Brewster
9. Andrew Morton   Chips McGuire
10. Lola-Lola   Erika von Schluetow

————points

(*Answers on page 272*)

NAME THE STAR—DUFFERS' TEE

If you found the Movie Buffs' version of NAME THE STAR too tough, then welcome to the Duffers' Tee. But if you came here directly, just check the names of the movie characters we've listed below. On each line, we list two characters played by the same star. And though these are the same stars suggested in the Movie Duffs' version, the character names shown here are probably better known. So for each star you identify, add 5 points to your score. (And for those of you who passed up the Movie Buffs' version, we hope you kick yourself after we've jogged your memory.)

1. Maria Walewska   Anna Karenina
2. Col. Ted Lawson   Lieut. Steve Maryk
3. "Blackie" Norton   Capt. Rhett Butler
4. Marshal Will Kane   Longfellow Deeds
5. Ulysses   Vincent Van Gogh
6. Robert Stroud   Elmer Gantry
7. Mr. Brink   Dr. Livingstone
8. Walter Burns   Ernie Mott
9. Capt. Philip M. Queeg   Fred C. Dobbs
10. Christine Vole   Madame Bertholt

————points

(*Answers on page 272*)

THE DIRECTORS

In the diagram following, we have included the last names of eighty directors. However, the names run forward and backward, up and down, and diagonally, in any direction—though always in a straight line. To assist you in finding them, we've alphabetized the directors below, by initial. We know you wouldn't want this to be too easy, so rather than giving you their names, we've used a title of a film each directed—though not necessarily his best-known film. You get 10 points for each name you ferret out—so we'll start you off with a free 10-point clue. If you start your word search in the upper left-hand corner of the chart, the first director you come across is represented by number 9 below. You remember—he helped to make the Mercouri rise . . .

B. 1. "Disputed Passage"
    2. "Subway in the Sky"
    3. "Take the High
        Ground"
    4. "Romance"
C. 5. "Broadway Bill"
    6. "It Happened
        Tomorrow"
    7. "Le Corbeau"
    8. "Son of Fury"
D. 9. "The Canterville
        Ghost"
   10. "3:10 to Yuma"
   11. "Bobbikins"
   12. "Java Head"
   13. "Male and Female"
   14. "After the Fox"
   15. "Dr. Socrates"
   16. "Fearless Fagan"
E. 17. "Operation Petticoat"
F. 18. "Mary of Scotland"
   19. "The Victors"
   20. "The Young Stranger"
   21. "Dr. Blood's Coffin"
G. 22. "Man of Iron"

   23. "Judith of Bethulia"
H. 24. "Trail of the Lonesome
        Pine"
   25. "The Last Movie"
   26. "Border Legion"
   27. "Across the Pacific"
J. 28. "Forty Pounds of Trouble"
K. 29. "Sea of Grass"
   30. "Gigot"
   31. "Tol'able David"
   32. "Not As a Stranger"
   33. "The Killing"
L. 34. "Oregon Passage"
   35. "Western Union"
   36. "The Blue Bird"
   37. "This Happy
        Breed"
   38. "Son of Frankenstein"
   39. "Top Speed"
   40. "The Bellboy"
   41. "East Lynne"
   42. "Ensign Pulver"
   43. "Ali Baba and the
        Forty Thieves"

```
S C H O E D S A C K I N G K C I R B U B K
F N C B B O R A P N O K S U G H D A V E L S A K
R E G N M B E R X P N H C I S E T T H R A L I Z Z
N A R A I M O E R A S N M H D T I S R N L E A Z Z
K T O R E M A P U D O X K A N M I C N T R J L D N
E S T I M F R E S A P B R S K A N M R O I E B R A
H G I G O R L A N G D L R G R F L K R O S R I L T O W N I
E R T W D R M A R Y T O G N L A N F N R D S I H O U
M D L D O E E D B A N Y O Z I E L G R I S R W A N R T T D U
I L U V I M E E D B D N O I B Z U L Y E L O M D R A N E P S Q
A W E L L U M B E E D R O O K S O A G C O M D R U N N E P S Q
D A I L V L U M D M A N N O N K N L O C L A S U O R A C D T C K
S L E E L A D M I M A R K I S O R H Y I D R A N T E P C
N S A N C L E W I S R E M A N K O R E M C L D O N R O E D D C C N I
I H L E V L A W S W I R S E P E N A R K I L Y O D S H Y N F D A C P N
N E L S O N S K M O R E L C O O Y R E H P E R A C C T E P S H
```

50

44. "Trouble in Paradise"
45. "The Last Gangster"
46. "Stage Struck"
47. "Never Fear"
48. "Crazylegs"
M. 49. "The Great Flamarion"
50. "About Mrs. Leslie"
51. "Quick Before It Melts"
52. "A Study in Scarlet"
53. "Gentle Annie"
54. "Gun the Man Down"
55. "I Dood It"
N. 56. "Soldier in the Rain"
P. 57. "Major Dundee"
58. "Mickey One"
59. "Whirlpool"
Q. 60. "Pushover"
61. "The Buccaneer"
R. 62. "No Down Payment"
63. "Isle of the Dead"
S. 64. "Barefoot in the Park"
65. "The Hounds of Zaroff"
66. "Kathy O' "
67. "Hitler's Madmen"
68. "Highway 301"
T. 69. "Broadway Melody of 1940"
V. 70. "The Night Heaven Fell"
71. "So Red the Rose"
W. 72. "Artists and Models"
73. "The Stranger"
74. "Central Airport"
75. "The Major and the Minor"
76. "One Minute to Play"
77. "Captive City"
Y. 78. "Come Blow Your Horn"
Z. 79. "The Taming of the Shrew"
80. "Eyes in the Night"

_____points

(*Answers on page 273*)

THE DIRECTORS—DUFFERS' TEE

In the diagram on the preceding page, we have included the names of eighty directors. The names, however, run backward and forward, up and down, and diagonally, in any direction—but always in a straight line. To assist you, we've alphabetized the directors below, but by initial only. So this shouldn't be too easy, the directors are represented by the title of one of the films they've directed. For the most part it is one of the director's better-known films. If you start in the upper left-hand corner of the chart, the first director you encounter is represented by number 9 below. You remember, he helped to make the Mercouri rise—and we've helped your score rise, since we're giving 10 points for each director's name you locate.

B.	1. "Seventh Heaven"		L.	34. "The Vampire"

B.
1. "Seventh Heaven"
2. "The Beachcomber"
3. "Elmer Gantry"
4. "Anna Christie"

C.
5. "Mr. Deeds Goes to Town"
6. "The Ghost Goes West"
7. "Diabolique"
8. "Anna and the King of Siam"

D.
9. "Never on Sunday"
10. "Broken Arrow"
11. "The Green Man"
12. "Lorna Doone"
13. "The Ten Commandments"
14. "Two Women"
15. "Portrait of Jennie"
16. "Charade"

E.
17. "Darling Lili"

F.
18. "Stagecoach"
19. "The Guns of Navarone"
20. "Seven Days in May"
21. "The Ipcress File"

G.
22. "Divorce—Italian Style"
23. "The Birth of a Nation"

H.
24. "Kiss of Death"
25. "Easy Rider"
26. "Fire over England"
27. "The Treasure of the Sierra Madre"

J.
28. "In the Heat of the Night"

K.
29. "On the Waterfront"
30. "Hello, Dolly!"
31. "The Snows of Kilimanjaro"
32. "Ship of Fools"
33. "2001: A Space Odyssey"

L.
34. "The Vampire"
35. "Fury"
36. "The King and I"
37. "Ryan's Daughter"
38. "The Bridge of San Luis Rey"
39. "Quo Vadis?"
40. "The Family Jewels"
41. "Mutiny on the Bounty"
42. "Picnic"
43. "Buck Privates"
44. "Ninotchka"
45. "Wake of the Red Witch"
46. "The Group"
47. "Outrage"
48. "The Great Locomotive Chase"

M.
49. "El Cid"
50. "Come Back, Little Sheba"
51. "Marty"
52. "Tall in the Saddle"
53. "Ben-Hur" (second unit)
54. "McLintock"
55. "Gigi"

N.
56. "Lilies of the Field"

P.
57. "Straw Dogs"
58. "Bonnie and Clyde"
59. "Anatomy of a Murder"

Q.
60. "Hotel"
61. "The Buccaneer"

R.
62. "Hud"
63. "Champion"

S.
64. "The Odd Couple"
65. "Mighty Joe Young"

66. "The Three Worlds of Gulliver"
67. "Written on the Wind"
68. "The Last Voyage"
T. 69. "Skippy"
V. 70. "La Ronde"
71. "Duel in the Sun"
W. 72. "White Heat"

73. "Citizen Kane"
74. "Wings"
75. "The Apartment"
76. "For Whom the Bell Tolls'
77. "The Sound of Music"
Y. 78. "Divorce American Style"
Z. 79. "Romeo and Juliet"
80. "From Here to Eternity"

_____points

(*Answers on page 273*)

HUBBIES

Below we list ten triplets of film actresses. The one thing they all have in common—as we focus on this exercise—is that they all appeared as wives to the same cinematic husband. In this one, we'll give 10 points for your coming up with the name of the actor who played the "common husband." Moreover, we'll let you have an additional 5 points for each film you can name in which the marital alliance was included. That's a possible 25 points per question—or hopefully, an additional 250 points for you.

1. Jan Sterling, Gina Lollobrigida, and Julie Bishop
2. Joan Bennett, Marjorie Steele, and Dorothy McGuire
3. Tallulah Bankhead, Vivian Vance, and Carole Lombard
4. Olivia de Havilland, Greer Garson, and Deborah Kerr
5. Jeanne Crain, June Allyson, and Grace Kelly
6. Ann Sheridan, Myrna Loy, and Paula Raymond
7. Lana Turner, Rita Johnson, and Joan Bennett
8. Evelyn Keyes, Jane Wyatt, and Gloria Grahame
9. Polly Bergen, Ann Todd, and Jane Wyman
10. Jeanne Moreau, Maureen O'Hara, and Lilli Palmer

_____points

(*Answers on page 274*)

HUBBIES—DUFFERS' TEE

Below we list ten triplets of actresses, and films in which they appeared. In these films, they had the same cinematic spouse. For each triplet, and the respective films listed, we ask you to name the actor involved in these marital alliances. Take 15 points for each one right.

1. Jan Sterling   "The Harder They Fall"
   Gina Lollobrigida   "Beat the Devil"
   Julie Bishop   "Action in the North Atlantic"

2. Joan Bennett   "The Macomber Affair"
   Marjorie Steele   "Face to Face"
   Dorothy McGuire   "The Dark at the Top of the Stairs"

3. Tallulah Bankhead   "The Devil and the Deep"
   Vivian Vance   "The Blue Veil"
   Carole Lombard   "They Knew What They Wanted"

4. Olivia de Havilland   "Not As a Stranger"
   Greer Garson   "Desire Me"
   Deborah Kerr   "The Sundowners"

5. Jeanne Crain   "Apartment for Peggy"
   June Allyson   "Executive Suite"
   Grace Kelly   "The Bridges at Toko-Ri"

6. Ann Sheridan   "I Was a Male War Bride"
   Myrna Loy   "Mr. Blandings Builds His Dream House"
   Paula Raymond   "Crisis"

7. Lana Turner   "Cass Timberlane"
   Rita Johnson   "Edison the Man"
   Joan Bennett   "Father of the Bride"

8. Evelyn Keyes   "Mrs. Mike"
   Jane Wyatt   "Pitfall"
   Gloria Grahame   "The Bad and the Beautiful"

9. Polly Bergen   "Cape Fear"
   Ann Todd   "The Paradine Case"
   Jane Wyman   "The Yearling"

10. Jeanne Moreau   "The Yellow Rolls-Royce"
    Maureen O'Hara   "The Foxes of Harrow"
    Lilli Palmer   "The Four-Poster"

———————**points**

(*Answers on page 275*)

TRUSTY STEED

This is a simple test, especially if you are—or were—a Western fan. In this exercise, we're looking for the names—not of stars or features—but the names of horses. And these shouldn't be too difficult, since the horses we're looking for are famous ones—often getting billing as prominent as that their owners enjoyed. So just give us the names of the horses of the Western stars listed below, and take 10 points for each one you get correct.

1. William S. Hart   F _ _ _ _ _
2. Tom Mix   T _ _ _
3. Buck Jones   S _ _ _ _ _ _
4. Ken Maynard   T _ _ _ _ _ _
5. Hopalong Cassidy   T _ _ _ _ _ _
6. Tex Ritter   W _ _ _ _ F _ _ _ _
7. Rex Allen   K _ _ _
8. Gene Autry   C _ _ _ _ _ _ _ _
9. Allan "Rocky" Lane   B _ _ _ _ _ _ _ _ _
10. Roy Rogers   T _ _ _ _ _ _
11. Smiley Burnette   R _ _ _ _ _ _
12. Dale Evans   B _ _ _ _ _ _ _ _ _ _

_____points

(*Answers on page 275*)

TRUSTY STEED—DUFFERS' TEE

This shouldn't be too difficult, especially if you are—or were—a Western fan. In this exercise, we're not looking for the names of stars or features, but are seeking to match up the famous Western horses with their star owners. The Western stars who relied on their trusty steeds are listed in Column One. Their horses—who often received the same screen billing as the human star—are listed, out of order, in Column Two. Your task is to match the horse with the owner; and receive 10 points for each correct pairing.

1. William S. Hart	a. Silver
2. Tom Mix	b. Tarzan
3. Buck Jones	c. Fritz
4. Ken Maynard	d. Koko
5. Hopalong Cassidy	e. Blackjack
6. Tex Ritter	f. Champion
7. Rex Allen	g. Buttermilk
8. Gene Autry	h. Ringeye
9. Allan "Rocky" Lane	i. Topper
10. Roy Rogers	j. Tony
11. Smiley Burnette	k. Trigger
12. Dale Evans	l. White Flash

————points

(*Answers on page 275*)

SPOT THE BIO: FEMALES

Each of the following actresses portrayed well-known female entertainers. For filling in the name of the entertainer portrayed, you get 5 points. However, if you can also name the film in which the portrayal was included, you get an additional 10 points. Get them all—15 points for each of the 15 names, or 225 points—and we'll toss in a bonus of 125 points. So for a possible score of 350 on this one, go—go—go!

	PERFORMER	FILM TITLE
1. Susan Hayward	———— ————	————————
2. Kim Novak	———— ————	————————
3. Eleanor Parker	———— ————	————————
4. Ann Blyth	———— ————	————————
5. Dorothy Malone	———— ————	————————
6. Luise Rainer	———— ————	————————
7. Doris Day	———— ————	————————
8. Barbra Streisand	———— ————	————————
9. Carroll Baker	———— ————	————————
10. Ginger Rogers	———— ————	————————

	PERFORMER	FILM TITLE
11. Vanessa Redgrave	_____ _____	_____
12. Susan Hayward (again!)	_____ _____	_____
13. Maria Tallchief	_____ _____	_____
14. Julie Andrews	_____ _____	_____
15. Alice Faye	_____ _____	_____

_____points

+ _____bonus = _____total

(*Answers on page 275*)

SPOT THE BIO: FEMALES—DUFFERS' TEE

In Column One below, we list actresses who portrayed well-known female entertainers. The entertainers portrayed are listed, out of order, in Column Two, and the films in which the portrayals were included are listed, also out of order, in Column Three. Make your selections on entertainers portrayed and the appropriate films to match with Column One. You get 5 points for selecting the entertainer portrayed and 5 for pegging the film title. Get both parts right and you can have 15 points per question. Get all 15 questions correct, for a total of 225 points, and take a bonus of 75 additional points. That's a possible grand total of 300 points, so think about it!

Susan Hayward	1. Ruth Etting	a. "The Great Ziegfeld"
Kim Novak	2. Jean Harlow	b. "The Story of Vernon and Irene Castle"
Eleanor Parker	3. Irene Castle	c. "Star!" (or "Those Were the Days")
Ann Blyth	4. Lillian Russell	d. "Love Me or Leave Me"
Dorothy Malone	5. Jane Froman	e. "Funny Girl"
Luise Rainer	6. Anna Pavlova	f. "Lillian Russell"
Doris Day	7. Isadora Duncan	g. "I'll Cry Tomorrow"
Barbra Streisand	8. Anna Held	h. "With a Song in My Heart"
Carroll Baker	9. Helen Morgan	i. "Million Dollar Mermaid"

57

Ginger Rogers	10. Marjorie Lawrence	j. "Jeanne Eagels"
Vanessa Redgrave	11. Jeanne Eagels	k. "Too Much, Too Soon"
Susan Hayward (again!)	12. Gertrude Lawrence	l. "Isadora" (or "The Loves of Isadora")
Maria Tallchief	13. Fanny Brice	m. "The Helen Morgan Story"
Julie Andrews	14. Diana Barrymore	n. "Harlow"
Alice Faye	15. Lillian Roth	o. "Interrupted Melody"

————points

+————bonus = ————total

(*Answers on page 275*)

OSCAR SHUFFLE—WILD CARD

This exercise is a wild card—the same version prevails for Buff and Duffer. Below we have scrambled the names of four Oscar winners. Unscramble them, and use the designated letters to arrive at the name of *another* Oscar winner. One clue: All of the winners below won in the same category. Take 5 points for each name you unscramble, and if you can deduce the hidden name, you win another 10 points. Potential score: 30 points!

1. D O N G U R T H O R
   (_) _ _ _ (_) _ _ (_) (_) (_)
2. S E P L A L E R S T O N E S
   _ (_) _ _ (_) _ (_) _ (_) _ _ _ _ _
3. A K A L I D R O V E L
   _ _ _ (_) _ (_) (_) (_) _ _ _
4. H A M E G A R L I A R G O
   _ _ _ _ _ (_) (_) _ _ _ _ _ _

And the hidden name:

_ _ _ _ _ _ _ _ _ _ _ _ _

————points

(*Answers on page 276*)

EVEN MORE RE-DOS

By now, you should know how the "re-dos" exercise goes—but we'll refresh your memory once again—and this *is* the last time. The next time re-dos come up, you're on your own. As with all re-dos, the titles didn't change in the later version, but the stars did. In Columns One and Two, we supply the film title and two stars of an earlier version. In Column Three, taking advantage of the initials we supply, you must provide the names of the two performers who portrayed the same parts in a later version. Take 10 points for each name you get correct. That's a possible 20 points per question, or a potential of 200!

1. "One Million B.C."	Victor Mature	J_____	R_____
	Carole Landis	R_____	W_____
2. "The Man Who Knew Too Much"	Leslie Banks	J_____	S_____
	Edna Best	D_____	D_____
3. "The Taming of the Shrew"	Douglas Fairbanks	R_____	B_____
	Mary Pickford	E_____	T_____
4. "The Prisoner of Zenda"	Raymond Massey	J_____	M_____
	Madeleine Carroll	D_____	K_____
5. "A Star Is Born"	Fredric March	J_____	M_____
	Janet Gaynor	J_____	G_____
6. "Rose Marie"	Nelson Eddy	H_____	K_____
	Jeanette MacDonald	A_____	B_____
7. "King Solomon's Mines"	Cedric Hardwicke	S_____	G_____
	Anna Lee	D_____	K_____
8. "Anna Karenina"	Fredric March	K_____	M_____
	Greta Garbo	V_____	L_____
9. "Mayerling"	Charles Boyer	O_____	S_____
	Danielle Darrieux	C_____	D_____
10. "Goodbye, Mr. Chips"	Robert Donat	P_____	O'_____
	Greer Garson	P_____	C_____

_____points

(Answers on page 277)

EVEN MORE RE-DOS—DUFFERS' TEE

Here are even more re-dos—all of which had later versions produced. As in all re-dos, the stars changed, even though the titles didn't. In Columns One and Two, we list the film title and two performers from an earlier version. In Column Three, we list, out of order, the performer combinations who portrayed the same parts in the later versions. You are to select the appropriate couple from Column Three, and match it correctly with the title and performer combinations of Columns One and Two. Take 15 points for each correct matching.

1.	"One Million B.C."	Victor Mature Carole Landis	a. James Stewart Doris Day
2.	"The Man Who Knew Too Much"	Leslie Banks Edna Best	b. John Richardson Raquel Welch
3.	"The Taming of the Shrew"	Douglas Fairbanks Mary Pickford	c. Peter O'Toole Petula Clark
4.	"The Prisoner of Zenda"	Raymond Massey Madeleine Carroll	d. Howard Keel Ann Blyth
5.	"A Star Is Born"	Fredric March Janet Gaynor	e. Kieron Moore Vivien Leigh
6.	"Rose Marie"	Nelson Eddy Jeanette MacDonald	f. Stewart Granger Deborah Kerr
7.	"King Solomon's Mines"	Cedric Hardwicke Anna Lee	g. Richard Burton Elizabeth Taylor
8.	"Anna Karenina"	Fredric March Greta Garbo	h. James Mason Deborah Kerr
9.	"Mayerling"	Charles Boyer Danielle Darrieux	i. James Mason Judy Garland
10.	"Goodbye, Mr. Chips"	Robert Donat Greer Garson	j. Omar Sharif Catherine Deneuve

———points

(*Answers on page 277*)

FEMALES' FIRST FILMS

Some stars have most auspicious debuts in the film world. Others begin with walk-ons, proceed to bits, then to supporting roles—then featured roles, and perhaps stardom! In this quiz, we're asking you to tell us the first feature film in which the following actresses appeared. We've supplied minimal clues, and you get 10 points for each correct answer.

1. Dorothy McGuire   "_ _ _ _ _ _ _"

2. Jane Russell   "_ _ _ _ _ _ _ _ _"

3. Jennifer Jones   "N _ _ F _ _ _ _ _ _ _"

4. Linda Darnell   "D _ _ _ _ _ _ W _ _ _"

5. Lauren Bacall   "_ _ _ _ _ _ _ _ _ _ _ _"

6. Jane Fonda   "_ _ _ _ _ _ _ _ _ _ _"

7. Marie Dressler   "_ _ _ _ _ _ _ ' _ _ _ _ _ _ _ _ _ _ _ _ _ _ _"

8. Leslie Caron   "_ _ _ _ _ _ _ _ _ _ _ _ _ _ _"

9. Grace Kelly   "F _ _ _ _ _ _ _ _ _ _ _ H _ _ _ _ _ _ _"

10. Greer Garson   "_ _ _ _ _ _ _ _ _ , _ _ . _ _ _ _ _ _ _ _"

11. Maureen O'Hara   "J _ _ _ _ _ _ _ _ _ I _ _ _ _ _"

12. Julie Andrews   "_ _ _ _ _ _ _ _ _ _ _ _ _"

13. Ruby Keeler   "_ _ _ _ _ _ _ _ _ _ _ _ _ _ _"

14. Jean Seberg   "_ _ _ _ _ _ _ _ _ _"

15. Kim Novak   "_ _ _ _ _ _ _ _"

16. Carmen Miranda   "D _ _ _ _ _ _ A _ _ _ _ _ _ _ _ _ _ _ W _ _ _"

17. Eva Marie Saint   "_ _ _ _ _ _ _ _ _ _ _ _ _ _"

18. Katharine Hepburn   "A _ _ _ _ _ _ of _ _ _ _ _ _ _"

19. Bette Davis   "B _ _ S _ _ _ _ _ _"

20. Olivia de Havilland   "A _ _ _ _ _ _ _ _ _ _ _ _ _ _ _ _ 's _ _ _ _ _ _ _ _"

_____points

(*Answers on page 277*)

FEMALES' FIRST FILMS—DUFFERS' TEE

Some stars have most auspicious debuts in the film world. Others begin with walk-ons, proceed to bits, then to supporting roles—then featured film roles, and perhaps stardom! In this quiz, we're looking for the first films of the actresses listed in Column One. Select the appropriate title from Column Two, match it to the correct actress, and take 10 points for each correct pairing.

1. Dorothy McGuire		a.	"Fourteen Hours"
2. Jane Russell		b.	"Tillie's Punctured Romance"
3. Jennifer Jones		c.	"Bad Sister"
4. Linda Darnell		d.	"Pushover"
5. Lauren Bacall		e.	"Claudia"
6. Jane Fonda		f.	"Jamaica Inn"
7. Marie Dressler		g.	"The Outlaw"
8. Leslie Caron		h.	"Down Argentine Way"
9. Grace Kelly		i.	"New Frontier"
10. Greer Garson		j.	"Mary Poppins"
11. Maureen O'Hara		k.	"Daytime Wife"
12. Julie Andrews		l.	"A Midsummer Night's Dream"
13. Ruby Keeler		m.	"On the Waterfront"
14. Jean Seberg		n.	"A Bill of Divorcement"
15. Kim Novak		o.	"To Have and Have Not"
16. Carmen Miranda		p.	"Saint Joan"
17. Eva Marie Saint		q.	"42nd Street"
18. Katharine Hepburn		r.	"Goodbye, Mr. Chips"
19. Bette Davis		s.	"An American in Paris"
20. Olivia de Havilland		t.	"Tall Story"

————points

(Answers on page 277)

THREE OF A KIND

In THREE OF A KIND we're looking for the three-part answers to each question. And to say you've answered each question correctly means you've answered *all* three parts. Do it, and take 15 points per question, for a possible 150 point addition to your score.

1. Name the three actors who portrayed "My Three Angels":
   _____ _____; _____ _____; and _____ _____.

2. Name the three actors who were victims of the lynch mob in "The Ox-Bow Incident":
   _____ _____; _____ _____; and _____ _____.

3. Name the three actors who broke into the vault in "The Asphalt Jungle":
   _____ _____; _____ _____; and _____ _____.

4. Name at least three of the Dead End Kids, as they appeared in "Dead End":
   _____ _____; _____ _____; and _____ _____.

5. Name the three films in which James Dean was featured:
   "_____"; "_____"; and "_____."

6. Name at least three of the seven actors who were the original (American version) "Magnificent Seven":
   _____ _____; _____ _____; and _____ _____.

7. Name three plays by Shakespeare which have been filmed:
   "_____"; "_____"; and "_____."

8. Give the first names of the three Ritz Brothers:
   _____; _____; and _____.

9. Name at least three biographical roles played by Marlon Brando (Note: We're not asking for the titles of the films, but the names of the characters.):
   _____; _____; _____.

10. Give us the first names of the three Lane sisters:
    _____; _____; and _____.

_____**points**

(*Answers on page 278*)

THREE OF A KIND—DUFFERS' TEE

In this exercise, we want three correct answers for each question. We have supplied five possible answers, and it is your task to *eliminate* those answers which are *incorrect*. If you retain the three correct answers—and we insist on all three—you may add 15 points for *each* question.

1. Name the three actors who portrayed "My Three Angels":
   a. Aldo Ray; b. Basil Rathbone; c. Humphrey Bogart; d. Peter Ustinov; e. Dewey Martin.

2. Name the three actors who were victims of the lynch mob in "The Ox-Bow Incident":
   a. Henry Fonda; b. Francis Ford; c. Harry Morgan; d. Dana Andrews; e. Anthony Quinn.

3. Name the three actors who broke into the vault in "The Asphalt Jungle":
   a. Sam Jaffe; b. James Whitmore; c. Louis Calhern; d. Sterling Hayden; e. Anthony Caruso.

4. Name three of the Dead End Kids, as they appeared in "Dead End":
   a. Bobby Jordan; b. Mickey Knox; c. Bernard Punsley; d. Billy Benedict; e. Huntz Hall.

5. Name the three films in which James Dean was featured:
   a. "East of Eden"; b. "Giant"; c. "The Young Stranger"; d. "Wild River"; e. "Rebel Without a Cause."

6. Name three of the following actors who were part of the original "Magnificent Seven" (American version):
   a. Charles Coburn; b. Brad Dexter; c. Robert Vaughn; d. Horst Buchholz; e. Eli Wallach.

7. Of the five listed, name the three of Shakespeare's plays which have been filmed:
   a. "Richard III"; b. "Love's Labour's Lost"; c. "Henry V"; d. "Coriolanus"; e. "Othello."

8. Give the first names of the three Ritz brothers:
   a. Harry; b. Fritzie; c. Frankie; d. Al; e. Jimmy.

9. Name three biographical roles played by Marlon Brando:
   a. Emiliano Zapata; b. Thomas Watson; c. Marc Antony; d. Napoleon; e. Disraeli.

10. Give us the first names of the three Lane sisters:
    a. Priscilla; b. Lily; c. Lola; d. Rosemary; e. Lois.

————**points**

(*Answers on page 278*)

MORE LINK-UPS—BUFFS AND DUFFERS

Let's relax for a moment, and have an exercise for Buffs and Duffers alike—no special versions. Okay? We're sure you remember how to play this. Recall the example of

Benjamin FRANKLIN Roosevelt? . . .

Just supply the missing name in Column Two which will serve as a correct surname for the actor or actress suggested in Column One, as well as serving as the appropriate first name for the actor or actress suggested in Column Three.

Put your mind to the task and take away 5 points for each correct answer.

1. Trevor _____ Duff
2. Doris _____ Digges
3. Robert _____ Taylor
4. Donna _____ Hadley
5. Gladys _____ Brent
6. Gene _____ Fitzgerald
7. Tony _____ Williams
8. Jean _____ Lake
9. Robert _____ Foster
10. Robert _____ Holmes

_____ points

(*Answers on page 279*)

AND YET MORE LINK-UPS—BUFFS AND DUFFERS

You did that so well, we think you're hot! And when you're hot—well, you know . . . So while the time is ripe, strike again—both Buffs and Duffers—and grab 5 points for each correct link-up. That's 50 for the quiz, but get 'em all—and double your score!

1. Jessie _____ Forbes
2. Edna May _____ Hardy
3. Warren _____ Gargan
4. H. B. _____ Oland
5. Billy _____ Roland

6. Kim _____ Ridges
7. Douglas _____ Powell
8. Mary _____ Aherne
9. Charlotte _____ Wilcoxon
10. Alice _____ Emerson

_____**points**

(*Answers on page 279*)

ODD MAN OUT #2

In each sequence of names below, all of the items included—save *one*—belong because of some common characteristic with the others. The common characteristic can be as far-reaching as parts played, specialties, color of eyes, origin, or any other factor of commonality. Your task is to eliminate the item which is therefore incompatible with the others. Add 10 points to your score for each "odd man" you correctly toss out!

1. John Wayne, Marc Lawrence, Donna Reed, Harry Langdon.
2. Don Ameche, Douglas Fairbanks, Walter Abel, Lex Barker, Gene Kelly.
3. Ronald Colman, William Powell, Gary Cooper, John Gilbert, Spencer Tracy.
4. Stephen Basustow, Ub Iwerks, Douglas Shearer, Max Fleischer, Walt Disney.
5. Dana Andrews, Kirk Douglas, Barry Fitzgerald, George Sanders, Frank McHugh.
6. Todd-AO, Cinerama, Panavision, VistaVision, CinemaScope.
7. "Wilson," "Crossfire," "The Snake Pit," "Gentleman's Agreement," "Pinky."
8. Humphrey Bogart, Cornel Wilde, Paul Muni, Joseph Schildkraut, Errol Flynn.
9. John Garfield, Lee J. Cobb, Walter Brennan, Franchot Tone, Luther Adler.
10. Vivien Leigh, Joan Crawford, Bette Davis, Luise Rainer.

_____**points**

(*Answers on page 280*)

ODD MAN OUT #2—DUFFERS' TEE

This form of ODD MAN OUT is a little different from the one you played before. Below we list a common trait or characteristic—then provide a number of names. Your task is to select the singular item from the group which does not have the commonality of the others. Take 10 points for each "odd man" you correctly toss out!

1. Which one was *not* born in Iowa:
   John Wayne, Marc Lawrence, Donna Reed, or Harry Langdon?

2. Which one did *not* play D'Artagnan in some version of "The Three Musketeers":
   Don Ameche, Douglas Fairbanks, Walter Abel, Lex Barker, or Gene Kelly?

3. Which one of the following did *not* appear first in silent films:
   Ronald Colman, William Powell, Gary Cooper, John Gilbert, or Spencer Tracy?

4. Which one was *not* a specialist in animated cartoon work:
   Stephen Basustow, Ub Iwerks, Douglas Shearer, Max Fleischer, or Walt Disney?

5. Which one did *not* have a brother who *also* worked in films:
   Dana Andrews, Kirk Douglas, Barry Fitzgerald, George Sanders, or Frank McHugh?

6. Which one of the following wide-screen processes operates with *more* than one projector required:
   Todd-AO, Cinerama, Panavision, VistaVision, or CinemaScope?

7. Which one of the following "socially significant" films was *not* a 20th Century-Fox production:
   "Wilson," "Crossfire," "The Snake Pit," "Gentleman's Agreement," or "Pinky"?

8. Which one of the following *never* played a biographical role:
   Humphrey Bogart, Cornel Wilde, Paul Muni, Joseph Schildkraut, or Errol Flynn?

9. Which one of the following was never a member of New York's Group Theatre:
   John Garfield, Lee J. Cobb, Walter Brennan, Franchot Tone, or Luther Adler?

10. Which one of the following won only *one* Oscar, whereas the others each won two:
    Vivien Leigh, Joan Crawford, Bette Davis, or Luise Rainer?

_____ **points**

(*Answers on page 280*)

MOVIE-MAKERS' CRISSCROSS

The MOVIE-MAKERS' CRISSCROSS should be simple enough for you. To complete it, merely fill in the blanks with the correct surname—and be sure the one you select is of the proper length. Complete it correctly and everything interlocks—including 500 points for your score. Sorry, but we're *not* supplying you with the names to be used for the fill-ins. Your movie expertise must do that. We have, however, given you the hints which should enable you to identify the movie-makers. Decipher the clue, identify the name, and the crisscross should be a cinch. We've even given you a start by filling in the name of that venerated cinemaster Melvin Harlonel! You say you've never heard of Melvin Harlonel? Hmmmm.

Three-Letter Names
A major studio still bears his name.
Tony was part of the act.

Four-Letter Names
She and sister Dorothy worked for D.W.
Once, he traded his saddle for a chariot.

Five-Letter Names
Frank lost a horizon.
His friends at 20th called him Andre.
He was part owner of the first California-made feature, "The Squaw Man."
L.B.
He and his *frères* were responsible for one of the first "foreign films."
He was the *S* in Essanay.
His was the name of royalty.
A big little man with Paramount, he said: "The public is never wrong."

Six-Letter Names
When Clarence Nash squawked to him, he was a happy employer.
Good Night, Sweet Prince.
"Hell's Angels."
His was probably the first American crime picture.
A director, he married Lillian Burns.
His nom de plume was Melvin Crossman.

Seven-Letter Names
He came to us from a British music hall troupe.
He parted the Red Sea—twice.
He changed his name from Goldfish.
He was the little big man of Universal, Uncle Carl.

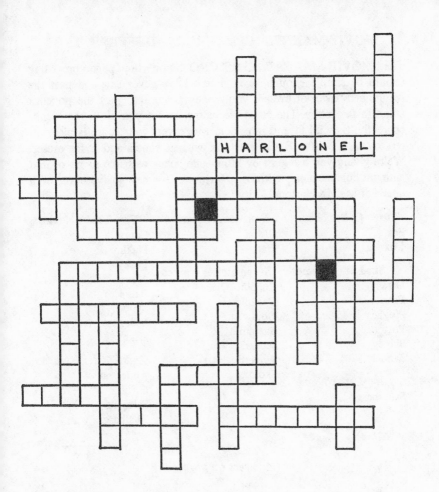

Nick or Joe.
He hired Gloria and Carole and Fatty and Bing.
He and Darryl F. had a falling-out.

Eight-Letter Names

He was the *A* in Essanay.
Billy Bitzer did his bidding.
Lewis, Myron, or David O.
They called him "genius"—Norma called him "dear."

Nine-Letter Name

B.P., or Budd.

(500)_____points?

(Answers on page 280)

MOVIE-MAKERS' CRISSCROSS—DUFFERS' TEE

The MOVIE-MAKERS' CRISSCROSS on the page preceding should be simple enough, even if you have never snapped past the Midnight Movie, or even if you've never ventured past the popcorn stand in the lobby. The clues are below, and if you fill in the blanks correctly, they all fit and interlock. Moreover, your score is also fatter, by 300 points. Better start off with a pencil and a fat eraser. We're giving you a leg up by filling one space with the name of that eminent cinema pioneer Melvin Harlonel. You say you've never even *heard* of Melvin Harlonel? Pity.

Three-Letter Names	Four-Letter Names	Five-Letter Names
Fox	Gish	Capra
Mix	Hart	Hakim
		Lasky
Six-Letter Names	Seven-Letter Names	Mayer
Disney	Chaplin	Pathé
Fowler	DeMille	Spoor
Hughes	Goldwyn	Vidor
Porter	Laemmle	Zukor
Sidney	Schenck	
Zanuck	Sennett	Eight-Letter Names
	Skouras	Anderson
Nine-Letter Name		Griffith
Schulberg		Selznick
		Thalberg

_____points

(Answers on page 281)

IMPROPER NAMES

When you stop to think about it, many movie personalities were known only by their nicknames. They retained their proper surnames, but their renown with the movie-going public was limited to the improper nickname. If the correct first name was mounted on the marquee, odds are that the majority of ticket buyers would not know whom the exhibitor was talking about. Below, we've listed a number of movie personalities who fall into this category. We ask you to give us the correct first name. Some are easy—and some are very difficult. But we'll award 15 points for each correct name you get.

1.	Bing Crosby	_____ Crosby
2.	Gabby Hayes	_____ Hayes
3.	Slim Summerville	_____ Summerville
4.	Bud Abbott	_____ Abbott
5.	Wild Bill Elliott	_____ Elliott
6.	Fuzzy Knight	_____ Knight
7.	Buddy Ebsen	_____ Ebsen
8.	Red Skelton	_____ Skelton
9.	Fatty Arbuckle	_____ Arbuckle
10.	Harpo Marx	_____ Marx
11.	Chico Marx	_____ Marx
12.	Groucho Marx	_____ Marx
13.	Hoot Gibson	_____ Gibson
14.	Buster Keaton	_____ Keaton
15.	Spike Jones	_____ Jones
16.	Buck Jones	_____ Jones

_____ **points**

(*Answers on page 282*)

IMPROPER NAMES—DUFFERS' TEE

When you stop to think about it, many movie personalities were known only by their nicknames. They retained their original surnames, but their renown with the movie-going public was limited to the audience's knowledge of the improper nickname. Below, in Column One, we list sixteen personalities who fall into this category. In Column Two, we list, out of order, the correct first names. Your task is to select the appropriate proper name for matching with the personality listed in Column One. You may take 15 points for each correct pairing.

1. Bing Crosby	a. Julius
2. Gabby Hayes	b. Charles
3. Slim Summerville	c. Richard
4. Bud Abbott	d. J. Forrest

71

5. Wild Bill Elliott	e. Roscoe
6. Fuzzy Knight	f. Harry
7. Buddy Ebsen	g. Leonard
8. Red Skelton	h. Lindley Armstrong
9. Fatty Arbuckle	i. George
10. Harpo Marx	j. Joseph
11. Chico Marx	k. William
12. Groucho Marx	l. Edward
13. Hoot Gibson	m. Gordon
14. Buster Keaton	n. Christian Rudolf
15. Spike Jones	o. George
16. Buck Jones	p. Adolph

And because you've been good guys and haven't squawked about being Duffers, here's one chance we *didn't* give to the Buffs—and it's your chance to surge ahead!

Tell us Spanky McFarland's proper name (sorry, no choices) and you can triple the score you've just earned on this exercise:
_____ McFarland

_____points (× 3?)

(*Answers on page 282*)

WILD CARD—BUFFS AND DUFFERS

These are questions selected at random—and they are for both Buffs and Duffers. You may ignore them, if you wish—and proceed to the next set of questions. These are included to give you a chance to sweeten your score. The questions may seem obscure—but with television giving us great old films, you may have seen some of these very films in the last few days. If you have been doing the Buffs' version, then take 15 points for each correct answer you get; but if you've been driving off the Duffers' Tee—and you are on your honor here—you may take 30 points for each correct answer!

1. "The boy next door"—give the title of the film which this phrase brings to mind.

2. Assuming you have the film title of Question One nailed down, give us *the address* of "the boy next door."

3. Two sets of real-life fathers and sons appeared in a film which dealt with Humphrey Bogart seeking gold in the remote mountains of Mexico. Who were they?

4. Give us the correct—and by this we mean *the exact*—title of the film referred to in Question Three.

5. One of the three films below was the first feature film to play the Radio City Music Hall on its opening in January 1933. Was it:
        a. "The Bitter Tea of General Yen";
        b. "Becky Sharp"; or
        c. "Barbary Coast"?

6. Mrs. Richard M. Nixon is purported to have worked as an extra in one of the three films mentioned in Question Five. Which one was it?

7. The little girl who danced the cakewalk with Judy Garland in "Meet Me in St. Louis"—give us her real-life name as well as her character name in the movie.

8. What dead animal was buried in the garden in "Sunset Boulevard"?

9. From the following list of names, select those which were the names of the Seven Dwarfs:
    a. Bashful   d. Stuffy   g. Happy   j. Sleepy
    b. Punchy   e. Doc   h. Sneezy   k. Rusty
    c. Dopey   f. Wacky   i. Grumpy   l. Pinky
    (*And you must get all seven . . .*)

10. Assuming you selected the Seven Dwarfs correctly in Question Nine, you are left with five character names which were *not* those of Disney's Seven Dwarfs. Yet, one screen comedian portrayed those five characters you're left with. Name him.

_____**points**

(*Answers on page 282*)

HEY, DADDY!

In each of the films below, a father-offspring relationship was evident. We provide the title and the actor or actress who portrayed the son or daughter. Your job: Tell us the name of the actor who was the cinematic father. Take 10 points for each correct answer.

1. "The Barretts of Wimpole
   Street"   Norma Shearer   _____
2. "Death of a Salesman"   Kevin McCarthy   _____
3. "Never Too Late"   Connie Stevens   _____
4. "Captains Courageous"   Freddie Bartholomew   _____
5. "The Actress"   Jean Simmons   _____
6. "Prince of Players"   Richard Burton   _____
7. "Captains Courageous"   Mickey Rooney   _____
8. "Gone with the Wind"   Vivien Leigh   _____
9. "Shane"   Brandon de Wilde   _____
10. "Hud"   Paul Newman   _____

_____points

(Answers on page 283)

HEY, DADDY—DUFFERS' TEE

In each of the films below, a father-offspring relationship was evident. We have provided the actor or actress who portrayed the son or daughter, and the title of the film in which this relationship existed. You have a multiple choice in Column Three, and your task is to select the actor who portrayed the father. 10 points for each correct selection.

1. "The Barretts of Wimpole Street"	Norma Shearer	a. Melville Cooper b. Charles Laughton c. Montagu Love
2. "Death of a Salesman"	Kevin McCarthy	a. Lee J. Cobb b. Thomas Mitchell c. Fredric March
3. "Never Too Late"	Connie Stevens	a. Paul Ford b. Paul Cavanaugh c. Wallace Ford
4. "Captains Courageous"	Freddie Bartholomew	a. Melvyn Douglas b. Lionel Barrymore c. Spencer Tracy
5. "The Actress"	Jean Simmons	a. Louis Calhern b. Walter Pidgeon c. Spencer Tracy

6. "Prince of Players"	Richard Burton	a. Torin Thatcher b. Sir Cedric Hardwicke c. Raymond Massey
7. "Captains Courageous"	Mickey Rooney	a. Lionel Barrymore b. Melvyn Douglas c. John Carradine
8. "Gone with the Wind"	Vivien Leigh	a. Edward Arnold b. Thomas Mitchell c. Grant Mitchell
9. "Shane"	Brandon de Wilde	a. Alan Ladd b. Elisha Cook, Jr. c. Van Heflin
10. "Hud"	Paul Newman	a. Melvyn Douglas b. Myron McCormick c. Ed Begley

_____points

(*Answers on page 283*)

TELL US WHO ⚹2

This exercise, TELL US WHO ⚹2, is played the same as the earlier TELL US WHO. We list below two incidents, or plot points, from two films in which the same player appeared. We ask you to identify the player—and if you correctly identify him, or her, you may take 15 points. Moreover, if you can also identify *both* films which are suggested in each question, you may add an additional 10 points for that question. Potential on this one: 250 points.

1. He threatened to throw himself from the top of City Hall, and— along with Ernest Truex—discovered spaghetti and firecrackers in ancient China.

2. He danced with Betsy Blair, and was thrown through a screen door by Spencer Tracy.

3. He attempted to jump a motorcycle over a barbed wire barricade, and engaged in a tire-screeching automobile chase through the streets of San Francisco.

4. He fenced with Eugene Pallette, and was sentenced to beheading at the order of Bette Davis.

5. His prize-fight career was managed by Adolphe Menjou, and he—along with Mickey Rooney—was shot to death in a North Korean gully.

6. She negotiated a divorce while Richard Basehart threatened to jump from the ledge of a tall building, and daringly invaded the apartment of Raymond Burr to search for clues to a suspected murder.

7. He was a Treasury agent who arrested Edmund Gwenn for counterfeiting, and later machine-gunned Paul Scofield alongside a crippled freight train in wartime France.

8. She lunched with her agent, Red Buttons, and then became the wife of retired fur trapper James Stewart.

9. He helped John Wayne and Richard Widmark defend the Alamo, and then committed suicide after shooting Angela Lansbury and James Gregory.

10. On the eve of attaining stardom in show business, he crippled his hand to avoid being drafted, and later he danced in a Mexican cantina on Olvera Street with child performer Sharon McManus.

———points

(*Answers on page 283*)

TELL US WHO #2—DUFFERS' TEE

As before, we have listed two incidents, or plot points, from two films in which the same player appeared. From your memory, tell us the actor or actress we're seeking. We have provided a list of answers, out of order, in Column Two. So for each player you can match with the incidents from his or her cinematic career, you will receive 15 points. If you can come up with the titles of both films suggested in each case—and it must be *both*—you may add another 15 points to your score for that question. That's a possible 30 points per question, or a total possibility of 300 points on this quiz.

1. He threatened to throw himself from the top of City Hall, and—along with Ernest Truex—discovered spaghetti and firecrackers in ancient China.   a. Errol Flynn

2. He danced with Betsy Blair, and was thrown through a screen door by Spencer Tracy.

    b. Laurence Harvey

3. He attempted to jump a motorcycle over a barbed wire barricade, and engaged in a tire-screeching auto chase through the streets of San Francisco.

    c. Burt Lancaster

4. He fenced with Eugene Pallette, and was sentenced to beheading at the order of Bette Davis.

    d. Carroll Baker

5. His prize-fight career was managed by Adolphe Menjou, and he—along with Mickey Rooney—was shot to death in a North Korean gully.

    e. Gary Cooper

6. She negotiated a divorce while Richard Basehart threatened to jump from the ledge of a tall building, and daringly invaded Raymond Burr's apartment to search for clues to a suspected murder.

    f. Gene Kelly

7. He was a Treasury agent who arrested Edmund Gwenn for counterfeiting, and later machine-gunned Paul Scofield alongside a crippled freight train in wartime France.

    g. Steve McQueen

8. She lunched with her agent, Red Buttons, and then became the wife of retired fur trapper James Stewart.

    h. Grace Kelly

9. He helped John Wayne and Richard Widmark defend the Alamo, and then committed suicide after shooting Angela Lansbury and James Gregory.

    i. William Holden

10. On the eve of attaining stardom in show business, he crippled his hand to avoid being drafted, and later he danced in a Mexican cantina on Olvera Street with child performer Sharon McManus.

    j. Ernest Borgnine

_____points

(*Answers on page 283*)

ON THE SIDE OF THE LAW

Below we list a number of well-known movie sleuths. We also supply the titles of films in which these master crime fighters appeared. And we ask you to tell us who played the detective in each film cited. Take 10 points for each correct answer.

1. Sam Spade	"The Maltese Falcon"	_____	_____
2. Mr. Wong	"Doomed to Die"	_____	_____
3. Mike Hammer	"Kiss Me Deadly"	_____	_____
4. Boston Blackie	"Meet Boston Blackie"	_____	_____
5. Philo Vance	"The Kennel Murder Case"	_____	_____
6. Perry Mason	"The Case of the Howling Dog"	_____	_____
7. Nick Carter	"Nick Carter, Master Detective"	_____	_____
8. Michael Shayne	"Michael Shayne, Private Detective"	_____	_____
9. Nero Wolfe	"Meet Nero Wolfe"	_____	_____
10. Father Brown	"Father Brown, Detective"	_____	_____
11. Inspector Maigret	"Man on the Eiffel Tower"	_____	_____
12. Hercule Poirot	"The Alphabet Murders"	_____	_____
13. Nancy Drew	"Nancy Drew, Detective"	_____	_____
14. Miss Marple	"Murder, She Said"	_____	_____
15. Matt Helm	"The Silencers"	_____	_____
16. The Lone Wolf	"The Lone Wolf Spy Hunt"	_____	_____
17. Inspector Clouseau	"A Shot in the Dark"	_____	_____
18. Derek Flint	"Our Man Flint"	_____	_____
19. Nick Charles	"The Thin Man"	_____	_____
20. Mr. Moto	"Thank You, Mr. Moto"	_____	_____

_____points

(*Answers on page 284*)

ON THE SIDE OF THE LAW—DUFFERS' TEE

Below we list a number of well-known sleuths, and titles of films in which these masterminds appeared. In Column Three, we supply a list of players who portrayed these famous movie detectives—albeit out of order—and we ask you to match the player with the sleuth. Take 10 points for each correct pairing.

1. Sam Spade	"The Maltese Falcon"	a. Warren William
2. Mr. Wong	"Doomed to Die"	b. Walter Connolly
3. Mike Hammer	"Kiss Me Deadly"	c. William Powell
4. Boston Blackie	"Meet Boston Blackie"	d. Boris Karloff
5. Philo Vance	"The Kennel Murder Case"	e. Peter Lorre
6. Perry Mason	"The Case of the Howling Dog"	f. Margaret Rutherford
7. Nick Carter	"Nick Carter, Master Detective"	g. Edward Arnold
8. Michael Shayne	"Michael Shayne, Private Detective"	h. Humphrey Bogart
9. Nero Wolfe	"Meet Nero Wolfe"	i. Peter Sellers
10. Father Brown	"Father Brown, Detective"	j. Bonita Granville
11. Inspector Maigret	"Man on the Eiffel Tower"	k. Chester Morris
12. Hercule Poirot	"The Alphabet Murders"	l. Charles Laughton
13. Nancy Drew	"Nancy Drew, Detective"	m. Warren William
14. Miss Marple	"Murder, She Said"	n. William Powell
15. Matt Helm	"The Silencers"	o. Lloyd Nolan
16. The Lone Wolf	"The Lone Wolf Spy Hunt"	p. James Coburn
17. Inspector Clouseau	"A Shot in the Dark"	q. Walter Pidgeon
18. Derek Flint	"Our Man Flint"	r. Ralph Meeker
19. Nick Charles	"The Thin Man"	s. Tony Randall
20. Mr. Moto	"Thank You, Mr. Moto"	t. Dean Martin

_____points

(Answers on page 284)

MORE "NAME THE STAR"

As before, we've listed on each line below two characters played by the same actor or actress. Either character name should be sufficient to jog your memory and spark your identification of the star we're seeking. But if our clues prove too obscure for you, feel free to move on to the Duffers' Tee on the page following. However, if you are that confident that you're staying with the Buffs' version, you'll be able to add 10 points to your score for each correct answer. Remember—we're seeking *only* the name of the star, and *not* the titles of the films represented.

1. The Dauphin   Lieut. Barney Greenwald
2. Blanche Hudson   Crystal Allen
3. Danny Wilson   Bennett Marco
4. Genl. Winfield Scott   The Dutchman
5. Patsy Barton   Irene Hoffman
6. David Larrabee   Joe Bonaparte
7. Dave Tolliver   Pres Dillard
8. Dan Hilliard   President Jordan Lyman
9. Wolf Larsen   Barton Keyes
10. C. C. Baxter   Harry Hinkle

———————points

(*Answers on page 285*)

MORE "NAME THE STAR"—DUFFERS' TEE

Well, look who's here. If the characters above didn't ring a bell loudly enough for you to identify the star, here are some more parts played by the stars we're asking you to identify. For those of you who came directly to the Duffers' Tee, the characters listed on each line below are very familiar ones, we think, and both were portrayed by the same star. Merely tell us the names of the stars suggested— don't bother with the titles of the features—and add 5 points to your score for each correct identification.

1. Henri de Toulouse-Lautrec   Cyrano de Bergerac
2. Flaemmchen   Mildred Pierce
3. Johnny Concho   Angelo Maggio

4. Señor Farrari   Kasper Gutman
5. Lily Mars   Esther Blodgett
6. Joe Gillis   Sefton
7. Chad Hanna   Tom Joad
8. Count Vronsky   Robert Browning
9. Johnny Rocco   Dr. Paul Ehrlich
10. Felix Unger   Ensign Frank Pulver

_____points

(*Answers on page 285*)

FILMS IN COMMON

In each coupling of Column One below, we list two films which had a similarity in plot points. For example, it might be said that "Mutiny on the Bounty" and "South Pacific" had a similarity by virtue of their geographical settings. In Column Two, we list two stars of a third picture which had the same commonality as the films in Column One. From these clues, you are to tell us the title we are seeking. In the example above, we might continue on with a listing of Max von Sydow and Julie Andrews as the clue for the *third* film. From the clue of these two stars, and the South Seas setting, you'd know the missing title to be "Hawaii." Take 10 points for ferreting out the common characteristic of the following questions—plus another 10 points for each correct title you come up with. Potential: 20 points a question, or a total of 200 points.

1. "Judith" "Exodus"	Kirk Douglas, Yul Brynner
2. "Little Old New York" "The Story of Alexander Graham Bell"	Spencer Tracy, Rita Johnson
3. "Suez" "Union Pacific"	Jack Hawkins, James Robertson Justice
4. "Leave Her to Heaven" "Black Widow"	Joan Crawford, Ann Blyth
5. "The Adventures of Marco Polo" "The Barbarian and the Geisha"	Tyrone Power, Cecile Aubry

6. "Madame Curie"   Edward G. Robinson, Ruth
   "The Story of Louis Pasteur"   Gordon
7. "The Prisoner of Shark   Frank Sinatra, Sterling Hayden
   Island"
   "We Were Strangers"
8. "Angel on My Shoulder"   Robert Montgomery, Claude Rains
   "The Angel Levine"
9. "The Bridge on the River   George Segal, Tom Courtenay
   Kwai"
   "Stalag 17"
10. "Green Dolphin Street"   Clark Gable, Jeanette MacDonald
    "The Hurricane"

_____points

(*Answers on page 286*)

FILMS IN COMMON—DUFFERS' TEE

In each question of Column One below, we list two films which had a similarity in plot points. For example, it might be said that "Hawaii" and "Mutiny on the Bounty" had a similarity because of the South Seas settings. In each question below, we ask you to determine the commonality, and then select the film title in Column Two which had the greatest similarity to those films of Column One. Take 10 points for each correct answer.

1. "Judith"   a. "Panic in the Streets"
   "Exodus"   b. "Cast a Giant Shadow"
            c. "Wild Is the Wind"

2. "Little Old New York"   a. "No Way to Treat a Lady"
   "The Story of Alexander   b. "The Magic Box"
   Graham Bell"   c. "The Professionals"

3. "Suez"   a. "Land of the Pharaohs"
   "Union Pacific"   b. "The Ten Commandments"
            c. "Wind Across the Everglades"

4. "Leave Her to Heaven"   a. "Cape Fear"
   "Mildred Pierce"   b. "Black Widow"
            c. "Operation Terror"

5. "The Adventures of Marco Polo"

   "The Barbarian and the Geisha"

   a. "Blood and Sand"
   b. "Seven Days' Leave"
   c. "The Black Rose"

6. "Madame Curie"

   "The Story of Louis Pasteur"

   a. "The Amazing Dr. Clitterhouse"
   b. "Doctor in the House"
   c. "Dr. Ehrlich's Magic Bullet"

7. "The Prisoner of Shark Island"

   "We Were Strangers"

   a. "Glory Alley"
   b. "Suddenly"
   c. "State of the Union"

8. "Angel on My Shoulder"

   "The Angel Levine"

   a. "Here Comes Mr. Jordan"
   b. "Nightmare Alley"
   c. "Lucky Jordan"

9. "The Bridge on the River Kwai"

   "Stalag 17"

   a. "What Price Glory?"
   b. "Devil's Canyon"
   c. "King Rat"

10. "Green Dolphin Street"

    "The Hurricane"

   a. "San Francisco"
   b. "A Tale of Two Cities"
   c. "Written on the Wind"

_____points

(Answers on page 287)

LA RONDE

It is possible to find a chain of connection between a star and almost any other star by films in which they have appeared. For example, should you want to link Humphrey Bogart with Robert Young—not a likely pairing, you'll admit—you might trace a linkage via this route:

Humphrey Bogart appeared with Ingrid Bergman ("Casablanca") who played with Gregory Peck ("Spellbound") who co-starred with Dorothy McGuire ("Gentleman's Agreement") who starred opposite Robert Young ("The Enchanted Cottage").

We admit that's a little like a Tinkers-to-Evers-to-Chance combination, but if you know your films, you can connect virtually anybody. Sometimes you can lead yourself right back to your starting point—a complete circle—as we have done in the diagram on the page following, which we have called "La Ronde."

To complete the wheel, supply the appropriate titles for the symbols—A through L—we've designated. Do this completely and you'll score 100 points. One rule is that no title may be used more than once. So be careful!

A. Robert Taylor and Greta
   Garbo: "_____"

B. Greta Garbo and Charles
   Boyer: "_____"

C. Charles Boyer and Hedy
   Lamarr: "_____"

D. Hedy Lamarr and Clark
   Gable: "_____"

E. Clark Gable and Grace Kelly: "_____"

F. Grace Kelly and Gary Cooper: "_____"

G. Gary Cooper and Audrey
   Hepburn: "_____"

H. Audrey Hepburn and
   Humphrey Bogart: "_____"

I. Humphrey Bogart and June
   Allyson: "_____"

J. June Allyson and William
   Holden: "_____"

K. William Holden and Barbara
   Stanwyck: "_____"

L. Barbara Stanwyck and Robert
   Taylor: "_____"

_____points

(Answers on page 288)

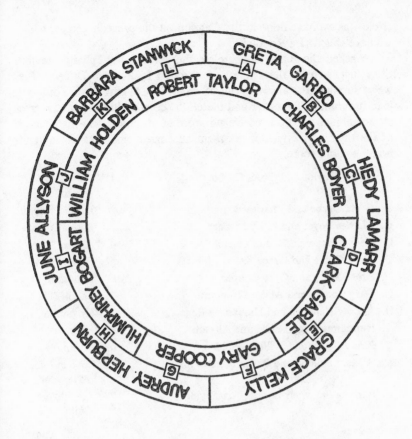

A (Greta Garbo)
B (Charles Boyer)
C (Hedy Lamarr)
D (Clark Gable)
E (Grace Kelly)
F (Gary Cooper)
G (Humphrey Bogart)
H (Audrey Hepburn)
I (June Allyson)
J (William Holden)
K (Barbara Stanwyck)
L (Robert Taylor)

LA RONDE—DUFFERS' TEE

It is possible to find a chain of connection between a star and almost any other star by films in which they have appeared. For example, should you want to link Humphrey Bogart and Robert Young—not a likely pairing, we admit—you might trace a linkage via this route:

Humphrey Bogart appeared with Ingrid Bergman ("Casablanca") who played with Gregory Peck ("Spellbound") who co-starred with Dorothy McGuire ("Gentleman's Agreement") who starred opposite Robert Young ("The Enchanted Cottage").

We admit that's a little like a Tinkers-to-Evers-to-Chance combination, but if you know your films, you can connect virtually anybody. Sometimes you can lead yourself right back to the start—a complete circle—as we have done in the diagram on the preceding page, which we have called "La Ronde."

We asked the Buffs to complete the wheel by supplying the film titles suggested by the symbols A through L. For the Duffers' Tee, we've supplied the answers, out of order, in Column Two. Your task is to unscramble the order and match the correct title with the correct star combination. You receive no score at all unless you match each of the titles correctly, but get them all correct and you can add 50 points to your score.

A. Robert Taylor and Greta Garbo

B. Greta Garbo and Charles Boyer
C. Charles Boyer and Hedy Lamarr
D. Hedy Lamarr and Clark Gable
E. Clark Gable and Grace Kelly
F. Grace Kelly and Gary Cooper
G. Gary Cooper and Audrey Hepburn
H. Audrey Hepburn and Humphrey Bogart
I. Humphrey Bogart and June Allyson
J. June Allyson and William Holden
K. William Holden and Barbara Stanwyck

L. Barbara Stanwyck and Robert Taylor

1. "This Is My Affair"

2. "Battle Circus"
3. "Boom Town"
4. "Algiers"
5. "Golden Boy"
6. "Conquest"
7. "Camille"
8. "Mogambo"
9. "High Noon"
10. "Sabrina"
11. "Love in the Afternoon"

12. "Executive Suite"

_____points

(*Answers on page 288*)

MORE RE-DOS YET

By now, we presume you know what we mean by "re-dos." Well, here are some more of them. But this time, we have a slight twist. Heretofore, we've given you the film title and stars of an *earlier* version, and have asked you to provide the star combinations who played the same parts in the *later* version. In this exercise, which is played essentially the same as the other "re-do" quizzes you've done, the star combinations listed in Column Two *might* represent a *later* version of the film, while the star combinations we're seeking in

Column Three *could* then represent an *earlier* version of the film. The factor which has not changed—and that which makes "re-dos" what they are—is that the film title did not change from version to version. So add the names indicated by initials in Column Three, and take 15 points for each name supplied.

1. "One Sunday Afternoon"	Gary Cooper	D_____	M_____
	Fay Wray	D_____	M_____
2. "Swiss Family Robinson"	Thomas Mitchell	J_____	M_____
	Edna Best	D_____	M_____
3. "The Adventures of Tom Sawyer"	Jack Pickford	T_____	K_____
	Edythe Chapman	M_____	R_____
4. "The Desert Song"	Dennis Morgan	J_____	B_____
	Irene Manning	C_____	K_____
5. "Ben-Hur"	Ramon Novarro	C_____	H_____
	May McAvoy	H_____	H_____
6. "Little Women"	Peter Lawford	P_____	L_____
	Janet Leigh	F_____	D_____
7. "The Maltese Falcon"	Ricardo Cortez	H_____	B_____
	Bebe Daniels	M_____	A_____
8. "Dr. Jekyll and Mr. Hyde"	Spencer Tracy	F_____	M_____
	Ingrid Bergman	M_____	H_____
9. "Raffles"	Ronald Colman	D_____	N_____
	Kay Francis	O_____	d_____
10. "Smilin' Through"	Brian Aherne	L_____	H_____
	Jeanette MacDonald	N_____	S_____

_____points

(Answers on page 288)

MORE RE-DOS YET—DUFFERS' TEE

By now, we presume you know what we mean by "re-dos." Well, here are some more of them. But this time, we have given them a slight twist. As before, Column One presents the title of the film re-done, which did not change. Column Two presents a star combination of that film, while Column Three represents, out of order, a star combination who took the same parts in another version of the film.

Unlike earlier "re-dos," the star combinations in Column Three could be from an *earlier or later* version of the film. So select the appropriate combination from Column Three which matches correctly with the title and combination of Columns One and Two. Remember, in this one, the vintage of the "re-do" is of no particular help to you. As before, take 15 points for each correct pairing.

1. "One Sunday Afternoon"	Gary Cooper Fay Wray	a. Paul Lukas Frances Dee
2. "Swiss Family Robinson"	Thomas Mitchell Edna Best	b. Charlton Heston Haya Harareet
3. "The Adventures of Tom Sawyer"	Jack Pickford Edythe Chapman	c. Fredric March Miriam Hopkins
4. "The Desert Song"	Dennis Morgan Irene Manning	d. David Niven Olivia de Havilland
5. "Ben-Hur"	Ramon Novarro May McAvoy	e. Leslie Howard Norma Shearer
6. "Little Women"	Peter Lawford Janet Leigh	f. Dennis Morgan Dorothy Malone
7. "The Maltese Falcon"	Ricardo Cortez Bebe Daniels	g. Tommy Kelly May Robson
8. "Dr. Jekyll and Mr. Hyde"	Spencer Tracy Ingrid Bergman	h. Humphrey Bogart Mary Astor
9. "Raffles"	Ronald Colman Kay Francis	i. John Mills Dorothy McGuire
10. "Smilin' Through"	Brian Aherne Jeanette MacDonald	j. John Boles Carlotta Kay

———points

(*Answers on page 288*)

ONCE MORE, WHO IS IT?

Again, you only have to fill in the name of the actor or actress who portrayed the character listed in Column One. All of these characters are from various "series" films. Getting all of the names correct, and

88

locating the right vertical column, will reveal to you the name of a famous movie character, *not* from a series. Once you ascertain the name of this character, you must then tell us the name of the star who portrayed this mystery character. Do it—and add 50 points to your total!

Scattergood Baines	_ _ _	_ _ _ _ _ _
Dr. Kildare	_ _ _	_ _ _ _ _
Dr. Watson	_ _ _ _	_ _ _ _ _
Dick Tracy	_ _ _ _	_ _ _ _
Bomba	_ _ _ _ _	_ _ _ _ _ _ _ _
Flash Gordon	_ _ _ _	_ _ _ _ _
James Bond	_ _ _	_ _ _ _ _ _ _
Inspector Lestrade	_ _ _ _ _	_ _ _ _
Baby Dumpling	_ _ _ _	_ _ _ _ _
Hopalong Cassidy	_ _ _ _ _ _	_ _ _ _
Mr. Moto	_ _ _ _	_ _ _ _ _
Charlie Chan	_ _ _ _ _	_ _ _ _ _ _
Ma Kettle	_ _ _ _ _ _ _	_ _ _ _
Larry Talbot	_ _ _	_ _ _ _ _ _

And the name of the star is: _ _ _ _ _ _ _ _ _ _ _ _ _ _ _ **!**

_ _ _ _ _ _ _**points**

(*Answers on page 289*)

ONCE MORE, WHO IS IT?—DUFFERS' TEE

Again, you only have to fill in the name of the actor or actress who portrayed the character in Column One. All of these characters are from well-known "series" films. Once you've completed this, elect the proper vertical column and you will find revealed to you the name of a well-known character from the Samuel Goldwyn film "Dead End." By telling us the name of the star who portrayed this well-known character you will add 25 points to your score. But since you're a Duffer, you may also find the name of the star by unscrambling the key letters we've earmarked for you.

89

Scattergood Baines   ()_() _ _ _ _ _ _
Dr. Kildare   _ _ _   _ _ _ _ _
Dr. Watson   _ _ _ _ _   _ _ ()_ _
Dick Tracy   _ _ _ _ () _ _ () _
Bomba   _ _ _ _ _ _   _ _ () _ _
Flash Gordon   _ _ _ _ _   _ _ _ () _ _
James Bond   _ _ _ _ _ _ _ _ _ _ () _
Inspector Lestrade _ _ _ _ _ _   _ () _ _
Baby Dumpling   _ () _ _ _   _ _ _ _ _
Hopalong Cassidy   _ _ _ _ _ _ () _ _ _ _
Mr. Moto   () _ _ _ _   _ _ () _ _
Charlie Chan   _ _ _ _ _ _ () _ _ _ _
Ma Kettle   _ _ _ _ _ _ _   _ _ _ _
Larry Talbot   _ _ _   _ () _ _ _ _

And the name of the star is: _ _ _ _ _ _ _ _ _ _ _ _ _ _ _!

_____points

(Answers on page 289)

CHARACTERS

Speaking of characters—uh, yes—we *were* speaking of characters—many films have produced many memorable characters. Often the name of the character is implanted in the memory of movie-goers long after the title of the film is forgotten. Below, we list a number of such characters, and ask you to tell us which film is suggested. Take 15 points for each correct answer:

1. President Merkin Muffley
2. John J. Macreedy
3. Cody Jarrett
4. Gold Hat
5. Gaylord Ravenal
6. Boss Jim Gettys
7. Henry Gondorff
8. Jett Rink
9. Addie Pray
10. Tommy Udo
11. J. J. Gittes

12. Max de Winter
13. Lina Lamont
14. Capt. Munsey
15. Hedley Lamarr

_____points

(*Answers on page 290*)

CHARACTERS—DUFFERS' TEE

Many films have produced memorable characters—with memorable names—and often the name of a character will trigger a memory even though the title of the film is forgotten. Below, in Column One, we list fifteen such character names. In Column Two, we list the film titles from which the character names were taken. Your task is to match the correct title to the appropriate character. Take 15 points for each correct answer.

1. President Merkin Muffley	a. "The Sting"
2. John J. Macreedy	b. "Citizen Kane"
3. Cody Jarrett	c. "Brute Force"
4. Gold Hat	d. "Blazing Saddles"
5. Gaylord Ravenal	e. "Kiss of Death"
6. Boss Jim Gettys	f. "Chinatown"
7. Henry Gondorff	g. "Dr. Strangelove"
8. Jett Rink	h. "White Heat"
9. Addie Pray	i. "Singin' in the Rain"
10. Tommy Udo	j. "Bad Day at Black Rock"
11. J. J. Gittes	k. "Show Boat"
12. Max de Winter	l. "Giant"
13. Lina Lamont	m. "Rebecca"
14. Capt. Munsey	n. "The Treasure of the Sierra Madre"
15. Hedley Lamarr	o. "Paper Moon"

_____points

(*Answers on page 290*)

AND MORE LINK-UPS—BUFFS AND DUFFERS

Time for a stretch, and an exercise for Buffs and Duffers alike. Again, we're asking you to supply the name in Column Two which will complete the names of the players suggested in Columns One and Three. As before, the name you must come up with will serve as a surname for the Column One player as well as the first name for the Column Two player. Set your mind to the task and take 5 points for each correct name you insert in Column Two.

1. Gloria _____ Muir
2. Edward _____ Stang
3. Paul _____ Korman
4. Marion _____ Thompson
5. Peggy _____ O'Neal
6. June _____ Price
7. Glenn _____ Sterling
8. Claire _____ Howard
9. Melvyn _____ Fairbanks
10. Jean _____ Hall

_____points

(*Answers on page 290*)

ORDER IN THE COURT

This quiz is an easy one—in form, anyway. Many films are set, or at least have a pivotal scene, in a courtroom. All we ask in this quiz is that you identify who was on trial in the film's courtroom scene. We're not looking for character names, but the actor(s) or actress(es) who took the role of the defendant. As a help, we have supplied the initials—so take 10 points for each correct answer, and tell us who was on trial in:

1. "A Place in the Sun"   M_____ C_____
2. "Witness for the Prosecution" T_____ P_____
3. "The Caine Mutiny"   V_____ J_____
4. "The Paradine Case"   A_____ V_____

5. "Trial"   R_____ C_____
6. "Anatomy of a Murder"   B_____ G_____
7. "Knock on Any Door"   J_____ D_____
8. "The Court-Martial of Billy Mitchell"   G_____ C_____
9. "Inherit the Wind"   D_____ Y_____
10. "They Won't Forget"   E_____ N_____
11. "The People Against O'Hara"   J_____ A_____
12. "Madame X"   L_____ T_____
13. "Cell 2455 Death Row"   W_____ C_____
14. "I Want to Live"   S_____ H_____
                                             B_____ D_____
                                                   and
15. "Compulsion"   D_____ S_____

                                             _____points

(Answers on page 291)

ORDER IN THE COURT—DUFFERS' TEE

This is relatively simple—as we told those who are playing the Film Buffs' version. Many films are set, or at least have a pivotal scene, in a courtroom. All we ask for in this quiz is that you identify the player(s) who were on trial. We're not seeking the character names. So to get 10 points for each correct answer, merely select the defendants from Column Two and match them with the appropriate film titles in Column One.

1. "A Place in the Sun"   a. James Arness
2. "Witness for the Prosecution"   b. William Campbell
3. "The Caine Mutiny"   c. Gary Cooper
4. "The Paradine Case"   d. Rafael Campos
5. "Trial"   e. John Derek
6. "Anatomy of a Murder"   f. Brad Dillman and Dean
                                        Stockwell
7. "Knock on Any Door"   g. Susan Hayward

8. "The Court-Martial of Billy Mitchell"
9. "Inherit the Wind"
10. "They Won't Forget"
11. "The People Against O'Hara"
12. "Madame X"
13. "Cell 2455 Death Row"
14. "I Want to Live"
15. "Compulsion"

h. Edward Norris
i. Ben Gazzara
j. Tyrone Power
k. Van Johnson
l. Montgomery Clift
m. Lana Turner
n. Dick York
o. Alida Valli

_____points

(*Answers on page 291*)

MUH-MUH-MUH-MUH-MOMMA

In each of the films below, the mother-child relationship was an important facet of the plot. We have provided the title and the name of the actor or actress who portrayed the offspring. You are to tell us who portrayed the mother. You may take 10 points for each correct answer.

1. "Gentleman's Agreement" Gregory Peck _____
2. "Somebody Up There Likes Me" Paul Newman _____
3. "I Remember Mama" Barbara Bel Geddes _____
4. "The Catered Affair" Debbie Reynolds _____
5. "The Best Years of Our Lives" Teresa Wright _____
6. "Citizen Kane" Orson Welles _____
7. "The Grapes of Wrath" Henry Fonda _____
8. "Ben-Hur" Cathy O'Donnell _____
9. "The Glass Menagerie" Arthur Kennedy _____
10. "King of Kings" Jeffrey Hunter _____

_____points

(*Answers on page 291*)

MUH-MUH-MUH-MUH-MOMMA— DUFFERS' TEE

In each of the films below, the mother-offspring relationship was an important facet of the plot. We have provided the actor or actress who portrayed the offspring (in Column Two) and the title of the film. From the choices we supply in Column Three, select the actress who played the mother. Take 10 points for each correct answer.

1. "Gentleman's Agreement"	Gregory Peck	a. Ann Shoemaker b. Ann Harding c. Anne Revere
2. "Somebody Up There Likes Me"	Paul Newman	a. Eileen Heckart b. Eileen Herlie c. Jo Van Fleet
3. "I Remember Mama"	Barbara Bel Geddes	a. Irene Dunne b. Ellen Corby c. Virginia Christine
4. "The Catered Affair"	Debbie Reynolds	a. Thelma Ritter b. Connie Gilchrist c. Bette Davis
5. "The Best Years of Our Lives"	Teresa Wright	a. Myrna Loy b. Fay Bainter c. Claudette Colbert
6. "Citizen Kane"	Orson Welles	a. Maria Ouspenskaya b. Agnes Moorehead c. Alma Kruger
7. "The Grapes of Wrath"	Henry Fonda	a. Zeffie Tilbury b. Beulah Bondi c. Jane Darwell
8. "Ben-Hur"	Charlton Heston	a. Dorothy Adams b. Olive Blakeney c. Martha Scott
9. "The Glass Menagerie"	Jane Wyman	a. Bette Davis b. Gertrude Lawrence c. Jessica Tandy
10. "King of Kings"	Jeffrey Hunter	a. Siobhan McKenna b. Dorothy McGuire c. Jennifer Jones

_____points

(*Answers on page 291*)

SPOT THE BIO: WRITERS

The form is simpler, but the quiz itself might prove more difficult than the earlier version of SPOT THE BIO, since here we're asking for information regarding well-known writers who have been portrayed in films. Below we list several actors and actresses who portrayed these literary greats, and the films in which the portrayals were included. You hay have 10 points for each correct identification you make of the writers portrayed.

1.	Burgess Meredith	"The Story of G.I. Joe"	_____	_____
2.	Gregory Peck	"Beloved Infidel"	_____	_____
3.	Sydney Greenstreet	"Devotion"	_____	_____
4.	Jack Lemmon	"Cowboy"	_____	_____
5.	Morris Carnovsky	"The Life of Emile Zola"	_____	_____
6.	Merle Oberon	"A Song to Remember"	_____	_____
7.	John Carradine	"The Adventures of Mark Twain"	_____	_____
8.	Ida Lupino	"Devotion"	_____	_____
9.	Jeffrey Lynn	"The Fighting 69th"	_____	_____
10.	Elsa Lanchester	"The Bride of Frankenstein"	_____	_____

_____ points

(*Answers on page 292*)

SPOT THE BIO: WRITERS—DUFFERS' TEE

Below we list several actors and actresses and the films in which they portrayed well-known writers out of our literary past. Because this is a bit tougher than the earlier version of SPOT THE BIO, we have made it a bit simpler—if that makes sense. In Column Three, we provide a list of literary luminaries, and we ask you to select the writers portrayed by the players of Column One in the films of Column Two. You may have 10 points for each correct matching.

1. Burgess Meredith	"The Story of G.I. Joe"	a. Mary Shelley
2. Gregory Peck	"Beloved Infidel"	b. Emily Brontë
3. Sydney Greenstreet	"Devotion"	c. Frank Harris
4. Jack Lemmon	"Cowboy"	d. Bret Harte
5. Morris Carnovsky	"The Life of Emile Zola"	e. George Sand
6. Merle Oberon	"A Song to Remember"	f. Joyce Kilmer
7. John Carradine	"The Adventures of Mark Twain"	g. Wm. Makepeace Thackeray
8. Ida Lupino	"Devotion"	h. F. Scott Fitzgerald
9. Jeffrey Lynn	"The Fighting 69th"	i. Anatole France
10. Elsa Lanchester	"The Bride of Frankenstein"	j. Ernie Pyle

_____points

(*Answers on page 292*)

WHAT'S MY LINE?

Select the correct occupation, or "line"—and correctly complete the following incomplete titles. One or two of these *are* posers, but the others are relatively easy. That's why we're allowing only 5 points for each correct answer.

1. "The _ _ _ _ _ _ _ _'s Paradise"
2. "The Big _ _ _ _ _ _ _ _ _"
3. "Death of a _ _ _ _ _ _ _ _ _"
4. "_ _ _ _ _ _ _ _ _ _ Story"
5. "The _ _ _ _ _ _ _ _ _ _ _ _ _ and the Lady"
6. "Diary of a _ _ _ _ _ _ _ _ _ _ _"
7. "The _ _ _ _ _ _ _ _ _ _ _'s Daughter"
8. "Test _ _ _ _ _ _"
9. "The Amazing _ _ _ _ _ _ _ Clitterhouse"
10. "_ _ _ _ _ _ _ _ in the Rain"
11. "The Nutty _ _ _ _ _ _ _ _ _ _"

12. "Two Girls and a _ _ _ _ _ _"
13. "_ _ _ _ _ _ _'s Pet"
14. "The _ _ _ Who Came In from the Cold"
15. "The _ _ _ _ _ _ _ Was Indiscreet"
16. "The _ _ _ _ _ _ Takes a Wife"
17. "Her Highness and the _ _ _ _ _ _ _"
18. "_ _ _ _ _ _ _ Creek"
19. "Mr. _ _ _ _ _ _ _ _ _ _"
20. "_ _ _ _ _ Hardy's Children"

_____points

(*Answers on page 292*)

WHAT'S MY LINE?—DUFFERS' TEE

We're asking you to complete the incomplete titles in Column One below. And to do it, all you have to do is select the appropriate occupation, or "line," from those we've listed in Column Two. You'll receive 5 points for each completion you get correct.

1. "The _____'s Paradise"   a. Professor
2. "The Big _____"   b. Spy
3. "Death of a _____"   c. Senator
4. "_____ Story"   d. Fisherman
5. "The _____ and the Lady"   e. Doctor
6. "Diary of a _____"   f. Bellboy
7. "The _____'s Daughter"   g. Salesman
8. "Test _____"   h. Judge
9. "The Amazing _____ Clitterhouse" i. Scoutmaster
10. "_____ in the Rain"   j. Chambermaid
11. "The Nutty _____"   k. Farmer
12. "Two Girls on a _____"   l. Coroner
13. "_____'s Pet"   m. Captain
14. "The _____ Who Came In from the
    Cold"   n. Sailor
15. "The _____ Was Indiscreet"   o. Ambassador
16. "The _____ Takes a Wife"   p. Detective

98

17. "Her Highness and the _____" q. Soldier
18. "_____ Creek" r. Teacher
19. "Mr. _____" s. Pilot
20. "_____ Hardy's Children" t. Prizefighter

_____points

(*Answers on page 292*)

WILD CARD—BUFFS AND DUFFERS

Here's another mental exercise for Buffs and Duffers alike. Again, movie knowledge might be of some help—but logic and keen observation are needed most. So analyze, think, deduce—and when you get it all sorted out—and correctly—then add 100 points to your score.

Script Doctor

The producer called in Gregg Pitman, known to many as Hollywood's cleverest script doctor. The producer needed help on the ending of his new private eye flick, "Sam Marlowe."

"It's the wind-up scene following the vault theft caper," the producer explained. "Sort of an 'Asphalt Jungle,' but the switch is, the gang doesn't make it. Now, we've established earlier that it's an inside job—and Marlowe gets there for the last confrontation scene in the owner's office."

"Who're the characters?" asked Pitman.

"Cook, Brophy, Jenkins, Tobias, and Calleia."

"What're they supposed to do?" asked Pitman.

"Well, one of 'em owns the jewelry firm. If the theft works, he's out a lot of dough, so we know *he's* innocent. The other four are: his crooked security head, his shyster lawyer, his sneaky assistant, and the shifty-eyed night watchman—but I'm not sure in what order."

"Seems simple enough," Pitman nodded.

"Not exactly," said the producer. "We know that, except for the owner, the other four all had a part in the caper. Now the scene I want you to write has to be full of accusations and cross-accusations. I want the finger of guilt pointing at everybody in the scene."

"Except for the owner," interjected Pitman.

"Right—*and* the actual ringleader. Keep him cool, because it's his plan, and he's being protected by the other three guilty ones."

"I got it," said Pitman. "And from just watching, Marlowe has to figure out who the ringleader is—right?"

"Right," said the producer—"as well as the lawyer, the assistant, the security head, and the shifty-eyed night watchman. Gregg, this scene has to be the shortest, tightest scene you can devise. And one other thing—don't give the guy playing the owner any lines. His throat's delicate, and I want to nurse him for some retakes."

"Got it," said Pitman. "I'll have it in an hour!" And here is what he delivered:

Scene 105: NIGHT—OWNER'S OFFICE: WIDE
SECURITY HEAD
Cook devised the whole caper, the rat!

Scene 106: SAME; DIFFERENT ANGLE
COOK
(*Yelling at security head*) Liar! You're pinning it on me to save your own neck. You know you're the brains behind it!
With this, COOK lashes out with a right jab, connecting with the SECURITY HEAD's nose. Blood is drawn. The SECURITY HEAD falls back against the OWNER.

Scene 107: MEDIUM BUST, SECURITY HEAD
SECURITY HEAD
(*Wiping blood from nose*) I tell yuh—Cook arranged the set-up. It's his plan!

Scene 108: FROM OWNER'S POINT OF VIEW
ASSISTANT
You're both crazy—we know who planned it. It was Jenkins!

Scene 109: WIDE-SHOT AGAIN
NIGHT WATCHMAN
(*Shouting*) Won't you believe me? I said it once and I'll say it again—Tobias was behind it all!

Scene 110: DIFFERENT ANGLE
LAWYER
(*Sucking on toothpick*) Well, *I'm* clean!

Scene 111: CLOSE-UP OF BROPHY
BROPHY
Don't you believe it! (*Points at lawyer*) He's your man!

(*More to Come*)

100

"This should do the job," wrote Pitman in a postscript. "Have your writer use this scene as is, and just let Marlowe observe. All the clues are here which your writer will need to develop Marlowe's last speech, where he steps in and figures out who each character is, as well as nabbing the real ringleader. I'm off to Palm Springs. Pitman."

"What the hell is this?" screamed the producer, as he and the writer looked at Pitman's work.

"I think I have it," smiled the writer.

Did he? Have you? Did Pitman do the job, or merely confuse the issue? From what you have here, figure out who is who, and put your finger on the ringleader. Get it right, and add 100 points.

_____points

(*Answers on page 293*)

ODD MAN OUT ⚡3

Again, we list a sequence of names, titles, articles, etc. All of the items included in a sequence—save one—have some characteristic in common with the others. The characteristic, as we've said before, can be "way out"—so be on your toes. Your task is to eliminate the item which does not have a commonality with the other items in the sequence. Take 10 points for each "odd man" you ferret out.

1. "The Apartment"; "Brigadoon"; "Nights of Cabiria"; "Miracle on 34th Street."

2. Herbert Stothart; Max Steiner; Van Nest Polglase; Erich Wolfgang Korngold.

3. James Stewart; Myron McCormick; Margaret Sullavan; Mildred Natwick; Jane Brian.

4. Tony Perkins; Jason Robards; Peter Fonda; Warren Beatty; Robert Walker.

5. "Tomorrow the World"; "Born Yesterday"; "Our Town"; "The Dirty Dozen"; "No Time for Sergeants."

6. "One Foot in Heaven"; "Come to the Stable"; "Happy Land"; "Going My Way"; "I'd Climb the Highest Mountain."

7. Larry; Moe; Curly; Shemp; Ted; Joe.

8. "Dial M for Murder"; "South Pacific"; "Bwana Devil"; "House of Wax"; "The Stewardesses."

9. "Sergeant Rutledge"; "In Cold Blood"; "Johnny Belinda"; "Town Without Pity"; "Death Wish."

10. "Pork Chop Hill"; "Time Limit"; "The Rack"; "The Green Berets."

_____points

(*Answers on page 294*)

ODD MAN OUT #3—DUFFERS' TEE

Again in this version of ODD MAN OUT, we list a sequence—and all items included save one belong because of some common characteristic. Your task is to eliminate the single item which does not have a commonality with the others. Take 10 points for each correct answer.

1. Which one of the following was *not* first a movie and later transformed into a Broadway musical:
   a. "The Apartment"; b. "Brigadoon"; c. "Nights of Cabiria" d. "Miracle on 34th Street"?

2. Which one of the following was *not* concerned with the musical aspect of the motion pictures on which he worked:
   a. Herbert Stothart; b. Max Steiner; c. Van Nest Polglase; d. Erich Wolfgang Korngold?

3. Which one of the following was *not* part of a summer theater group, formed during their college days, and prior to their entrance into films:
   a. James Stewart; b. Myron McCormick; c. Margaret Sullavan; d. Mildred Natwick; e. Jane Brian?

4. Which one of the following actors was *not* the son of a film actor:
   a. Tony Perkins; b. Jason Robards, Jr.; c. Peter Fonda; d. Warren Beatty; e. Robert Walker, Jr.?

5. Which one of the following films was *not* a Broadway play from which a film was later produced:
   a. "Tomorrow the World"; b. "Born Yesterday"; c. "Our Town"; d. "The Dirty Dozen"; e. "No Time for Sergeants"?

6. Which one of the following did *not* have a member of the clergy as its protagonist:
   a. "One Foot in Heaven"; b. "Come to the Stable"; c. "Happy Land"; d. "Going My Way"; e. "I'd Climb the Highest Mountain"?

7. Which of the following was *not* one of the Three Stooges—ever:
   a. Larry; b. Moe; c. Curly; d. Ted; e. Shemp; f. Joe?

8. Which one of the following was *not* originally shot in 3-D:
   a. "Dial M for Murder"; b. "South Pacific"; c. "Bwana Devil"; d. "House of Wax"; e. "The Stewardesses"?

9. Which one of the following did not include the commission of rape as a plot point:
   a. "Sergeant Rutledge"; b. "In Cold Blood"; c. "Johnny Belinda"; d. "Town Without Pity"; e. "Death Wish"?

10. Which one of the following films was *not* concerned with the Korean conflict:
   a. "Pork Chop Hill"; b. "Time Limit"; c. "The Rack"; d. "The Green Berets"?

_____points

(*Answers on page 295*)

FROM SHUBERT ALLEY TO THE SUNSET STRIP

Hollywood has long drawn upon the Broadway stage, both for scripts and talent. Frequently, the original Broadway star or featured player was used in the same role when the film was made. But, more frequently, the co-star from the stage version was replaced by a Hollywood "name." Below we list several Broadway shows which were filmed, and two stars of the Broadway production. However, only one of the stars was used in the Hollywood version. Your task is to tell the Hollywood "name" who served as replacement. Take 10 points for each correct answer:

1. "Our Town"	Martha Scott John Craven	_____
2. "Night Must Fall"	Dame May Whitty Emlyn Williams	_____
3. "The Farmer Takes a Wife"	June Walker Henry Fonda	_____
4. "The Gay Divorce"	Clare Luce Fred Astaire	_____
5. "Cabin in the Sky"	Ethel Waters Dooley Wilson	_____

6. "Claudia"	Dorothy McGuire Donald Cook	_____
7. "The Man Who Came to Dinner"	Carol Goodner Monty Woolley	_____
8. "Louisiana Purchase"	Victor Moore William Gaxton	_____
9. "The Little Foxes"	Tallulah Bankhead Charles Dingle	_____
10. "Harvey"	Josephine Hull Frank Fay	_____

_____points

(*Answers on page 295*)

FROM SHUBERT ALLEY TO THE
SUNSET STRIP—DUFFERS' TEE

Below we demonstrate the thesis that Hollywood has long looked to the Broadway stage for both scripts and talent. We have listed a number of Broadway shows which were later translated into motion pictures. We list the title and one of the stars of the Broadway production. From the multiple choices in Column Three, you are to select the Hollywood actor or actress who, in the film version, played the part originally played by the Broadway actor/actress listed in Column Two. Take 10 points for each correct answer.

1. "Our Town"	John Craven	a. Frank Craven b. William Holden c. Paul Newman
2. "Night Must Fall"	Emlyn Williams	a. Robert Montgomery b. Douglass Montgomery c. Rhys Williams
3. "The Farmer Takes a Wife"	June Walker	a. Gloria Holden b. Sara Holden c. Janet Gaynor

		a. Betty Field
4. "The Gay Divorce"	Clare Luce	b. Ginger Rogers
		c. Joan Fontaine

		a. Cab Calloway
5. "Cabin in the Sky"	Dooley Wilson	b. Mantan Moreland
		c. Eddie "Rochester" Anderson

		a. Robert Young
6. "Claudia"	Donald Cook	b. Reginald Gardiner
		c. Richard Haydn

		a. Bette Davis
7. "The Man Who Came to Dinner"	Carol Goodner	b. Ann Sheridan
		c. Billie Burke

		a. Allyn Joslyn
8. "Louisiana Purchase"	William Gaxton	b. Bob Hope
		c. Bing Crosby

		a. Nancy Coleman
9. "The Little Foxes"	Tallulah Bankhead	b. Bette Davis
		c. Patricia Neal

		a. James Stewart
10. "Harvey"	Frank Fay	b. Frank Faylen
		c. Jesse White

_____points

(*Answers on page 295*)

SOME MORE "WHO KILLED . . . ?"

As before, we've listed some cinematic "victims" and the films in which the players met their violent end. Your task is to tell us who the killer was. As was the case in the earlier version, take 10 points for each correct answer.

1. Cecil Kellaway, in "The Postman Always Rings Twice"?
2. Lionel Barrymore, in "Rasputin and the Empress"?
3. Sessue Hayakawa, in "The Bridge on the River Kwai"?
4. John Barrymore, in "Romeo and Juliet"?
5. William Holden, in "Sunset Boulevard"?

6. Kirk Douglas, in "The Brotherhood"?

7. Howard Da Silva, in "Unconquered"?

8. Elisha Cook, Jr., in "Shane"?

9. Suzanne Cloutier, in "Othello"?

10. Rod Steiger, in "Oklahoma!"?

11. Burt Lancaster, in "The Killers"?

12. Sam Levene, in "Crossfire"?

13. Akim Tamiroff, in "Touch of Evil"?

14. Charles McGraw, in "Spartacus"?

15. Anthony Dawson, in "Dial M for Murder"?

_____points

(*Answers on page 296*)

SOME MORE "WHO KILLED . . . ?"—DUFFERS' TEE

As before, we've listed some cinematic "victims" and the films in which they met their violent end. Your task is to select the killer from Column Two, and match him (or her) appropriately with the film title and victim from Column One. Take 5 points for each correct answer.

1. Cecil Kellaway, in "The Postman Always Rings Twice"?

    a. Grace Kelly

2. Lionel Barrymore, in "Rasputin and the Empress"?

    b. Jack Palance

3. Sessue Hayakawa, in "The Bridge on the River Kwai"?

    c. Orson Welles

4. John Barrymore, in "Romeo and Juliet"?

    d. Charles McGraw and William Conrad

5. William Holden, in "Sunset Boulevard"?

    e. Gordon Macrae

6. Kirk Douglas, in "The Brotherhood"?

    f. John Garfield

7. Howard Da Silva, in "Unconquered"?

    g. John Barrymore

8. Elisha Cook, Jr., in "Shane"?

    h. Orson Welles

9. Suzanne Cloutier, in "Othello"?

    i. Kirk Douglas

10. Rod Steiger, in "Oklahoma!"?

    j. Basil Rathbone

11. Burt Lancaster, in "The Killers"?

    k. Robert Ryan

12. Sam Levene, in "Crossfire"?
13. Akim Tamiroff, in "Touch of Evil"?
14. Charles McGraw, in "Spartacus"?
15. Anthony Dawson, in "Dial M for Murder"?

l. Geoffrey Horne
m. Alex Cord
n. Gary Cooper
o. Gloria Swanson

_____points

(Answers on page 296)

WHAT ARE THEY TRYING TO SAY? PART II

Again we present some brief excerpts from books about films or filmmakers. Somehow or other, a gremlin got into the author's typewriter, and what ended up in the book seems to be at odds with what the fact really was. Spot the error, and give yourself 20 points for each error you detect.

1. From *The New York Times Guide to Movies on TV*, concerning "Witness for the Prosecution":
   ". . . and especially Charles Laughton, in a richly succulent and amusing portrait of the trial judge."

2. From *The Garden of Allah*, by Sheilah Graham:
   "The other two [pictures which lost money during World War II] were 'Wilson and 'Orlando and the Thief.'"

3. From *Billy Wilder*, by Axel Madsen, concerning "Sunset Boulevard":
   "Cecil B. DeMille, Wilder's confrere at Paramount, plays himself as the director phoning [Gloria Swanson] to ask her whether he can rent the Isotta Fraschini."

4. From *The Movies*, by Richard Griffith and Arthur Mayer, concerning "G-Men":
   "Barton MacLane and Russell Hopton torment a captured Fed, William Harrigan, while their molls look on."

5. From *The Name Above the Title*, by Frank Capra:
   "But in 1935, the labor was in full cry. Actor Ronald Reagan, writer John Howard Lawson, and director King Vidor led the fight for their respective guilds."

_____points

(Answers on page 296)

WHAT ARE THEY TRYING TO SAY?
PART II–DUFFERS' TEE

Again, we present some brief excerpts from books about films or filmmakers. Somehow or other, a gremlin got into the author's typewriter, and what ended up in the book seems to be at odds with what the fact really was. If you've gone through the Buffs' version of this exercise, you may have already detected the errors. But in this Duffers' Tee, we present you with multiple-choice answers. Refer to the Movie Buffs' version of WHAT ARE THEY TRYING TO SAY PART II, immediately preceding, and then select your answer. Take 20 points for each error you detect.

1. From *The New York Times Guide to Movies on TV*, concerning "Witness for the Prosecution":

   (a) Charles Laughton was not in the film; (b) Charles Laughton played the prosecuting attorney; or (c) Charles Laughton played the defense attorney.

2. From *The Garden of Allah*, by Sheilah Graham:

   (a) The film "Wilson" was made during World War I; (b) she is really referring to *one* film entitled "Orlando Wilson"; or (c) the correct title of the second film is "Yolanda and the Thief."

3. From *Billy Wilder*, by Axel Madsen, concerning "Sunset Boulevard":

   (a) DeMille did not do the phoning. This was done by a member of the staff. Swanson bumped into DeMille merely by accident; (b) the studio in question was not Paramount, but Warner Brothers; or (c) the automobile in question was not an Isotta Fraschini, but a Rolls-Royce.

4. From *The Movies*, by Richard Griffith and Arthur Mayer, concerning "G-Men":

   (a) Barton MacLane was not in the film. The authors have confused him with George Bancroft; (b) William Harrigan was not a captured Fed, but a rival gang chieftain; or (c) William Harrigan was not a federal officer, but a county sheriff.

5. From *The Name Above the Title*, by Frank Capra:

   (a) John Howard Lawson was not a writer, but a composer; (b) Mr. Capra should have written "Charles Vidor," rather than "King Vidor"; or (c) in 1935, Ronald Reagan was not yet in motion pictures, but was still a radio announcer in Iowa.

————points

(*Answers on page 296*)

RE-DOS, THE MALE SIDE

Here again are some films which have had newer versions produced—but in this instance, we are only dealing with male performers. When the films were redone, their titles did not change, though their performers did. Columns One and Two have the titles and the male performer combinations of the earlier version. In Column Three, you must supply the names of the male performers who portrayed the same parts in the re-do. You make 15 points for each correct name—30 points a question, or a possible 300-point increase for this quiz.

1. "A Christmas Carol"	Reginald Owen	A_____	S_____
	Gene Lockhart	M_____	J_____
2. "The Killers"	Charles McGraw	L_____	M_____
	William Conrad	C_____	G_____
3. "King of Kings"	H. B. Warner	J_____	H_____
	Victor Varconi	H_____	H_____
4. "Kid Galahad"	Edward G. Robinson	G_____	Y_____
	Wayne Morris	E_____	P_____
5. "Les Miserables"	Fredric March	M_____	R_____
	Charles Laughton	R_____	N_____
6. "Oliver Twist"	Irving Pichel	A_____	G_____
	Dickie Moore	J_____H_____D_____	
7. "Romeo and Juliet"	Leslie Howard	L_____	H_____
	Henry Kolker	M_____	J_____
8. "Julius Caesar"	Louis Calhern	J_____	G_____
	John Gielgud	R_____	J_____
9. "Stagecoach"	Donald Meek	R_____	B_____
	Berton Churchill	R_____	C_____
10. "Dawn Patrol"	Neil Hamilton	B_____	R_____
	Douglas Fairbanks, Jr.	D_____	N_____

_____points

(Answers on page 297)

RE-DOS, THE MALE SIDE—DUFFERS' TEE

Here again are some pictures which have had newer versions produced. This quiz is played exactly the same as the earlier re-do quizzes. The only difference is that we have limited our questioning to the male members of the various casts. Again, the film title and performer combinations are listed in Columns One and Two. Column Three lists—out of order, of course—the performer combination who played the same parts in the later version. Select the proper combination from Column Three to correspond with those in Column Two, and take 15 points for each correct pairing. Unlike the last re-do quiz, the combinations in Column Two *are* from an earlier version. Good luck for a possible 150 points.

1. "A Christmas Carol"	Reginald Owen Gene Lockhart	a. Michael Rennie Robert Newton
2. "The Killers"	Charles McGraw William Conrad	b. John Gielgud Richard Johnson
3. "King of Kings"	H. B. Warner Victor Varconi	c. Basil Rathbone David Niven
4. "Kid Galahad"	Edward G. Robinson Wayne Morris	d. Alec Guinness John Howard Davies
5. "Les Miserables"	Fredric March Charles Laughton	e. Laurence Harvey Mervyn Johns
6. "Oliver Twist"	Irving Pichel Dickie Moore	f. Red Buttons Robert Cummings
7. "Romeo and Juliet"	Leslie Howard Henry Kolker	g. Lee Marvin Clu Gulager
8. "Julius Caesar"	Louis Calhern John Gielgud	h. Gig Young Elvis Presley
9. "Stagecoach"	Donald Meek Berton Churchill	i. Alastair Sim Mervyn Johns
10. "Dawn Patrol"	Neil Hamilton Douglas Fairbanks, Jr.	j. Jeffrey Hunter Hurd Hatfield

————points

(*Answers on page 297*)

THE STATE OF THINGS

This might be a little sticky—so if you don't feel too sharp in movie memory, or geography, move on to the Duffers' Tee. But if you think you're up to it, just think of the state some things are in, and complete the following titles. Take 10 points for each answer you get correct.

1. "In Old _ _ _ _ _ _ _ _ _ _ "
2. "_ _ _ _ _ _ _ Trail"
3. "_ _ _ _ _ _ _ _ _ _ _ Gambler"
4. "_ _ _ _ _ _ _ _ _ Territory"
5. "_ _ _ _ _ _ _ _ _ Johnson"
6. "_ _ _ _ _ _ _ Mail"
7. "Little Old _ _ _ _ _ _ _ "
8. "The _ _ _ _ _ _ Rangers"
9. "_ _ _ _ _ _ _ Pacific"
10. "Bad Men of _ _ _ _ _ _ _ _ "
11. "_ _ _ _ _ _ _ Smith"
12. "Badlands of _ _ _ _ _ _ _ _ "
13. "The _ _ _ _ _ _ _ _ _ Traveler"
14. "_ _ _ _ _ _ _ _ _ Rifle"
15. "_ _ _ _ _ _ _ _ _ City"
16. "The _ _ _ _ _ _ _ _ Kid"
17. "North to _ _ _ _ _ _ _ "
18. "_ _ _ _ _ _ _ _ _ _ Purchase"
19. "The Baron of _ _ _ _ _ _ _ "
20. "_ _ _ _ _ _ _ Lil"

_____points

(Answers on page 297)

THE STATE OF THINGS—DUFFERS' TEE

This is the Duffers' Tee version of the preceding quiz. Movie memory and geography might help. All we're asking here is that you match the state name from Column Two to the appropriate titles in Column One. Take 5 points for each correct answer.

1. "In Old _____ "   a. Arkansas
2. "_____ Trail"   b. Texas
3. "_____ Gambler"   c. California
4. "_____ Territory"   d. New York

5. "_____ Johnson"

6. "_____ Mail"

7. "Little Old _____"

8. "The _____ Rangers"

9. "_____ Pacific"

10. "Bad Men of _____"

11. "_____ Smith"

12. "Badlands of _____"

13. "The _____ Traveler"

14. "_____ Rifle"

15. "_____ City"

16. "The _____ Kid"

17. "North to _____"

18. "_____ Purchase"

19. "The Baron of _____"

20. "_____ Lil"

e. Oklahoma

f. Dakota

g. Kansas

h. Alaska

i. Wyoming

j. Arizona

k. Virginia

l. Montana

m. Oregon

n. Missouri

o. Nevada

p. Tennessee

q. Kentucky

r. Mississippi

s. Louisiana

t. Colorado

_____ points

(*Answers on page 297*)

MORE CAREERS IN COMMON

As before, we have listed below in Column One, two stars and films in which they appeared in which they both pursued the same career, or occupation. In Column Two, we list another performer who, in one of his (or her) roles, pursued the same career. Tell us *both* the career common to all three films, as well as the title of the film in which the performer of Column Two pursued that career. Answers are in two parts, and you receive 10 points for each part you get correct—for a possible 200 points.

1. Adolphe Menjou—"The Front Page"
   James Cagney—"Come Fill the Cup"

   Humphrey Bogart

   _____   _____

2. Cary Grant—"Arsenic and Old Lace"
   Joseph Cotten—"Citizen Kane"

   George Sanders

   _____   _____

112

3. Henry Fonda—"Fail Safe"   Polly Bergen
   Walter Huston—"Gabriel
   over the White House"   _____   _____

4. Barbara Stanwyck—"Lady of   Natalie Wood
   Burlesque"
   Joanne Woodward—"The   _____   _____
   Stripper"

5. Joseph Cotten—"The Third   Peter Lorre
   Man"
   Dick Powell—"The Bad and   _____   _____
   the Beautiful"

6. Tony Curtis—"Sweet Smell of   Edmond O'Brien
   Success"
   Jack Carson—"A Star Is   _____   _____
   Born"

7. Walter Brennan—"The   Joseph Welch
   Westerner"
   Spencer Tracy—"Judgment at   _____   _____
   Nuremberg"

8. Ingrid Bergman—"Spellbound"   Leo Genn
   Lee J. Cobb—"The Dark Past"   _____   _____

9. Paul Douglas—"Fourteen   Milton Berle
   Hours"
   Jack Carson—"Arsenic and   _____   _____
   Old Lace"

10. Barry Fitzgerald—"Naked   Kirk Douglas
    City"
    Dana Andrews—"Laura"   _____   _____

                                              _____ points

(Answers on page 298)

MORE CAREERS IN COMMON—DUFFERS' TEE

As before, we have listed pairs of film players in Column One below,
along with the films in which they pursued the same occupation, or
career. In Column Two, we list three more performers and films in
which they appeared. Only one of the three (in the film listed) had
the same occupation as the players in Column One. Your task is to
select the player in Column Two who pursued the same occupation as

the players in Column One within the films designated. Take 15 points for each correct answer.

1. Adolphe Menjou—"The Front Page"
   James Cagney—"Come Fill the Cup"

   Humphrey Bogart—"Chicago Deadline"
   Mel Ferrer—"Lili"
   Gregory Peck—"Man with a Million"

2. Cary Grant—"Arsenic and Old Lace"

   Joseph Cotton—"Citizen Kane"

   William Holden—"Apartment for Peggy"
   George Sanders—"All About Eve"
   Lyle Bettger—"The Carnival Story"

3. Henry Fonda—"Fail Safe"

   Walter Huston—"Gabriel over the White House"

   Myrna Loy—"The Ambassador's Daughter"
   Frank Lovejoy—"Goodbye, My Fancy"
   Polly Bergen—"Kisses for My President"

4. Barbara Stanwyck—"Lady of Burlesque"

   Joanne Woodward—"The Stripper"

   Kim Novak—"Five Against the House"
   Natalie Wood—"Gypsy"
   Marilyn Monroe—"We're Not Married"

5. Joseph Cotton—"The Third Man"
   Dick Powell—"The Bad and the Beautiful"

   John Ericson—"Teresa"

   Peter Lorre—"Mask of Dimitrios"
   Maurice Evans—"Kind Lady"

6. Tony Curtis—"Sweet Smell of Success"

   Jack Carson—"A Star Is Born"

   Robert Young—"The Enchanted Cottage"
   Henry Fonda—"The Lady Eve"
   Edmond O'Brien—"A Double Life"

7. Walter Brennan—"The Westerner"
   Spencer Tracy—"Judgment at Nuremberg"

   Joseph Welch—"Anatomy of a Murder"
   Rex Harrison—"Major Barbara"
   James Gleason—"Here Comes Mr. Jordan"

8. Ingrid Bergman—"Spellbound"
   Lee J. Cobb—"The Dark Past"

   Roman Bohnen—"Brute Force"
   Frank Morgan—"The Great Ziegfeld"
   Leo Genn—"The Snake Pit"

9. Paul Douglas—"Fourteen Hours"

Jack Carson—"Arsenic and Old Lace"

10. Barry Fitzgerald—"Naked City"
Dana Andrews—"Laura"

Humphrey Bogart—"They Drive by Night"
Danny Thomas—"Big City"
Milton Berle—"Margin for Error"

Kirk Douglas—"Detective Story"
Glenn Langan—"Dragonwyck"
Lew Ayres—"The Dark Mirror"

_____points

(*Answers on page 298*)

THE LADIES

In the diagram following, we have included the last names of over 100 female movie performers—from *all* eras. The names run up and down, backward and forward, and diagonally—but always in a straight line. We've given you some clues on the names you're looking for below. In the diagram, you're dealing with surnames only—so by using the first-name clues in the alphabetical categories below, it shouldn't be too difficult. Credit your score with 5 points for each surname you drag out of the myriad of letters. A clue: 112 is not Miss West!

1. A _ _ _ _ _, Elizabeth
2. B _ _ _ _ _ _, Lauren
3. B _ _ _ _ _ _ _, Fay
4. B _ _ _, Lucille
5. B _ _ _ _ _ _, Anne
6. B _ _ _ _ _ _ _, Louise
7. B _ _ _ _ _ _ _ _ _, Bea
8. B _ _ _ _ _ _ _, Ingrid
9. B _ _ _ _ _ _, Jacqueline
10. B _ _ _ _ _ _, Vivian
11. B _ _ _ _ _, Janet
12. B _ _ _ _ _, Ann
13. B _ _ _ _ _ _, Mary
14. B _ _ _ _ _, Beulah
15. B _ _ _ _ _, Shirley

16. B _ _ _ _ _, Alice
17. B _ _ _ _ _, Mary
18. C _ _ _ _ _, Leslie
19. C _ _ _ _ _ _ _, Madeleine
20. C _ _ _ _ _ _ _, Janis
21. C _ _ _ _ _ _ _, Claudette
22. C _ _ _ _ _, Jeanne
23. D _ _ _ _, Patricia
24. D _ _ _ _ _, Bette
25. D _ _, Doris
26. D _ _, Laraine
27. D _ _ _ _ _ _, Yvonne
28. D _ _, Frances
29. D _ _ _ _ _, Dolores
30. D _ _ _ _, Patty

115

31. D _ _ _ _ _ _ , Ann
32. E _ _ _ _ _ , Samantha
33. E _ _ _ _ _ _ , Sally
34. F _ _ _ _ , Alice
35. F _ _ _ _ _ , Jane
36. F _ _ _ , Sidney
37. G _ _ _ _ , Franceska
38. G _ _ _ _ _ , Greta
39. G _ _ _ _ _ _ , Janet
40. G _ _ _ _ _ _ , Betty
41. G _ _ _ _ _ _ _ , Kathryn
42. G _ _ _ _ _ _ _ _ _ , Charlotte
43. G _ _ _ _ , Nan
44. G _ _ _ _ _ _ , Anne
45. H _ _ _ _ _ , Jean
46. H _ _ _ _ _ _ , Jean
47. H _ _ _ _ , Dolores
48. H _ _ _ _ _ , June
49. H _ _ _ _ _ , Helen
50. H _ _ _ _ _ _ _ , Katharine
51. H _ _ _ _ _ _ , Eileen
52. H _ _ _ _ , Marianna
53. H _ _ _ _ , Celeste
54. K _ _ _ _ _ _ , Aliza
55. K _ _ _ _ , Dorothea
56. K _ _ _ _ , Deborah
57. L _ _ _ _ , Priscilla
58. L _ _ _ _ , June
59. L _ _ _ _ _ , Hope
60. L _ _ , Dixie
61. L _ _ _ _ _ , Doris
62. L _ _ _ _ , Marjorie
63. L _ _ _ _ _ , Sophia
64. L _ _ , Myrna
65. L _ _ _ _ , Diana
66. L _ _ _ _ , Sue
67. M _ _ _ _ , Marjorie
68. M _ _ _ _ _ _ , Dorothy
69. M _ _ _ _ , Adele

70. M _ _ _ _ _
71. M _ _ _ _ _ , Mona
72. M _ _ _ _ _ _ _ , Marilyn
73. M _ _ _ , Elaine
74. M _ _ _ _ , Virginia
75. M _ _ _ _ , Georgia
76. M _ _ _ _ _ _ , Marilyn
77. M _ _ _ _ _ , Constance
78. M _ _ _ _ , Jean
79. N _ _ _ _ , Patricia
80. N _ _ _ _ _ _ _ , Mabel
81. N _ _ _ _ _ , Kim
82. O _ _ _ _ _ _ , Susan
83. P _ _ _ _ _ _ _ , Estelle
84. P _ _ _ _ _ _ , Jean
85. P _ _ _ _ _ _ , Eleanor
86. R _ _ _ _ , Barbara
87. R _ _ _ _ _ _ , Ruth
88. R _ _ _ _ _ , Ruth
89. R _ _ _ _ , Rossana
90. R _ _ _ _ _ , Françoise
91. R _ _ _ _ , Katharine
92. R _ _ _ _ _ , Barbara
93. R _ _ _ _ , Barbara
94. R _ _ _ _ _ _ _ , Jane
95. R _ _ _ _ , Peggy
96. S _ _ _ _ _ _ _ , Anne
97. S _ _ _ _ _ _ _ _ , Simone
98. S _ _ _ _ _ , Gale
99. S _ _ _ _ _ _ _ , Gloria
100. T _ _ _ _ _ _ , Elizabeth
101. T _ _ _ _ _ _ , Lana
102. T _ _ _ _ _ , Beverly
103. V _ _ _ _ _ , Alida
104. V _ _ _ _ _ , Diane
105. W _ _ _ _ _ , Jacqueline
106. W _ _ _ _ _ _ _ , Marie
107. W _ _ _ _ , Toby
108. W _ _ _ _ , Natalie

109. W _ _ _ _ _ _, Jo Anne   111. W _ _ _ _, Jane
110. W _ _ _ _ _ _, Teresa   112. W _ _ _, May
                113. Y _ _ _ _, Loretta

_____ **points**

(*Answers on page 299*)

```
H A R G D Y N D E L L R I O I R B H T O O B D
R A F Y R G L A N D R E L O L T E N O R S A L Y H R E T G H H O O D
T R B O L A I C E D R Y O L E R O L T E N A D O E R I
Y F O X A R I B Y L O R O N I V A D R S M A R L N I D W O
E B B C D D V O R R C A B K A N M A R A D A R M L I N
B L A I N E C A B E D I S S E T X Y M N Y B L E I G R E E N
O R Y O L M L R A C E B D D R M A X W E L B O A N G R
Y G R A M I N F G R O E N D A V E I G A R B O L S O R G
A W O L U R A H H R O D A V H S L E G I N Y R A O S Y A R
D Y N O S S E W L H B M P Y B A R A C L S G T H I R M I R L O S
E O R A S N R W S U H U R A T B A G L Y R M Y O M L F E N O
E N A L O R E R O L Y S U R A R S A Y R B L E Y A L A L R H I
N N E O N E K U D S E N O L B V A L O R I C T R S
G I N W O R L E Y O A R H R N H A M S U E N E L R O H
H A L M P O E T U R E I B E R N O R M A N D S O R D U I C K A
```

Here's one to test your eagle-eye, and your patience. In the diagram on the page preceding, we have buried the last names of over 100 female movie performers—from *all* eras. The names run up and down, backward and forward, and even diagonally, in any direction—but always in a straight line. To assist you, we've even listed the names below and leave it to you to do the spotting. You may take 5 points for each surname you isolate in the myriad of letters. Good luck—and remember, neatness counts!

1. Allen, Elizabeth
2. Bacall, Lauren
3. Bainter, Fay
4. Ball, Lucille
5. Baxter, Anne
6. Beavers, Louise
7. Benadaret, Bea
8. Bergman, Ingrid
9. Bisset, Jacqueline
10. Blaine, Vivian
11. Blair, Janet
12. Blyth, Ann
13. Boland, Mary
14. Bondi, Beulah
15. Booth, Shirley
16. Brady, Alice
17. Brian, Mary
18. Caron, Leslie
19. Carroll, Madeleine
20. Carter, Janis
21. Colbert, Claudette
22. Crain, Jeanne
23. Dane, Patricia
24. Davis, Bette
25. Day, Doris
26. Day, Laraine
27. De Carlo, Yvonne
28. Dee, Frances
29. Del Rio, Dolores
30. Duke, Patty
31. Dvorak, Ann
32. Eggar, Samantha
33. Eilers, Sally
34. Faye, Alice
35. Fonda, Jane
36. Fox, Sidney
37. Gaal, Franceska
38. Garbo, Greta
39. Gaynor, Janet
40. Grable, Betty
41. Grayson, Kathryn
42. Greenwood, Charlotte
43. Grey, Nan
44. Gwynne, Anne
45. Hagen, Jean
46. Harlow, Jean
47. Hart, Dolores
48. Haver, June
49. Hayes, Helen
50. Hepburn, Katharine
51. Herlie, Eileen
52. Hill, Marianna
53. Holm, Celeste
54. Kashi, Aliza
55. Kent, Dorothea
56. Kerr, Deborah
57. Lane, Priscilla
58. Lang, June

59. Lange, Hope
60. Lee, Dixie
61. Lloyd, Doris
62. Lord, Marjorie
63. Loren, Sophia
64. Loy, Myrna
65. Lynn, Diana
66. Lyon, Sue
67. Main, Marjorie
68. Malone, Dorothy
69. Mara, Adele
70. Margo
71. Maris, Mona
72. Maxwell, Marilyn
73. May, Elaine
74. Mayo, Virginia
75. Moll, Georgia
76. Monroe, Marilyn
77. Moore, Constance
78. Muir, Jean
79. Neal, Patricia
80. Normand, Mabel
81. Novak, Kim
82. Oliver, Susan
83. Parsons, Estelle
84. Peters, Jean
85. Powell, Eleanor

86. Read, Barbara
87. Roland, Ruth
88. Roman, Ruth
89. Rori, Rossana
90. Rosay, Françoise
91. Ross, Katharine
92. Ruick, Barbara
93. Rush, Barbara
94. Russell, Jane
95. Ryan, Peggy
96. Shirley, Anne
97. Signoret, Simone
98. Storm, Gale
99. Swanson, Gloria
100. Taylor, Elizabeth
101. Turner, Lana
102. Tyler, Beverly
103. Valli, Alida
104. Varsi, Diane
105. Wells, Jacqueline
106. Windsor, Marie
107. Wing, Toby
108. Wood, Natalie
109. Worley, Jo Anne
110. Wright, Teresa
111. Wyman, Jane
112. Wynn, May

113. Young, Loretta

_____points

(*Answers on page 299*)

FIRST FILMS, THE MEN

As we were concerned earlier with the debuts of females in films, so now are we seeking the first films of these well-known actors. Use the rather vague clues we provide, and give us the first film of each of the stars. Take 10 points for each correct answer.

1. Spencer Tracy   "__ ___ _____"

2. Gregory Peck   "D _ _ _ o _ G _ _ _ _ _"

3. Claude Rains   "The _ _ _ _ _ _ _ _ _ Man"

4. Paul Newman   "_ _ e _ _ _ _ _ r _ _ _ _ _ _ e"

5. James Stewart   "M_____ M___"

6. Gene Kelly   "_ _ _ _ _ _ _ _ _ _ _ _"

7. Steve McQueen   "The _ _ _ _"

8. Kirk Douglas   "The _ _ _ _ _ _ _ Love of _ _ _ _ _ _ _ _ _ _"

9. Tony Curtis   "C_____ _____ the R_____"

10. Marlon Brando   "_____ ____"

11. Jack Lemmon   "It_____ _ _ _"

12. Dean Martin   "____ _____"

13. Lee. J. Cobb   "G _ _ _ _ _ _ B _ _"

14. José Ferrer   "J_____ _ _ _ _"

15. Richard Widmark   "_ _ _ _ _ _ _ _ _"

16. Walter Matthau   "The _ _ _ _ _ _ _ _ _ n"

17. Eli Wallach   "_ _ _ _ _ _ _ _"

18. Danny Kaye   "_ _ _ _ _ _ _ s"

19. Van Johnson   "Murder _ _ _ _ _ _ _ _ _ _ _ _"

20. Burt Lancaster   "The _ _ _ _ _ _ _ _"

_____**points**

(*Answers on page 300*)

FIRST FILMS, THE MEN—DUFFERS' TEE

As we were concerned earlier with the debut films of female stars, so now are we seeking the first films of some well-known actors. Select the appropriate film title from Column Two, and match it as the first film for the actor in Column One. You may take 10 points for each correct pairing.

1. Spencer Tracy   a. "Baby Doll"
2. Gregory Peck   b. "The Men"
3. Claude Rains   c. "Joan of Arc"

4. Paul Newman	d. "Up the River"
5. James Stewart	e. "Murder in the Big House"
6. Gene Kelly	f. "Days of Glory"
7. Steve McQueen	g. "My Friend Irma"
8. Kirk Douglas	h. "It Should Happen to You"
9. Tony Curtis	i. "The Silver Chalice"
10. Marlon Brando	j. "Up in Arms"
11. Jack Lemmon	k. "Golden Boy"
12. Dean Martin	l. "The Kentuckian"
13. Lee J. Cobb	m. "The Strange Love of Martha Ivers"
14. José Ferrer	n. "The Killers"
15. Richard Widmark	o. "City Across the River"
16. Walter Matthau	p. "The Invisible Man"
17. Eli Wallach	q. "For Me and My Gal"
18. Danny Kaye	r. "The Blob"
19. Van Johnson	s. "Murder Man"
20. Burt Lancaster	t. "Kiss of Death"

_____points

(Answers on page 300)

SOME MORE "NAME THE STAR"

Once again, we list two characters played by the same star. Either one should give you the identity of that star, and enable you to add 10 points to your score for each correct answer. But if you find these too obscure, or your memory befogged, then move on to the next page, and the Duffers' Tee. There the drives are shorter and the clues more obvious.

1. Rupert Cadell	John "Scottie" Ferguson
2. Norman Cass, Sr.	Levasseur
3. Arnold Boult	Joe Wheeler
4. Hector David	Boats Gilhooley
5. Ivy Peterson	Alicia Huberman
6. Queen Guinevere	Sarah, Wife of Abraham
7. Fred Demara	Albert DeSalvo

8. C. R. MacNamara	Jim Kincaid
9. Jo Marsh	Amanda Bonner
10. Eileen Tyler	Julie Ann Warren

————points

(*Answers on page 301*)

SOME MORE "NAME THE STAR"—DUFFERS' TEE

Again we list two characters played by the same star. Your task is to identify the star. If you've already pegged the stars in question by the clues on the Buffs' version of this quiz, you've added 10 points to your score for each correct answer. But if the clues on the Buffs' version were too faint, these are a bit better-known. Because this Duffers' version is easier, we're allowing only 5 points for each correct answer in this version of the quiz.

1. Tom Jeffords	Jefferson Smith
2. Mr. Murdstone	Sir Guy of Guisbourne
3. Matt Drayton	Henry Drummond
4. Liberty Valance	Kid Shelleen
5. Cleo Dulaine	Isla Laszlo
6. Lady Brett	The Duchess of Alba
7. Sidney Falko	Harry Houdini
8. Jerry Plunkett	Eddie Bartlett
9. Rose Sayer	Tracy Lord
10. Kitty Twist	Barbarella

————points

(*Answers on page 302*)

THE TEENY-TINY MARQUEE ⚡2

This is another version of THE TEENY-TINY MARQUEE you played earlier. It is played the same way—except in the first version of this exercise, we gave you all kinds of help. Remember, the name

122

in the clue may be either a player's first name or surname. Whichever you determine it to be, use the opposite. If it's a surname, use the first name, and vice versa. Get the substitute name correct, and you'll correctly complete the film titles suggested below. Since this exercise isn't the easiest, we're giving 10 points for each correct answer.

1. "Mrs. M _ z _ _ k i"
2. "D _ w _ s Apollo"
3. "The Tower of J _ l _ e"
4. "Champagne for S _ d"
5. "The Diary of Anne M _ H _ g _ "
6. "The Private Life of T _ a _ e _ s VIII"
7. "What Ever Happened to Baby D _ r _ e _ l?"
8. "Bonnie Prince B _ t t _ _ w _ _ t _ "
9. "Harriet J _ m _ s"
10. "Citizen R _ c _ m _ n _ "
11. "C _ r _ o _ Boulevard"
12. "G _ e _ n Cargo"

_____points

(Answers on page 302)

THE TEENY-TINY MARQUEE #2—DUFFERS' TEE

This is merely another version of THE TEENY-TINY MARQUEE, and it's played in the same way—except in the earlier version, the going was easier. Remember that what seems to be a film title is incorrect, in particular that name which is a first name or surname of a film player. If it is the first name, insert the appropriate surname which correctly completes the suggested title—and if it is a surname, insert the appropriate first name which correctly, etc. We've made this a bit more difficult, but we're allowing 10 points for each correct answer. Of course, if you're really stuck, the correct answers are listed, out of order, in Column Two.

1. "Mrs. M _ z _ _ k i"   a. Craig
2. "D _ w _ s Apollo"   b. Caesar
3. "The Tower of J _ l _ e "   c. Kane
4. "Champagne for S _ d "   d. Strange

123

5. "The Diary of Anne M _ H _ g _ "   e. Mike
6. "The Private Life of T _ a _ e _ s VIII"   f. Johnny
7. "What Ever Happened to Baby
   D _ r _ e _ 1?"   g. Frank
8. "Bonnie Prince B _ tt _ _ w _ _ t _ "   h. Sunset
9. "Harriet J _ m _ s"   i. Henry
10. "Citizen R _ c _ m _ n _ "   j. Charlie
11. " C _ r _ o _ Boulevard"   k. Jane
12. " G _ e _ n Cargo"   l. London

_____points

(*Answers on page 302*)

MORE REDOS, THE MALE SIDE

Here are some more films which were re-dos—and we've been
through all that. If you can't remember how this exercise is played,
then look back to the earlier re-dos. These are *all* male, and, as
before, we're seeking the male performer combination in Column
Three that corresponds to the combination of Column Two. However, the combination represented in Column Two might be from an
earlier version of the film, *or* a later version. You get 15 points for
each correct name of you come up with—for a potential total of 300
points.

1. "The Front Page"	Walter Matthau	A_____	M_____
	Jack Lemmon	P_____	O_____
2. "The Prince and the Pauper"	William Sorrell	E_____	F_____
	William Barrons	C_____	R_____
3. "The Adventures of Huckleberry Finn"	Eddie Hodges	M_____	R_____
	Tony Randall	W_____	C_____
4. "M"	Peter Lorre	D_____	W_____
	Gustaf Grundgens	M_____	G_____
5. "Great Expectations"	Phillips Holmes	A_____	G_____
	Henry Hull	F_____	C_____
6. "The Virginian"	Joel McCrea	G_____	C_____
	Sonny Tufts	R_____	A_____

7. "Lost Horizon"	Peter Finch	R_____	C_____
	Charles Boyer	S_____	J_____
8. "What Price Glory?"	James Cagney	V_____	M_____
	Dan Dailey	E_____	L_____
9. "The Buccaneer"	Fredric March	Y_____	B_____
	Akim Tamiroff	C_____	B_____
10. "Billy the Kid"	Johnny Mack Brown	R_____	T_____
	Wallace Beery	B_____	D_____

_____points

(Answers on page 303)

MORE RE-DOS, THE MALE SIDE—DUFFERS' TEE

Here are some more films which were re-dos—and we've been through all that before. Again, these deal with only male performers. Columns One and Two give the title and a male performer combination which starred in one version of the film. Column Three provides, out of order, male performer combinations who portrayed the same parts in another version of the film—not necessarily a *later* version. Select the appropriate male performer combination and match it correctly with the title and combination of Columns One and Two—and take 20 points for each correct pairing.

1. "The Front Page"	Walter Matthau Jack Lemmon	a. Alec Guinness Finlay Currie
2. "The Prince and the Pauper"	William Sorrell William Barrons	b. Mickey Rooney Walter Connolly
3. "The Adventures of Huckleberry Finn"	Eddie Hodges Tony Randall	c. Yul Brynner Charles Boyer
4. "M"	Peter Lorre Gustaf Grundgens	d. Robert Taylor Brian Donlevy
5. "Great Expectations"	Phillips Holmes Henry Hull	e. Gary Cooper Richard Arlen
6. "The Virginian"	Joel McCrea Sonny Tufts	f. Victor McLaglen Edmund Lowe

7. "Lost Horizon"	Peter Finch Charles Boyer	g. David Wayne Martin Gabel
8. "What Price Glory?"	James Cagney Dan Dailey	h. Ronald Colman Sam Jaffe
9. "The Buccaneer"	Fredric March Akim Tamiroff	i. Errol Flynn Claude Rains
10. "Billy the Kid"	Johnny Mack Brown Wallace Beery	j. Adolphe Menjou Pat O'Brien

———points

(*Answers on page 303*)

MULTIPLE RE-DOS

You did great on that last one! So while you're hot, let's hit some more—fast! As you know, there were a number of re-do films which were done more than once. Here we list eleven such films. Column One lists the title. Column Two lists the player combination who played in an early version. In columns Three and Four, you are to tell us who played the same parts in later versions of the film. Take 15 points for each name you get correct, and rack up 660 points for getting them all!

1. "Back Street"	Irene Dunne John Boles	Margaret _____ Charles _____	S_____ H_____ J_____ G_____
2. "Beau Geste"	Ronald Colman Noah Beery, Sr.	Gary _____ Brian _____	G_____ S_____ T_____ S_____
3. "Madame X"	Ruth Chatterton Raymond Hackett	Gladys _____ John _____	L_____ T_____ K_____ D_____
4. "The Merry Widow"	Mae Murray John Gilbert	Jeanette _____ Maurice _____	L_____ T_____ F_____ L_____
5. "The Phan- tom of the Opera'"	Mary Philbin Lon Chaney	Susanna _____ Claude _____	H_____ S_____ H_____ L_____
6. "Show Boat"	Laura la Plante Joseph Schildkraut	Irene _____ Allan _____	K_____ G_____ H_____ K_____

126

7. "State Fair"	Janet Gaynor Will Rogers	Jeanne _____	P_____	T_____
		Charles _____	T_____	E_____
8. "Kid- napped"	Freddie Bartholomew Warner Baxter	Roddy _____	J_____	M_____
		Dan _____	P_____	F_____
9. "Of Human Bond- age"	Bette Davis Leslie Howard	Eleanor _____	K_____	N_____
		Paul _____	L_____	H_____
10. "The Hunch- back of Notre Dame"	Patsy Ruth Miller Lon Chaney	Maureen _____	G_____	L_____
		Charles _____	A_____	Q_____
11. "Treasure Island"	Shirley Mason Charles Ogle	Jackie _____	B_____	D_____
		Wallace _____	R_____	N_____

_____points

(Answers on page 304)

MULTIPLE RE-DOS—DUFFERS' TEE

Here are some films, re-dos, which were redone more than once. Columns One and Two list titles and the star combination of an early version. Columns Three and Four list star combinations from a subsequent version of the film, and an even later version. Columns One and Two correspond, but Columns Three and Four are wildly out of order. Your task is to arrange Columns Three and Four to match correctly with the first two columns. On this one, we're offering 25 points for each correct pairing, or 50 points per question. Here's your chance to boom ahead with 550 points total for the exercise. One tip: We suggest wrestling with Column Three first, and when you've exhausted possibilities there, move on to rearranging Column Four. Good luck!

| 1. "Back Street" | Irene Dunne John Boles | A. Jeanette MacDonald Maurice Chevalier | a. Kathryn Grayson Howard Keel |

2. "Beau Geste"	Ronald Colman Noah Beery, Sr.	B. Gladys George John Beal	b. Gina Lollo-brigida Anthony Quinn
3. "Madame X"	Ruth Chatterton Raymond Hackett	C. Eleanor Parker Paul Henreid	c. Guy Stockwell Telly Savalas
4. "The Merry Widow"	Mae Murray John Gilbert	D. Jackie Cooper Wallace Beery	d. Susan Hayward John Gavin
5. "The Phan-tom of the Opera"	Mary Philbin Lon Chaney	E. Maureen O'Hara Charles Laughton	e. Kim Novak Laurence Harvey
6. "Show Boat"	Laura la Plante Joseph Schildkraut	F. Gary Cooper Brian Donlevy	f. Heather Sears Herbert Lom
7. "State Fair"	Janet Gaynor Will Rogers	G. Susanna Foster Claude Rains	g. James MacArthur Peter Finch
8. "Kid-napped"	Freddie Bartholomew Warner Baxter	H. Irene Dunne Allan Jones	h. Bobby Driscoll Robert Newton
9. "Of Human Bond-age"	Bette Davis Leslie Howard	I. Jeanne Crain Charles Winninger	i. Lana Turner Keir Dullea
10. "The Hunch-back of Notre Dame"	Patsy Ruth Miller Lon Chaney	J. Roddy McDowall Dan O'Herlihy	j. Pamela Tiffin Tom Ewell
11. "Treasure Island"	Shirley Mason Charles Ogle	K. Margaret Sullavan Charles Boyer	k. Lana Turner Fernando Lamas

———points

(Answers on page 304)

SISTERS, SISTERS

In each of the films below, there was a "sister" relationship as part of the plot. We have provided a film title and the name of the actor or actress who portrayed the brother or sister of the actress in question. You must tell us who played the sister. Take 10 points for each correct answer.

1. "The Hard Way"   Joan Leslie   _____
2. "Psycho"   Vera Miles   _____
3. "Since You Went
   Away"   Shirley Temple   _____
4. "Picnic"   Susan Strasberg   _____
5. "Love Finds Andy
   Hardy"   Mickey Rooney   _____
6. "The Cardinal"   Tom Tryon   _____
7. "Dead End"   Billy Halop   _____
8. "The Diary of
   Anne Frank"   Diane Baker   _____
9. "White Christmas"   Vera-Ellen   _____
10. "A Tree Grows in
    Brooklyn"   Ted Donaldson   _____

_____points

(*Answers on page 305*)

SISTERS, SISTERS—DUFFERS' TEE

In each of the films listed in Column One below, a "sister" relationship was part of the plot. We have provided the actor or actress who portrayed the sister or brother of the actress in question. You have a multiple choice in Column Three from which to select the actress who portrayed the sister. Take 5 points for each correct answer.

1. "The Hard   Joan Leslie   a. Jane Wyatt
   Way"   b. Priscilla Lane
                                             c. Ida Lupino

2. "Psycho"   Vera Miles   a. Sylvia Miles
                                             b. Janet Leigh
                                             c. Teresa Wright

3. "Since You Went Away"	Shirley Temple	a. Jennifer Jones b. Phyllis Kirk c. Marcia Mae Jones
4. "Picnic"	Susan Strasberg	a. Rosalind Russell b. Betty Field c. Kim Novak
5. "Love Finds Andy Hardy"	Mickey Rooney	a. Cecilia Parker b. Dorris Bowdon c. June Preisser
6. "The Cardinal"	Tom Tryon	c. Carroll Baker b. Carol Lynley c. Carole Lombard
7. "Dead End"	Billy Halop	a. Sylvia Sidney b. Mayo Methot c. Iris Adrian
8. "The Diary of Anne Frank"	Diane Baker	a. Audrey Hepburn b. Millie Perkins c. Carrie Snodgress
9. "White Christmas"	Vera-Ellen	a. Marjorie Reynolds b. Marie Wilson c. Rosemary Clooney
10. "A Tree Grows in Brooklyn"	Ted Donaldson	a. Peggy Ann Garner b. Dorothy McGuire c. Janet Blair

————points

(Answers on page 305)

OSCAR SHUFFLE #2—WILD CARD

Another wild card! This exercise is for Buff and Duffer alike. As before, we have scrambled the names of three Oscar winners. Your task is to unscramble them, and thus arrive at the name of *another* Oscar winner. The same clue we gave you before holds in this exercise as well—all winners, including the hidden winner, are from the same category of the Oscar sweepstakes. You receive 5 points for each name you unscramble—plus 10 points for unearthing the hidden winner. Got it? So good luck in knocking off 25 points on this one.

1. H I N Q U N T A N Y O N
   (_) (_) (_) _ _ _ _   _ _ _ (_) (_)
2. N E W D U D E M N G N
   (_) _ _ _ _ _   _ (_) _ _ _
3. G Y A A D Z T I R B R F L E R
   (_) (_) _ (_) _   _ _ _ _ _ (_) (_) _ (_) _

Hidden name: _ _ _ _ _ _   _ _ _ _ _ _

_____points

(*Answers on page 305*)

THREE OF A KIND, AGAIN

You've played THREE OF A KIND before—and now we ask you to play it again. As before, each question has three answers, and you must answer *all three* parts in order to score the 20 points we're allowing on each question. So for a total of 200 points on this quiz, 'op to it!

1. "Gunga Din" was the film. Now, tell us the three actors who played the three leads. But just naming the three actors won't do. You must have each actor properly assigned to his particular character. So, who played: Cutter, Ballantine, and MacChesney?

2. As long as we're on the "three soldiers" kick, let's do it again. The film was "The Lives of a Bengal Lancer." The characters were: Lieut. Stone, Lieut. Forsythe, and Capt. McGregor. Name the actors.

3. There have been four films which co-starred Jackie Cooper and Wallace Beery. Name three of them.

4. There have been three versions of the film "State Fair." Name the three actors who played the reporter with whom the family's daughter falls in love.

5. Those desperadoes, the Dalton Boys, have been portrayed in a number of films. There were *four* Daltons—but we're asking you to give us the first names of three of them.

6. Actor Richard Bennett had three daughters. All of them appeared in films, though with varying degrees of success. Give us the first names of the three Bennett daughters.

7. Name three biographical roles played by Gary Cooper.

8. Name three of the actors or actresses interviewed by the newsreel reporter in "Citizen Kane."

9. The film was "A Letter to Three Wives." Who played the three wives?

10. Name at least three films in which Ginger Rogers and Fred Astaire appeared together.

————points

(*Answers on page 306*)

THREE OF A KIND, AGAIN—DUFFERS' TEE

In this exercise, as before, there are three correct answers for each question. We supply five possible answers, and it is your task to eliminate those two answers which are incorrect. You will receive 20 points for each question—providing you have eliminated *both* incorrect answers.

1. Name the three actors who portrayed the swashbuckling soldiers in "Gunga Din":
   a. David Niven; b. Victor McLaglen; c. Errol Flynn; d. Cary Grant; e. Douglas Fairbanks, Jr.

2. Name the three actors who portrayed the swashbuckling soldiers in "The Lives of a Bengal Lancer":
   a. Franchot Tone; b. Cary Grant; c. Victor McLaglen; d. Richard Cromwell; e. Gary Cooper.

3. Name the three films which co-starred Jackie Cooper and Wallace Beery:
   a. "The Champ"; b. "Stand Up and Fight"; c. "The Bowery"; d. "Treasure Island"; e. "The Devil Is a Sissy."

4. There have been three versions of the film "State Fair." Name the three actors who played the reporter with whom the daughter falls in love:
   a. Lew Ayres; b. John Payne; c. Russ Tamblyn; d. Dana Andrews; e. Bobby Darin.

5. As every Western fan knows, there were *four* Dalton Boys. Three of them were:
   a. Cole; b. Frank; c. Grat; d. Bob; e. Emmett.

6. Actor Richard Bennett had three daughters, all of whom appeared in films—though with varying degrees of success. Their names:
   a. Polly; b. Constance; c. Barbara; d. Joan; e. Billie.

7. A number of actors or actresses were interviewed by the newsreel reporter in "Citizen Kane." Three of them were:
   a. Paul Stewart; b. Agnes Moorehead; c. Harry Shannon; d. Everett Sloane; e. Joseph Cotten.
8. Name at least three biographical roles played by Gary Cooper:
   a. Dr. Corydon Wassell; b. Robert Oppenheimer; c. Lou Gehrig; d. James Forrestal; e. Billy Mitchell.
9. The film was "A Letter to Three Wives." The wives were played by:
   a. Celeste Holm; b. Linda Darnell; c. Jeanne Crain; d. June Haver; e. Ann Sothern.
10. Choose the three films in which Ginger Rogers and Fred Astaire appeared together:
    a. "Carefree"; b. "A Damsel in Distress"; c. "Follow the Fleet"; d. "Dancing Lady"; e. "Swing Time."

_____points

(*Answers on page 306*)

DOUBLE DUTY

Frequently, the Hollywood thinking is that if a script delivers a good film once, it can do it again. Consequently, an old script is dusted off, recast, retitled, reshot, and emerges as a new film. Unlike the earlier re-dos, these remakes were usually less obviously based on the earlier films. Below, we list some well-known films which were *remade* into equally well-known second versions. Tell us the title of the *remake* and for each correct title you get, take 15 points.

1. "Little Miss Marker" _____
2. "Charley's Aunt" _____
3. "Four Daughters" _____
4. "It Happened One Night" _____
5. "Outward Bound" _____
6. "These Three" _____
7. "The Front Page" _____
8. "Ruggles of Red Gap" _____
9. "The Sea Beast" _____
10. "The Matchmaker" _____

11. "The More the Merrier"   _____
12. "The Milky Way"   _____
13. "An American Tragedy"   _____
14. "House of Strangers"   _____
15. "Broadway Bill"   _____

_____points

(*Answers on page 307*)

DOUBLE DUTY—DUFFERS' TEE

Remakes are different than re-dos, we maintain. For example, in a remake, even the title is changed—unlike re-dos. Below, all of the films in Column One were *remade* into the films listed in Column Two. The only problem is that Column Two is out of order. If you can match the proper remake title with the original title of Column One, you may take 10 points for each correct answer.

1. "Little Miss Marker"   a. "Fancy Pants"
2. "Charley's Aunt"   b. "Moby Dick"
3. "Four Daughters"   c. "Sorrowful Jones"
4. "It Happened One Night"   d. "The Kid from Brooklyn"
5. "Outward Bound"   e. "Broken Lance"
6. "These Three"   f. "Hello, Dolly!"
7. "The Front Page"   g. "Walk, Don't Run!"
8. "Ruggles of Red Gap"   h. "A Place in the Sun"
9. "The Sea Beast"   i. "Ridin' High"
10. "The Matchmaker"   j. "Where's Charley?"
11. "The More the Merrier"   k. "Young at Heart"
12. "The Milky Way"   l. "You Can't Run Away from It"
13. "An American Tragedy"   m. "Between Two Worlds"
14. "House of Strangers"   n. "The Children's Hour"
15. "Broadway Bill"   o. "His Girl Friday"

_____points

(*Answers on page 307*)

DOUBLE DUTY: CASTING

Earlier, we asked the Buffs to supply remake titles of some of Hollywood's well-known films. Assuming you're the movie buff you should be (after the tons of buttered popcorn you've no doubt consumed), we're sure you correctly supplied each remake title. Now, stretching your movie memory one notch more, we're using the same batch of films and supplying one of the stars of the original film. Your task is to supply the name of the Hollywood luminary who played the same part in the remake. To give you a leg up, we've supplied the initials. Take 15 points for each one you get correct.

1. "Little Miss Marker" Adolphe Menjou B_____ H_____

2. "Charley's Aunt" Jack Benny R_____ B_____

3. "Four Daughters" John Garfield F_____ S_____

4. "It Happened One Night" Clark Gable J_____ L_____

5. "Outward Bound" Leslie Howard J_____ G_____

6. "These Three" Joel McCrea J_____ G_____

7. "The Front Page" Pat O'Brien R_____ R_____

8. "Ruggles of Red Gap" Charles Laughton B_____ H_____

9. "The Sea Beast" John Barrymore G_____ P_____

10. "The Matchmaker" Paul Ford W_____ M_____

11. "The More the Merrier" Charles Coburn C_____ G_____

12. "The Milky Way" Harold Lloyd D_____ K_____

13. "House of Strangers" Edward G. Robinson S_____ T_____

14. "An American Tragedy" Phillips Holmes M_____ C_____

15. "Broadway Bill" Warner Baxter B_____ C_____

_____points

(*Answers on page 308*)

DOUBLE DUTY: CASTING—DUFFERS' TEE

Earlier, we asked you to supply the remake titles of some of Hollywood's well-known films. Because these are remakes—and not redos—when the star changed, so did the title. Below, we're using the same batch of films and supply, in Column Two, one of the stars of the earlier version. In Column Three, we have listed, out of order, the stars who played the same parts in a later version. Your task is to match the star of Column Three correctly with the original title and star of Columns One and Two. Take 10 points for each correct answer.

1. "Little Miss Marker"	Adolphe Menjou	a. Danny Kaye
2. "Charley's Aunt"	Jack Benny	b. Bob Hope
3. "Four Daughters"	John Garfield	c. Spencer Tracy
4. "It Happened One Night"	Clark Gable	d. Cary Grant
5. "Outward Bound"	Leslie Howard	e. James Garner
6. "These Three"	Joel McCrea	f. John Garfield
7. "The Front Page"	Pat O'Brien	g. Gregory Peck
8. "Ruggles of Red Gap"	Charles Laughton	h. Bing Crosby
9. "The Sea Beast"	John Barrymore	i. Ray Bolger
10. "The Matchmaker"	Paul Ford	j. Montgomery Clift
11. "The More the Merrier"	Charles Coburn	k. Rosalind Russell
12. "The Milky Way"	Harold Lloyd	l. Frank Sinatra
13. "House of Strangers"	Edward G. Robinson	m. Bob Hope
14. "An American Tragedy"	Phillips Holmes	n. Jack Lemmon
15. "Broadway Bill"	Warner Baxter	o. Walter Matthau

————points

(Answers on page 308)

MORE FIRST FILMS (TOUGHIES)

Earlier we asked for the first films of celebrated stars. In this quiz we're asking for the first films of another group of stars; however, these movie debuts were far less spectacular. In fact, if you know these debut films, count yourself as a Movie Buff with Clusters. Since these are tough, take 25 points for each one you get right.

1. Robert Mitchum   "_____ _____ ___ _____"
2. Marilyn Monroe   "_____ _____"
3. Ronald Reagan   "_____ _____ ___ _____"
4. Deborah Kerr   "_____ ____"
5. Yul Brynner   "_____ ___ __ _____"
6. Teresa Wright   "_____ _____"
7. Bob Hope   "_____ _____ _____"
8. Rita Hayworth   "_____ , _____"
9. Rock Hudson   "_____ _____"
10. Betty Hutton   "_____ _____ , __ ____"

_____points

(Answers on page 309)

MORE FIRST FILMS (TOUGHIES)—DUFFERS' TEE

Earlier we asked for the first films of celebrated stars, and most of those first films were rather auspicious debuts. The ten stars listed below had somewhat less spectacular entries into the film world—as witness the list of film titles in Column Two. However, if you can match up the correct title from Column Two as the debut film of the stars in Column One, you may have 20 points for each correct answer.

1. Robert Mitchum
2. Marilyn Monroe
3. Ronald Reagan
4. Deborah Kerr
5. Yul Brynner
6. Teresa Wright
7. Bob Hope

a. "Fighter Squadron"
b. "The Fleet's In"
c. "Dante's Inferno"
d. "The Little Foxes"
e. "Love Is on the Air"
f. "Dangerous Years"
g. "Hoppy Serves a Writ"

137

9. Rock Hudson   i. "Major Barbara"
8. Rita Hayworth   h. "Port of New York"
10. Betty Hutton   j. "Big Broadcast of 1938"

_____points

(*Answers on page 309*)

FIRST, THE WORD ⚹2

This exercise has to do with literary origin. In Column One, we have listed two films which can be traced to the same author, and in Column Two, we ask you to name the author. Get the author correct and take 10 points. Then, from the multiple choice in Column Three, you are to select the film which *also* came from the pen of the author in that question. Each title correctly selected brings you 5 points. And, in the same generous mood as before, we do not require that you get both parts right in order to score.

1. "Major Barbara"

"Caesar and Cleopatra"
_____

  a. "Drums Along the Mohawk"
  b. "The Devil's Disciple"
  c. "Salome"

2. "The Long Hot Summer"

"The Sound and the Fury"
_____

  a. "Tobacco Road"
  b. "Wuthering Heights"
  c. "The Story of Temple Drake"

3. "Penrod and Sam"

"Seventeen"
_____

  a. "The Magnificent Ambersons"
  b. "Young and Willing"
  c. "What a Life!"

4. "South Pacific"

"Return to Paradise"
_____

  a. "The Bridges at Toko-Ri"
  b. "The Bridge on the River Kwai"
  c. "Destination Tokyo"

138

5. "20,000 Leagues Under the Sea" "Five Weeks in a Balloon" _____

a. "Destination Moon"

b. "City Beneath the Sea"

c. "Journey to the Center of the Earth"

6. "Frenchman's Creek" _____ "Rebecca"

a. "The Birds"

b. "Psycho"

c. "M"

7. "The Matchmaker" _____ "Our Town"

a. "State Fair"

b. "The Towering Inferno"

c. "The Bridge of San Luis Rey"

8. "Kidnapped" _____ "The Master of Ballantrae"

a. "The Black Knight"

b. "Seven Keys to Baldpate"

c. "The Strange Door"

9. "The Adventures of Tom Sawyer" _____ "A Connecticut Yankee in King Arthur's Court"

a. "One Million B.C."

b. "Thanks a Million"

c. "Man with a Million"

10. "The Little Foxes" _____ "The Children's Hour"

a. "Night Must Fall"

b. "Toys in the Attic"

c. "The Time of Your Life"

_____points

(*Answers on page 309*)

FIRST, THE WORD ⚹2—DUFFERS' TEE

This exercise has to do with the literary origin of films. In Column One, we have listed two films which came originally from the pen of the same author. In Column Two, we list, out of order (what else?), the authors in question. And in Column Three, we list—also out of order—another film made from the work of the same author. If you can match the correct author from Column Two to the two films of Column One, take 5 points. If you can select the appropriate *third* film of the author's—from the list in Column Three—and match it correctly, you may have an additional 5 points. On this exercise, you score even though you might not get both parts of the question.

1. "Major Barbara"

            A. James Michener   a. "The Strange Door"

   "Caesar and Cleopatra"

2. "The Long Hot Summer"

            B. Thornton Wilder   b. "The Devil's Disciple"

   "The Sound and the Fury"

3. "Penrod and Sam"

            C Mark Twain   c. "Journey to the Center of the Earth"

   "Seventeen"

4. "South Pacific"

            D. Robert Louis Stevenson   d. "Toys in the Attic"

   "Return to Paradise"

5. "Five Weeks in a Balloon"

            E. Lillian Hellman   e. "The Magnificent Ambersons"

   "20,000 Leagues Under the Sea"

6. "Frenchman's
   Creek"

   F. George Bernard   f. "The Bridges at
         Shaw   Toko-Ri"

   "Rebecca"

7. "The
   Matchmaker"

   G. Booth Tarkington   g. "The Story of Temple
   "Our Town"   Drake"

8. "Kidnapped"

   H. Jules Verne   h. "Man with a Million"

   "The Master
   of Ballantrae"

9. "The Adventures
   of Tom
   Sawyer"

   I. Daphne du   i. "The Bridge of San
   "A Connecticut   Maurier   Luis Rey"
   Yankee in
   King Arthur's
   Court"

10. "The Little
    Foxes"

   J. William Faulkner   j. "The Birds"

    "The Children's
    Hour"

                 _____**points**

(*Answers on page 309*)

READING THE CREDITS

We're often amazed at people who profess to be Movie Buffs, but who usually fail to read the credits—particularly those credits devoted to the players. Similarly, we are always chagrined when the cast credits to the film are incomplete. It's no great feat for the tried-and-true Movie Buff to identify the movie in question from the several top entries of the cast credits. But below, we've provided you with the bottom of the cast credits. From these credits, identify (a) the film, (b) the producer, and (c) the two main stars. Do it, and add 50 points to your score—by answering (a), (b), *and* (c).

The Sergeant	Ed Chandler
A Wounded Soldier	George Hackathorne
A Convalescent Soldier	Roscoe Ates
A Dying Soldier	John Arledge
Amputation Case	Eric Linden
A Commanding Officer	Tom Tyler
A Mounted Officer	William Bakewell
A Hungry Soldier	Louis Jean Heydt
Emmy Slattery	Isabel Jewell
Yankee Major	Robert Elliott
Johnny Gallagher	J. M. Kerrigan
Yankee Business Man	Olin Howland
Tom, Yankee Captain	Ward Bond
Nurse	Lillian Kemble Cooper

_____points

(*Answers on page 311*)

READING THE CREDITS—DUFFERS' TEE

We're often amazed at people who think they know motion pictures, but who usually fail to read the credits—even when the producer is kind enough to provide *complete* credits! It's no great feat for the tried-and-true Movie Buff—or even the dedicated Duffer—to identify a film from its top stars. But below, we've provided instead the *bottom* of the cast credits. From this, we're asking you to identify the film. The character names may be of help to you, or perhaps the players who were further down in the cast may be a tip-off. Get the title, and add 20 points to your score. Get the two top stars of the film, and add 5 points for each. And if you can pin down the producer, add another 10 points!

The Sergeant	Ed Chandler
A Wounded Soldier	George Hackathorne
A Convalescent Soldier	Roscoe Ates
A Dying Soldier	John Arledge
Amputation Case	Eric Linden
A Commanding Officer	Tom Tyler
A Mounted Officer	William Bakewell

A Hungry Soldier	Louis Jean Heydt
Emmy Slattery	Isabel Jewell
Yankee Major	Robert Elliott
Johnny Gallagher	J. M. Kerrigan
Yankee Business Man	Olin Howland
Tom, Yankee Captain	Ward Bond
Nurse	Lillian Kemble Cooper

TITLE:

a. "So Red the Rose"; b. "Drango"; c. "Whistling in Dixie"; d. "Gone with the Wind"; e. "Reap the Wild Wind."

STARS:

a. Ray Milland; b. John Wayne; c. Clark Gable; d. James Stewart; e. Audie Murphy; f. Paulette Goddard; g. Miriam Hopkins; h. Norma Shearer; i. Vivien Leigh; j. Susan Hayward.

PRODUCER:

a. David O. Selznick; b. Irving Thalberg; c. Dore Schary; d. Darryl F. Zanuck; e. Herbert Yates.

_____**title points**
_____**star points**
_____**producer points**
_____**total points**

(*Answers on page 311*)

SOME MORE DOUBLE DUTY

Here are some more films which were remade into films *with different titles*. These, however, are a little more difficult. To show what nice guys we are, we are giving you some clues which should help you come up with the remake title we're seeking. As before, you may have 15 points for each correct answer.

1. "Blind Alley"   "_____ Dark _____"
2. "The Sea Wolf"   "_____ Larsen"
3. "Roberta"   "_____ to _____ ____"
4. "Valley of the
   Giants"   "_____ Big _____"
5. "A Slight Case
   of Murder"   "_____, _____' Killing _____"
6. "Gunga Din"   "_____ Three"

143

7. "Ah,
Wilderness"   "_____ Holiday"

8. "The Man Who
Played God"   "Sincerely _____"

9. "The Paleface"   "____ _____ ____ ____ ____ West"

10. "The Petrified
Forest"   "Escape ____ _____ _____"

11. "The Awful
Truth"   "_____,__ ____ ____ _____"

12. "The Black
Watch"   "_____ ____ _____ Khyber _____"

13. "The Major and
the Minor"   "_____,__ ____ ____ ____ _____"

14. "The Crowd
Roars"   "_____ McCoy"

15. "One Way
Passage"   "T_____ We M_____ A_____"

_____points

(*Answers on page 311*)

SOME MORE DOUBLE DUTY—DUFFERS' TEE

Here are some more films which have been remade into films using
different titles. These, however, are a little more difficult than those
you waded through before. Column One again has the title of the
original version, while (out of order) the remake titles are listed in
Column Two. Your task is to match the title in Column Two with the
earlier title of Column One. You may have 12 points for each correct
pairing.

1. "Blind Alley"   a. "Killer McCoy"

2. "The Sea Wolf"   b. "Sergeants Three"

3. "Roberta"   c. "Summer Holiday"

4. "Valley of the Giants   d. "Sincerely Yours"

5. "A Slight Case of Murder" e. "The Shakiest Gun in the
                                 West"

6. "Gunga Din"   f. "Lovely to Look At"

7. "Ah, Wilderness"   g. "You're Never Too Young"

144

8. "The Man Who Played God"
9. "The Paleface"
10. "The Petrified Forest"
11. "The Awful Truth"
12. "The Black Watch"
13. "The Major and the Minor"
14. "The Crowd Roars"
15. "One Way Passage"

h. "Till We Meet Again"
i. "Wolf Larsen"
j. "The Dark Past"
k. "The Big Trees"
l. "Stop, You're Killing Me"
m. "Escape in the Desert"
n. "Let's Do It Again"
o. "King of the Khyber Rifles"

_____points

(*Answers on page 311*)

SOME MORE DOUBLE DUTY: CASTING

You've been through this list of remake titles, and of course you made yourself a pile of points by recalling the title of the remade versions. But again, we're demanding even more of your movie memory. We again provide the list of titles and one player from the earlier version. You're asked to supply the name of the star who played the same part in the remake. Again, we've given you the initials of the name we're seeking, so you do have some help. Take 20 points for each correct answer.

1. "Blind Alley"	Chester Morris	W_____	H_____
2. "The Sea Wolf"	Edward G. Robinson	B_____	S_____
3. "Roberta"	Fred Astaire	H_____	K_____
4. "Valley of the Giants"	Wayne Morris	K_____	D_____
5. "A Slight Case of Murder"	Edward G. Robinson	B_____	C_____
6. "Gunga Din"	Robert Coote	J_____	B_____
7. "Ah, Wilderness"	Lionel Barrymore	W_____	H_____
8. "The Man Who Played God"	George Arliss	L_____	
9. "The Paleface"	Bob Hope	D_____	K_____
10. "The Petrified Forest"	Humphrey Bogart	H_____	D_____

145

11. "The Awful Truth"	Ralph Bellamy	A_____ R_____
12. "The Black Watch"	Victor McLaglen	T_____ P_____
13. "The Major and the Minor"	Ginger Rogers	J_____ L_____
14. "The Crowd Roars"	Frank Morgan	J_____ D_____
15. "One Way Passage"	William Powell	G_____ B_____

_____points

(Answers on page 311)

SOME MORE DOUBLE DUTY: CASTING—DUFFERS' TEE

You've been through this list of titles which have been remade. And we're confident that you figured out which title of the list we provided was the remake title. (If your memory is faulty, then turn back to SOME MORE DOUBLE DUTY—DUFFERS' TEE.) As we did earlier, we've listed the original title and a player from the earlier version (Columns One and Two). In Column Three—again, out of order—we have listed the players who limned the same parts in the remakes. Your task is to match the player from Column Three with the original title and star. You've already figured out the title of the remake, so tax your memory to remember the star of that film—and perhaps some of the supporting cast. These are a bit more difficult, so take 15 points for each correct answer.

1. "Blind Alley"	Chester Morris	a. Tyrone Power
2. "The Sea Wolf"	Edward G. Robinson	b. Jerry Lewis
3. "Roberta"	Fred Astaire	c. Broderick Crawford
4. "Valley of the Giants"	Wayne Morris	d. Liberace
5. "A Slight Case of Murder"	Edward G. Robinson	e. Don Knotts
6. "Gunga Din"	Sam Jaffe	f. William Holden

146

7. "Ah, Wilderness"	Lionel Barrymore	g. George Brent
8. "The Man Who Played God"	George Arliss	h. Kirk Douglas
9. "The Paleface"	Bob Hope	i. James Dunn
10. "The Petrified Forest"	Humphrey Bogart	j. Barry Sullivan
11. "The Awful Truth"	Ralph Bellamy	k. Helmut Dantine
12. "The Black Watch"	Victor McLaglen	l. Howard Keel
13. "The Major and the Minor"	Ginger Rogers	m. Aldo Ray
14. "The Crowd Roars"	Frank Morgan	n. Sammy Davis, Jr.
15. "One Way Passage"	William Powell	o. Walter Huston

_____points

(*Answers on page 312*)

AND SOME MORE "NAME THE STAR"

Once again we ask you to name the star from the clues we've supplied below. On each line, we've provided the names of two of the characters portrayed by that star during his or her career. From these, you are to identify the star in question. You'd have a good argument if you claimed that these characters were not the best-known characters in the careers of the stars we're seeking. If you don't feel confident, move on to the Duffers' Tee. But if you identify the star from these clues, you can have 10 points for each correct answer.

1. Sir Humphrey Pengalten	Seab Cooley
2. Ugarte	Hans Beckert
3. Rosa Moline	Maggie Cutler
4. Capt. Kirby York	"Ole" Olsen
5. Amy March	Leslie Lynton
6. Maj. Rama Sefti	Chuck Palmer

7.	Janet Ames	Sylvia Fowler
8.	Dr. John Pearly	Lemuel Morehouse
9.	Anthony Keane	Jimmy Ringo
10.	Fritz von Tarlenheim	David Slater

_____points

(*Answers on page 313*)

AND SOME MORE "NAME THE STAR"— DUFFERS' TEE

Once again you're asked to name the star who portrayed the two characters listed on each line below. If you're here from the Buffs' version, the stars are the same, though the characters we give as clues are a little more obvious. That's why, on this Duffers' Tee, we're only giving 5 points for the star identified. So jog your memory —remember the characters—and name the star.

1.	Sir Wilfred Robards	Capt. William Bligh
2.	"Dr. Einstein"	Joel Cairo
3.	Lily Moffatt	Margot Channing
4.	Frank "Spig" Wead	The Ringo Kid
5.	Rebecca, The Jewess	Maggie, the Cat
6.	Juan Galardo	Marty Maher
7.	Lavinia Mannon	Elizabeth Kenny
8.	Judge "Billy" Priest	David Harum
9.	Atticus Finch	Capt. Ahab
10.	Maj. Pollock	Phileas Fogg

_____points

(*Answers on page 313*)

FUNNY FOLKS CRISSCROSS

Here's a crisscross made up entirely of the last names of some great comedy characters of the movies. We've done this a little differently, since in this crisscross, we supply you with the first name, and you

148

must come up with the surname. Using the diagram following, put *each* surname into its proper slot, and you'll have completed the crisscross! And you'll have added 300 points to your score. We caution you to use a pencil in this diagram, and keep an eraser handy. Use ball-points at your own risk. And to show you what dandy guys we are, we've started you out with the first comedian under "Four-Letter Names" below. That should give you the clue that we've alphabetized the comedians by their missing surnames under each classification. Got that? Good.

Four-Letter Names	Five-Letter Names	Six-Letter Names
Sig (Arno)	Gracie	Bud
Mischa	Leon	Margaret
Willie	Chester	Edward Everett
Herman	Cass	Shemp
Ben	Joan	Pert
Charlie	Frank	Ernie
Karl	Patsy	Frank
Fritz	Victor	Jack
Willy	Polly	Edna May
Bob	Jack	Joe
Gil	Ole	May
Marjorie	ZaSu	Will
Zeppo	Renie	Sig
Frank	Larry	Grady
Martha	William	Ben
Harry		
Thelma		
Joe		

Seven-Letter Names	Eight-Letter Names	Nine-Letter Names
Chester	Leo	Jimmie
Louise	Lou	Nat
Jay C.	Sterling	Alison
Billy	Eddie	
Hugh	Mantan	
Edgar	Franklin	
Carmen		
Bert		
Robert		

_____points

(*Answers on page 314*)

FUNNY FOLKS CRISSCROSS—DUFFERS' TEE

Here's a crisscross made up entirely of the last names of some great comedy characters of the movies. As before, insert the appropriate surname into the diagram above, and every name will interlock— provided you plan ahead. One tip: Use a pencil with a good eraser. Or if you're really confident, use a ball-point, and buy several more copies of the book! To show you what dandy guys we are, we've started you off on the right foot with our beloved headwaiter and maître d', Sig ARNO. So, get it right, and add 300 points to your score!

Four-Letter Names

Arno	Bing	Dane	Hope	Marx	Ritz
Auer	Blue	Feld	Lamb	Orth	Todd
Best	Dale	Fung	Main	Raye	Yule

Five-Letter Names

Allen	Jenks	Olsen
Askin	Kelly	Pitts
Clute	Moore	Riano
Daley	Moran	Semon
Davis	Oakie	Tracy

Six-Letter Names

Abbott	Kovacs	Robson
Dumont	Morgan	Rogers
Horton	Norton	Rumann
Howard	Oliver	Sutton
Kelton	Penner	Turpin

Seven-Letter Names

Conklin	Gilbert	Miranda
Fazenda	Herbert	Wheeler
Flippen	Kennedy	Woolsey

Eight-Letter Names

Carrillo	Mayehoff
Costello	Moreland
Holloway	Pangborn

Nine-Letter Names

Finlayson Pendleton Skipworth

_____points

(*Answers on page 315*)

SPOT THE BIO: COMPOSERS

Each of the actors listed below portrayed well-known composers (or lyricists). In some of the films, the creative effort was a partnership, or even a *team* effort. Where such is the case, we have listed the two or more involved. For filling in the names of the composers portrayed by those players listed in Column One, you receive 5 points. If you can also name the film in which the portrayal was included, you get another 10 points. Get all 15 points on *each* of the fifteen questions, and we'll toss in a bonus of 75 points—for a possible 300! We wish you luck—and only require the last name of the composer portrayed. It's the least we can do . . .

	COMPOSER(S)	FILM TITLE
1. Cornel Wilde	_____	_____
2. Clifton Webb	_____	_____

151

3. Cary Grant   _____   _____

4. Danny Thomas   _____   _____

5. Red Skelton and   _____and   _____
    Fred Astaire   _____

6. Robert Alda   _____   _____

7. Don Ameche   _____   _____

8. Gordon Macrae,   _____,
    Ernest Borgnine,   _____,
    and Dan Dailey   and_____   _____

9. Robert Walker   _____   _____

10. Dirk Bogarde   _____   _____

11. José Ferrer   _____   _____

12. Maurice Evans and   _____and   _____
    Robert Morley   _____

13. Stewart Granger   _____   _____

14. Tom Drake and   _____and   _____
    Mickey Rooney   _____

15. Richard   _____   _____
    Chamberlain

_____points

_____bonus?

total_____

(*Answers on page 316*)

SPOT THE BIO: COMPOSERS—DUFFERS' TEE

In Column One below, we list actors who have played composers (or lyricists). If the particular creative effort was the work of a team of composers, then we list the actors in such fashion—as in question 5, 12, and 14. In Column Two, out of order, are the music creators portrayed. And in Column Three, also out of order, are those films in which the portrayals were included. Match the composer to the actor—and then, to *that* pairing, match the correct film title. For each pairing of composer to actor, you get 5 points. If you can then pair up the title from Column Three, that's 10 more points. Get both parts correct and it's worth 15 points per question. Get them all correct, for 225 points, and we'll throw in a bonus of 75 points—for a fat 300 on this exercise.

1. Cornel Wilde	A. Franz Liszt	a. "Song of Love"
2. Clifton Webb	B. Harry Ruby and Bert Kalmar	b. "A Song to Remember"
3. Cary Grant	C. Sigmund Romberg	c. "Song Without End"
4. Danny Thomas	D. Peter I. Tchaikovsky	d. "Swanee River"
5. Red Skelton and Fred Astaire	E. Frédéric Chopin	e. "The Great Victor Herbert"
6. Robert Alda	F. Johannes Brahms	f. "Deep in My Heart"
7. Don Ameche	G. John Philip Sousa	g. "Three Little Words"
8. Walter Connolly	H. Richard Rodgers and Lorenz Hart	h. "The Great Gilbert and Sullivan"
9. Robert Walker	I. George Gershwin	i. "The Magic Bow"
10. Dirk Bogarde	J. Gilbert and Sullivan	j. "The Music Lovers"
11. José Ferrer	K. Niccolò Paganini	k. "I'll See You in My Dreams"
12. Maurice Evans and Robert Morley	L. Victor Herbert	l. "Rhapsody in Blue"
13. Stewart Granger	M. Cole Porter	m. "Words and Music"
14. Tom Drake and Mickey Rooney	N. Stephen Foster	n. "Stars and Stripes Forever"
15. Richard Chamberlain	O. Gus Kahn	o. "Night and Day"

_____points
_____bonus?
total_____

(*Answers on page 316*)

THE TEENY-TINY MARQUEE ✻3

We're not about to explain the TEENY-TINY MARQUEE exercise again. If you're not quite sure how to play it, then for heaven's sake, look back at THE TEENY-TINY MARQUEE ✻1 or ✻2. It's exactly the same except for two points: (1) These are tougher, and (2) we're giving 15 points for each correct answer:

1. "M _ L _ _ d the Great"
2. "After the S _ d _ _ y"
3. "The N _ d Key"
4. "East O _ _ r m _ n"
5. "The War Against Mrs. R _ _ d"
6. "The Pied L _ u _ i _ "
7. "The M _ _ z i Years"
8. "C _ l _ n of India"
9. "G _ _ l the Great"
10. "Roxie D _ l _ r _ s"
11. "Four Flags M _ e"
12. "Baby Face B _ r _ y"

_____points

(*Answers on page 317*)

THE TEENY-TINY MARQUEE ✻3—DUFFERS' TEE

We're not about to explain the TEENY-TINY MARQUEE exercise again—even for you Duffers. If you can't remember how it is played, check back with THE TEENY-TINY MARQUEE ✻1 or ✻2. This is played exactly the same way, and is just the same except for two points: (1) These are tougher, and (2) we're giving 15 points for each correct answer:

1. "M _ L _ _ d the Great"	a. Green
2. "After the S _ d _ _ y "	b. Lynne
3. "The N _ d Key"	c. Hart
4. "East O _ _ r m _ n"	d. Clive
5. "The War Against Mrs. R _ _ d "	e. Catherine
6. "The Pied L _ u _ i _ "	f. Patrick
7. "The M _ _ z i Years"	g. Fox

154

8. "C _ 1 _ n of India"   h. West
9. "G _ _ l the Great"   i. Nelson
10. "Roxie D _ l _ r _ s"   j. Piper
11. "Four Flags M _ e"   k. Glass
12. "Baby Face B _ r _ y"   l. Hadley

_____points

(*Answers on page 317*)

MORE TYPE-CASTING

Again we list four "occupations" which a player represented in four of his or her films. Your task is to name the actor or actress in the questions—and also to give us the titles of the four films. You get 5 points for the name of the player, plus 5 points for *each* correct film title you can recall. The possible score on this is 375 points.

1. Detective's wife; plantation owner's wife; ambassador's daughter; junkie's wife.
2. First Lady; lady doctor; unscrupulous model; actress.
3. College professor; movie star; Nazi field marshal; Irish revolutionary.
4. Eurasian doctor; Red Cross nurse; Cuban revolutionary; schoolteacher.
5. Side-show proprietress; nineteenth-century guerrilla; housekeeper; actress.
6. Publishing tycoon; Roman senator; schoolmaster; naval captain.
7. Brothel madam; stockholder and board member; stripper; backwoods sharpshooter.
8. Musketeer; movie star; reporter; aspiring artist.
9. Fashion designer; psychiatrist; governess; hotel proprietress.
10. Prize fighter; screenwriter; jet pilot; furniture designer.
11. Personal secretary; schoolmistress; British queen; street peddler.
12. Pool shark; private eye; convict; lawyer.
13. Elevator operator; schoolteacher; gangster's moll; prostitute.
14. Gangster; medical professor; governor; junk tycoon.
15. Arab monarch; British king; prime minister; ferryboat captain.

_____points

(*Answers on page 318*)

MORE TYPE-CASTING—DUFFERS' TEE

Again we present four "occupations" which a player represented in four of his or her films. In Column Two, we list these players, out of order, and ask you to match the player with the grouping in Column One. We'll give you 5 points for each correct matching—and if you can get the titles of three of the four films in each grouping, you may add an additional 20 points. So with 15 questions, and a possible 25 points on each, here's your chance to rack up another 375 points.

1. Detective's wife; plantation owner's wife; ambassador's daughter; junkie's wife.

   a. Broderick Crawford

2. First Lady; lady doctor; unscrupulous model; actress.

   b. Bette Davis

3. College professor; movie star; Nazi field marshal; Irish revolutionary.

   c. Alec Guinness

4. Eurasian doctor; Red Cross nurse; Cuban revolutionary; schoolteacher.

   d. Charles Laughton

5. Side-show proprietress; nineteenth-century guerrilla; housekeeper; actress.

   e. Barbara Stanwyck

6. Publishing tycoon; Roman senator; schoolmaster; naval captain.

   f. Eleanor Parker

7. Brothel madam; stockholder and board member; stripper; backwoods sharpshooter.

   g. Jennifer Jones

8. Musketeer; movie star; reporter; aspiring artist.

   h. Shirley MacLaine

9. Fashion designer; psychiatrist; governess; hotel proprietress.

   i. William Holden

10. Prize fighter; screenwriter; jet pilot; furniture designer.

   j. Susan Hayward

11. Personal secretary; schoolmistress; British queen; street peddler.

   k. Gene Kelly

12. Pool shark; private eye; convict; lawyer.

   l. Sophia Loren

13. Elevator operator; schoolteacher; gangster's moll; prostitute.

   m. James Mason

14. Gangster; medical professor; governor; junk tycoon.

   n. Lauren Bacall

15. Arab monarch; British king; prime minister; ferryboat captain.

o. Paul Newman

_____points

(*Answers on page 318*)

OH, BROTHER

Again we're concerned with family relationships in films—and this time we're looking at brothers. In each of the films below, a "brother" relationship was part of the plot. We have provided the film title and the name of the actor or actress who played the brother or sister. You must tell us who played the brother—and then take 10 points for each correct answer.

1. "Sweet Bird of Youth"   Shirley Knight   _____

2. "A Thousand Clowns"   Jason Robards   _____

3. "Bonnie and Clyde"   Gene Hackman   _____

4. "City for Conquest"   Arthur Kennedy   _____

5. "The Glass Menagerie"   Jane Wyman   _____

6. "A Hole in the Head"   Frank Sinatra   _____

7. "Royal Wedding"   Keenan Wynn   _____

8. "The Human Comedy"   Mickey Rooney   _____

9. "Public Enemy"   Donald Cook   _____

10. "Sunday in New York"   Jane Fonda   _____

_____points

(*Answers on page 319*)

OH, BROTHER—DUFFERS' TEE

Again we're concerned with family relationships in films—and this time we're looking at brothers—though not Warner, Ritz, or Marx. In each of the films below, a brother relationship was part of the film, and in Column Two, we have listed the names of the actors or actresses who portrayed the brother or sister of the actor in question. You have a multiple choice in Column Three from which you must select the actor who played the brother. Take 5 points for each correct answer.

1. "Sweet Bird of Youth"   Shirley Knight
   a. Ben Gazzara
   b. Pat Hingle
   c. Rip Torn

2. "A Thousand Clowns"   Jason Robards
   a. Martin Balsam
   b. Gene Hackman
   c. Gene Saks

3. "Bonnie and Clyde"   Gene Hackman
   a. Stacy Keach
   b. Michael J. Pollard
   c. Warren Beatty

4. "City for Conquest"   Arthur Kennedy
   a. Jeffrey Lynn
   b. Pat O'Brien
   c. James Cagney

5. "The Glass Menagerie"   Jane Wyman
   a. Arthur Kennedy
   b. Marlon Brando
   c. Kirk Douglas

6. "A Hole in the Head"   Frank Sinatra
   a. Luther Adler
   b. Zero Mostel
   c. Edward G. Robinson

7. "Royal Wedding"   Keenan Wynn
   a. Keenan Wynn
   b. Fred Astaire
   c. Robert Coote

8. "The Human Comedy"   Mickey Rooney
   a. Barry Nelson
   b. Robert Mitchum
   c. Jackie "Butch" Jenkins

9. "Public Enemy"   Donald Cook
   a. Eddie Woods
   b. William Lundigan
   c. James Cagney

10. "Sunday in
    New York"   Jane Fonda

    a. Peter Fonda
    b. Rod Taylor
    c. Cliff Robertson

_____points

(*Answers on page 319*)

WILD CARD—BUFFS AND DUFFERS

Here's another wild-card exercise for Buffs and Duffers. It's an exercise in mental gymnastics, logic, patience, exasperation, and downright hard-nose stick-to-itiveness. Take your time, and watch your profanity in front of the children. When you have it all finished—correctly, we presume—you may add 100 points to your score.

Dear Gopher

To: Gopher
From: Stu Pendas, Exec. VP, Miracle Studios
Subj.: Casting

Dear Gopher:
By the time you read this, I'll be jetting to Europe, either for cocktails with Grace and Phil, or dinner with Ingmar, or both. But over the weekend, I had a hot flash for the new Stu Pendas-Miracle production, "Hat in the Ring." The writer and I have figured to sketch in five cameo roles —one for a SWASHBUCKLER, one for a great CHARACTER ACTOR, one for a great COMEDIAN, one for a great TRAGEDIAN, and one for a really beloved WESTERN HERO. Off the top of my head, I see Flynn, Laughton, Lahr, Barrymore, and Bill Hart—but since they've all passed on to the Great Producer in the sky, that's not a viable idea.

Irving Tithe, the agent, has suggested a bunch of names to me: SAMUEL HILL, ROLAND STONE, RICK WRAQUE, LES DANTS, and LODEN ZOAHN. Now, these guys sure the hell ain't Flynn, Laughton, and so on—but Tithe tells me they were all big in the forties . . . and with the nostalgia kick everyone's hot for now, we might give our b.o. a hefty hype by using them. But to level with you, I'm not sure which guy *is* the SWASHBUCKLER, the CHARACTER ACTOR, and so on. All I know is that they've retired, and none of them have even been near a studio in the last twenty years.

159

I had a list of where they all lived, but you know *me* with details. More-over, I was never much at geography, so I'll put down what I know of where the five have scattered to—that is, where they're *now* living—in terms of what I *can* remember.

One of them lives in the city that was the background for THE ST. VALENTINE'S DAY MASSACRE. Another of them lives in the city which they used for location in THREE COINS IN THE FOUNTAIN. A third guy lives in the city which was featured in Hellinger's NAKED CITY. A fourth lives in the town where they shot those great chase scenes in BULLITT, and the other one lives in the burg that was home base for the detective series with Basil Rathbone. You know, the flicks where Nigel Bruce was Rathbone's second banana.

Let's see—oh, yeah, I had Research get to work, and they'll pass on to you some stuff that might help you out. From the information above, and what Research will provide, I want you to figure out which actor lives in which city, and what his special talent is—COMEDIAN, TRAGE-DIAN, that sort of thing. I'll be back day after tomorrow, and I want to get on the horn and nail these guys down before Irving Tithe gets a line on what I'm up to. Ciao, sweetie!

(Signed) *Stu Pendas*

To: Gopher
From: Research Dept., Miracle Studios
Subj.: Casting

Mr. Pendas asked us to provide reserch data on the following talents:

SAMUEL HILL, ROLAND STONE, RICK WRAQUE, LES DANTS, and LODEN ZOAHN.

As you may or may not be aware, these talents have not been prom-inent in motion pictures for nearly twenty-five years. We have combed available files, and have come up with the sketchy data we list below. We have not listed the various sources, since Mr. Pendas advised this was not necessary. Hope this information is helpful, however brief.

SAMUEL HILL:
   a. Has a deep-seated fear resulting from an unhappy childhood; as a result he has always refused to work in films which require him to handle swords or horses.
   b. Has never appeared in a film with any of the other four actors.

RICK WRAQUE:
   c. (Quote) "God spare me from character actors. Every one of them is 100 per cent pure ham, and I can't stand being around them."

d. It has been established that the actor now residing on the East Coast has the same prejudice against Mr. Wraque that Mr. Wraque has for character actors.

e. The WESTERN HERO now lives east of Rick Wraque.

LODEN ZOAHN:

f. Mr. Zoahn and the CHARACTER ACTOR now reside in Europe.

g. Mr. Zoahn has never worn a ten-gallon hat or handled a six gun in his entire cinematic career.

h. Only if the TRAGEDIAN now lives in the city where Charles Laughton's first film was shot is Mr. Zoahn the SWASHBUCKLER.

ROLAND STONE:

i. Mr. Stone lives west of the COMEDIAN.

LES DANTS:

j. Mr. Dants once appeared in a film with the TRAGEDIAN.

MISCELLANEOUS/UNIDENTIFIED:

k. The actor now living in southern Europe once made a film with the CHARACTER ACTOR.

l. The actor now residing in the Midwest once suffered a black eye in a barroom brawl with the COMEDIAN.

P.S. The above information is all we have been able to turn up. While this was being prepared, Mr. Pendas radioed from his private jet. We reviewed the above information for him, and he opined that this should be sufficient to enable you to deduce the respective names, particular specialties, and cities of residence by the time he returns.

(Signed) Helena Morg, Research Asst.

_____**points**

(Answers on page 319)

AND AGAIN, WHO IS IT?

Once more you only have to fill in the name of the player who portrayed the well-known movie character listed in Column One. Getting all the names right, and finding the right vertical column, will reveal to you the name of a well-remembered character from an early crime classic. Tell us the name of the star who portrayed this cinematic criminal, and add 50 points to your score!

161

Spats Colombo	_ _ _ _ _ _ _ _ _
Doc Boone	_ _ _ _ _ _ _ _ _ _
Cody Jarrett	_ _ _ _ _ _ _ _ _
Col. Clint Maroon	_ _ _ _ _ _ _ _ _
Peter Warne	_ _ _ _ _ _ _ _
Doc Erwin Riedenschneider	_ _ _ _ _ _ _ _
Lina Lamont	_ _ _ _ _ _ _ _ _
Diamond Jim Brady	_ _ _ _ _ _ _ _ _ _ _
Charlie Allnut	_ _ _ _ _ _ _ _ _ _ _ _ _
Boss Jim Gettys	_ _ _ _ _ _ _ _ _ _
Victor Laszlo	_ _ _ _ _ _ _ _ _ _ _
Genl. Buck Turgidson	_ _ _ _ _ _ _ _ _ _ _ _

And the name of the star who played this character is

_____

_____points

(Answers on page 323)

AND AGAIN, WHO IS IT?—DUFFERS' TEE

And again you only have to fill in the name of the actor or actress
who portrayed the movie character listed in Column One. Once
you've done all of these, you'll find revealed (in the proper vertical
column) the title and leading character of a well-known early
gangster classic. By telling us who portrayed this character, you can
add 25 points to your score. But since, after all, you are still a
Duffer, you can also find the name of the actor by unscrambling the
key letters we've earmarked for you.

Rhett Butler	_ _ _ _ _ _ _(_)_ _
Willy Loman	_ _(_)_ _ _ _ _ _ _ _ _
Gerald O'Hara	_ _ _ _ _ _ _ _(_)_ _ _
Father Flanagan	(_)_ _ _ _ _ _ _(_)_ _ _
Charles Foster Kane	_(_)_ _ _
Minnesota Fats	_(_)_ _ _ _ _ _ _ _ _(_)
The Virginian	_ _ _ _ _ _(_)_ _ _
Capt. Bat Guano	_ _(_)_ _ (_)_ _ _
Duke Mantee	_ _ _ _ _ _ _ _ _ _ _ _ _
Genl. George Patton	(_)_ _ _ _ _ _ _ _(_)_ _
Mrs. Danvers	_ _(_)_ _ _ _ _(_)_ _ _ _
Willy Stark	_ _ _ _ _ _ _ _ _ _ _ _ _ _ _ _ _

And the name of the star is

— — — — — — — — — — — — — — !

——————points

(Answers on page 324)

AND SOME MORE DOUBLE DUTY

Once again, we are looking at some films which were remade into films with different titles. If you have the hang of it by now, you know we're looking for the titles of the remakes, and these shouldn't be all that tough. But since these are just a trifle more obscure, we're providing you with the smallest of hints. Give us the remake title, and take 15 points for each correct answer.

 1. "Nights of Cabiria"   "S_____ C_____"
 2. "The Women"   "The O_____ S_____"
 3. "Sentimental Journey"   "The G_____ of L_____"
 4. "Red Dust"   "C_____ M_____"
 5. "Rain"   "M_____ S_____ T_____"
 6. "The Philadelphia Story"   "H_____ S_____"
 7. "No, No, Nanette"   "T_____ f_____ T_____"
 8. "The Informer"   "U_____ T_____"
 9. "Waterloo Bridge"   "G_____"
10. "Destry Rides Again"   "F_____"
11. "Ninotchka"   "S_____ S_____"
12. "The Maltese Falcon"   "S_____ M_____ a L_____"
13. "My Favorite Wife"   "M_____ O____, D_____"
14. "Love Is News"   "T____ W_____ U_____"
15. "Love Affair"   "An A_____ t__ R_____"

——————points

(Answers on page 325)

163

AND SOME MORE DOUBLE DUTY—DUFFERS' TEE

Once again we're looking at some films which were remade into films with different titles. Column One again has the earlier film titles, and you'll find that Column Two has a list of the remake titles, which again are out of order. Match up the title of Column Two with the correct title in Column One, and take 12 points for each correct answer.

1. "Nights of Cabiria"
2. "The Women"
3. "Sentimental Journey"
4. "Red Dust"
5. "Rain"
6. "The Philadelphia Story"
7. "No, No, Nanette"
8. "The Informer"
9. "Waterloo Bridge"
10. "Destry Rides Again"
11. "Ninotchka"
12. "The Maltese Falcon"
13. "My Favorite Wife"
14. "Love Is News"
15. "Love Affair"

a. "That Wonderful Urge"
b. "Up Tight"
c. "Silk Stockings"
d. "The Gift of Love"
e. "Gaby"
f. "Sweet Charity"
g. "Satan Met a Lady"
h. "An Affair to Remember"
i. "The Opposite Sex"
j. "Miss Sadie Thompson"
k. "Tea for Two"
l. "Frenchie"
m. "High Society"
n. "Move Over, Darling"
o. "Congo Maisie"

_____points

(*Answers on page 325*)

AND SOME MORE DOUBLE DUTY: CASTING

We're certain you scored well on that last additional list of pictures which have been remade. And we're equally certain your movie memory extends to the stars of both the original and remake versions. However, just to be absolutely sure, we've listed the earlier films, and one of the stars. In Column Three, we're asking you to supply the name of the star who played the same part in the remake version. You may, of course, head straight for the answers—but then you won't be able to take 15 points for each correct one.

1. "Nights of Cabiria"   Giulietta Masina   _____y   _____e
2. "The Women"   Joan Crawford   _____n   _____s
3. "Sentimental
   Journey"   Maureen O'Hara   _____n   _____l
4. "Red Dust"   Jean Harlow   _____n   _____n
5. "Rain"   Joan Crawford   _____a   _____h
6. "The Philadelphia
   Story"   Ruth Hussey   _____e   _____m
7. "No, No, Nanette"   Anna Neagle   _____s   _____y
8. "The Informer"   Margot Grahame   _____y   _____e
9. "Waterloo Bridge"   Vivien Leigh   _____e   _____n
10. "Destry Rides
    Again"   Marlene Dietrich   _____y   _____s
11. "Ninotchka"   Greta Garbo   _____d   _____e
12. "The Maltese
    Falcon"   Bebe Daniels   _____e   _____s
13. "My Favorite
    Wife"   Irene Dunne   _____s   _____y
14. "Love Is News"   Loretta Young   _____e   _____y
15. "Love Affair"   Irene Dunne   _____h   _____r

_____**points**

(*Answers on page 325*)

AND SOME MORE DOUBLE DUTY:
CASTING—DUFFERS' TEE

We're certain you scored well on AND SOME MORE DOUBLE
DUTY—and now let's get to the casts of those very films. Since
we're sure you matched up the original and the remake, it should be
a snap for you to determine who played the same part in both versions. Once again, we list the title and one star from the earlier version in Columns One and Two, and we're asking you to pick out the
appropriate star who did the *same* part from Column Three. And
now that you are getting more proficient at this, we're only awarding
12 points for each correct matching.

1.	"Nights of Cabiria"	Giulietta Masina	a. Shelley Winters
2.	"The Women"	Joan Crawford	b. Doris Day
3.	"Sentimental Journey"	Maureen O'Hara	c. Ruby Dee
4.	"Red Dust"	Jean Harlow	d. Shirley MacLaine
5.	"Rain"	Joan Crawford	e. Cyd Charisse
6.	"The Philadelphia Story"	Ruth Hussey	f. Deborah Kerr
7.	"No, No, Nanette"	Anne Neagle	g. Joan Collins
8.	"The Informer"	Margot Grahame	h. Bette Davis
9.	"Waterloo Bridge"	Vivien Leigh	i. Rita Hayworth
10.	"Destry Rides Again"	Marlene Dietrich	j. Celeste Holm
11.	"Ninotchka"	Greta Garbo	k. Gene Tierney
12.	"The Maltese Falcon"	Bebe Daniels	l. Lauren Bacall
13.	"My Favorite Wife"	Irene Dunne	m. Leslie Caron
14.	"Love Is News"	Loretta Young	n. Ann Sothern
15.	"Love Affair"	Irene Dunne	o. Doris Day

————points

(*Answers on page 325*)

SENSATIONAL COLOR!

Now we are looking for film titles—twenty of them—and each of those we are seeking has a color as part of its title. As clues for you, we list two or three of the film's stars, the year of its release, and a key word or phrase as an additional clue. Come up with the proper title, and add 15 points to your score for each one you get correct.

1. Edward G. Robinson, Joan Bennett, Dan Duryea (1945)—Murder.
2. Alec Guinness, Stanley Holloway (1952)—Robbery.

3. Judy Holliday, Paul Douglas, Fred Clark (1956)—Stockholder.

4. Ray Milland, Joan Collins, Farley Granger (1955)—Evelyn Nesbitt.

5. David Niven, Peter Sellers, Capucine (1964)—Mancini's theme.

6. Gregory Peck, Jennifer Jones, Fredric March (1956)—Madison Avenue.

7. Alec Guinness, Joan Greenwood, Cecil Parker (1952)—Miracle fabric.

8. Douglas Fairbanks, Jr., Joan Bennett, Vincent Price (1940)—Inca treasure.

9. Paul Newman, Virginia Mayo, Jack Palance (1955)—The Last Supper.

10. Linda Darnell, Cornel Wilde, Richard Greene (1947)—Charles II.

11. Gregory Peck, Anne Baxter, Richard Widmark (1948)—Sixguns.

12. Jennifer Jones, Charlton Heston (1952)—Social climber.

13. Shirley Temple, Spring Byington, Nigel Bruce (1940)—Maeterlinck.

14. Gene Kelly, J. Carrol Naish (1950)—Extortion and murder.

15. Tyrone Power, Maureen O'Hara, Donald Crisp (1955)—West Point.

16. Alastair Sim, Terry-Thomas, George Cole (1957)—Assassination.

17. Anthony Quinn, Sophia Loren (1960)—Frontier theatricals.

18. Gregory Peck, Win Min Than, Bernard Lee (1955)—The R.A.F. in Burma.

19. Anna Magnani, Burt Lancaster, Marisa Pavan (1955)—Tennessee Williams.

20. Robert Young, James Stewart, Tom Brown (1937)—Annapolis.

_____points

(*Answers on page 326*)

SENSATIONAL COLOR!—DUFFERS' TEE

Color plays a major part in these film titles. Supply the color, and you'll complete the titles of the following films. If that's too difficult, then merely complete the titles and you'll have the color we're looking for! Through either simple method, you will have added 5 points to your score for each complete, and correct, film title. As additional clues, we've given you a couple of the stars of the film.

1. Edward G. Robinson, Joan Bennett: "_ _ _ _ _ _ _ Street"

2. Alec Guinness, Stanley Holloway: "The _ _ _ _ _ _ _ _ Hill Mob"

3. Judy Holliday, Paul Douglas: "The Solid _ _ _ _ _ Cadillac"

4. Ray Milland, Joan Collins: "The Girl in the _ _ _ Velvet Swing"

5. David Niven, Peter Sellers: "The _ _ _ _ _ Panther"

6. Gregory Peck, Jennifer Jones: "The Man in the _ _ _ _ Flannel Suit"

7. Alec Guinness, Joan Greenwood: "The Man in the _ _ _ _ _ Suit"

8. Douglas Fairbanks, Jr., Joan Bennett: "_ _ _ _ _ _ Hell"

9. Paul Newman, Virginia Mayo: "The _ _ _ _ _ _ _ Chalice"

10. Linda Darnell, Cornel Wilde: "Forever _ _ _ _ _ _"

11. Gregory Peck, Richard Widmark: "_ _ _ _ _ _ Sky"

12. Jennifer Jones, Charlton Heston: "_ _ _ _ Gentry"

13. Shirley Temple, Spring Byington: "The _ _ _ _ _ Bird"

14. Gene Kelly, J. Carrol Naish: "_ _ _ _ _ _ Hand"

15. Tyrone Power, Maureen O'Hara: "The Long _ _ _ _ Line"

16. Alastair Sim, Terry-Thomas: "The _ _ _ _ _ _ Man"

17. Anthony Quinn, Sophia Loren: "Heller in _ _ _ _ Tights"

18. Gregory Peck, Win Min Than: "The _ _ _ _ _ _ _ Plain"

19. Anna Magnani, Burt Lancaster: "The _ _ _ _ _ Tattoo"

20. Robert Young, James Stewart: "Navy _ _ _ _ _ and _ _ _ _ _"

_____ points

(*Answers on page 326*)

ODD MAN OUT #4

On each line below, we list a quartet of actors or actresses. Three of those listed all portrayed, at one time or another, the *same* movie character. The remaining player did *not*. Your task is to provide a two-part answer: (a) the character portrayed by the trio who properly belong in the group, and (b) the actor or actress who did not play the character, and who is therefore the "odd man." Take 10 points for each correct answer, but only if you have *both* parts correct.

1. Eddie Quillan   Dan Duryea   Ralph Bellamy   William Gargan
2. Elizabeth   Vivien Leigh   Claudette   Lynn Redgrave
   Taylor   Colbert
3. Boris Karloff   Charles Ogle   Glenn Langan   Glenn Strange
4. Kirk Douglas   Victor   Cesar Romero   Burt Lancaster
                      Mature
5. Roland   J. Carrol   Sidney Toler   Warner Oland
   Winters   Naish
6. Michael   Ronald   John Howard   Walter Pidgeon
   Rennie   Colman
7. John   Clive Brook   Basil Rathbone   William Powell
   Barrymore
8. Leo Gordon   Harold Huber   Nick Adams   Lawrence
                                                          Tierney
9. Robert   Richard   Dick Powell   Humphrey
   Montgomery   Conte   Bogart
10. Elmo K.   Johnny   Chuck Connors   Glenn Morris
    Lincoln   Weissmuller

_____points

(Answers on page 327)

ODD MAN OUT #4—DUFFERS' TEE

On each line below, we list a well-known movie character, as well as four actors or actresses. Three of those names in each list portrayed the character indicated, at one time or another, while the fourth did *not*. For 10 points each, tell us which player is out of place.

169

1. ELLERY QUEEN	Eddie Quillan Ralph Bellamy	Dan Duryea William Gargan
2. CLEOPATRA	Elizabeth Taylor Claudette Colbert	Vivien Leigh Lynn Redgrave
3. FRANKENSTEIN'S MONSTER	Boris Karloff Glenn Langan	Charles Ogle Glenn Strange
4. DOC HOLLIDAY	Kirk Douglas Cesar Romero	Victor Mature Burt Lancaster
5. CHARLIE CHAN	J. Carrol Naish Sidney Toler	Roland Winters Warner Oland
6. BULLDOG DRUMMOND	Michael Rennie John Howard	Ronald Colman Walter Pidgeon
7. SHERLOCK HOLMES	John Barrymore Basil Rathbone	Clive Brook William Powell
8. JOHN DILLINGER	Leo Gordon Nick Adams	Harold Huber Lawrence Tierney
9. PHILIP MARLOWE	Robert Montgomery Humphrey Bogart	Richard Conte Dick Powell
10. TARZAN	Johnny Weissmuller Chuck Connors	Elmo K. Lincoln Glenn Morris

———points

(*Answers on page 327*)

NAMES IN COMMON

Below, we list pairs of film players who have the same surname. The only problem is that we have neglected to tell you what the surname is. The other striking fact about these couples is that some of them *are* related, while the rest only have the commonality of the same surname by reasons "purely coincidental." As the first part of your answer, you are to provide the correct surname—and for each of those you get correct, you receive 5 points. In addition, you are to enter in either of the columns at the right your answer as to whether the couples are *related* or *unrelated*. If they are related, you must provide the relationship. For each correct answer regarding the relationship, or non-relationship, you may have another 10 points.

170

1. Bruce and Ruth G _ _ _ _ _
2. Etienne and Annie G _ _ _ _ _ _ _
3. Robert and Elizabeth M _ _ _ _ _ _ _ _ _
4. James and Lucille G _ _ _ _ _ _
5. Ben and Celia J _ _ _ _ _ _
6. Gene and June L _ _ _ _ _ _ _
7. Marlon and Jocelyn B _ _ _ _ _
8. Donald and Dolores G _ _ _
9. John and Hayley M _ _ _ _
10. Mervyn and Glynis J _ _ _ _
11. Rick and Sybil J _ _ _ _
12. Frank and Nancy S _ _ _ _ _ _
13. Michael and Joan C _ _ _ _ _ _ _
14. Edgar and Candice B _ _ _ _ _
15. Edmond and Margaret O ' _ _ _ _ _
16. Donald and Una O ' _ _ _ _ _ _
17. Conrad and Elsie J _ _ _ _
18. Hoot and Virginia G _ _ _ _ _
19. Cary and Kathryn G _ _ _ _
20. Dennis and Hedda H _ _ _ _ _

_____**points**

(*Answers on page 328*)

NAMES IN COMMON—DUFFERS' TEE

Below, in Column One, we list pairs of players who have the same surname. In the two columns at the right of the page, we ask you to tell us if there *is* or *is not* a relationship. If you can distinguish correctly, you may have 5 points. In those cases where there *is* some familial connection, you can win another 5 points by telling us *what* the relationship is.

1. Bruce and Ruth Gordon
2. Etienne and Annie Girardot
3. Robert and Elizabeth Montgomery

4. James and Lucille Gleason
5. Ben and Celia Johnson
6. Gene and June Lockhart
7. Marlon and Jocelyn Brando
8. Donald and Dolores Gray
9. John and Hayley Mills
10. Mervyn and Glynis Johns
11. Rick and Sybil Jason
12. Frank and Nancy Sinatra
13. Michael and Joan Crawford
14. Edgar and Candice Bergen
15. Edmond and Margaret O'Brien
16. Donald and Una O'Connor
17. Conrad and Elsie Janis
18. Hoot and Virginia Gibson
19. Cary and Kathryn Grant
20. Dennis and Hedda Hopper

————points

(*Answers on page 328*)

THE VIOLENT END

All of the players below, in the films we've specified, portrayed characters who came to a violent end. For 15 points each—assuming you have the correct answer—approach these questions gingerly . . . and tell us the manner of death!

1. James Cagney, in "White Heat"?
2. Kenneth Spencer, in "Bataan"?
3. Orson Welles, in "The Stranger"?
4. Van Heflin, in "Airport"?
5. Spencer Tracy, in "Captains Courageous"?
6. Jane Darwell, in "Jesse James"?
7. Susan Hayward, in "Reap the Wild Wind"?
8. Robert Wilke, in "The Magnificent Seven"?
9. James Coburn, in "Charade"?

10. Louis Calhern, in "The Asphalt Jungle"?
11. Charles McGraw, in "Spartacus"?
12. Edmund Gwenn, in "Foreign Correspondent"?
13. Norman Lloyd, in "Saboteur"?
14. Ernest Borgnine, in "The Vikings"?
15. Tyrone Power, in "Blood and Sand"?

_____points

(*Answers on page 329*)

THE VIOLENT END—DUFFERS' TEE

Below we list a number of players. In the films we've specified, the characters they portrayed all met violent deaths. In Column Two, out of order, we've supplied the manner of these deaths, and we ask you to match these correctly with the players of Column One. Take 15 points for each correct answer.

1. James Cagney, in "White Heat" . . .

    a. Jumped into a pit of wild animals.

2. Kenneth Spencer, in "Bataan" . . .

    b. Drowned in a pot of hot soup.

3. Orson Welles, in "The Stranger" . . .

    c. Killed by self-inflicted gunshot.

4. Van Heflin, in "Airport" . . .

    d. Suffocated by plastic bag.

5. Spencer Tracy, in "Captains Courageous" . . .

    e. Gored by bull in the bull ring.

6. Jane Darwell, in "Jesse James" . . .

    f. Impaled by sword on mechanical clock.

7. Susan Hayward, in "Reap the Wild Wind" . . .

    g. Fell from Statue of Liberty.

8. Robert Wilke, in "The Magnificent Seven" . . .

    h. Killed by explosion of gasoline tank.

173

9. James Coburn, in
   "Charade" . . .

10. Louis Calhern, in "The Asphalt
    Jungle" . . .

11. Charles McGraw, in
    "Spartacus" . . .

12. Edmund Gwenn, in "Foreign
    Correspondent" . . .

13. Norman Lloyd, in
    "Saboteur" . . .

14. Ernest Borgnine, in "The
    Vikings" . . .

15. Tyrone Power, in "Blood and
    Sand" . . .

i. Beheaded by Japanese
   soldier.

j. Fell from high building.

k. Killed by bomb thrown into
   house.

l. Drowned in a shipwreck.

m. Blown out of jetliner by a
   bomb he triggered.

n. Maimed and drowned by
   accident at sea.

o. Killed by thrown knife.

_____points

(Answers on page 329)

MORE QUOTABLES

Again, we give you some rather well-known lines of dialogue from a
number of well-known films. And again, we ask you to identify the
films from which the dialogue is taken. You may have 15 points for
each correct answer.

1. "Of all the gin joints in all
   the towns in all the world,
   she walks into mine."

   "_ _ _ _ _ _ _ _ _ _ _"

2. "Well, nobody's perfect."

   "_ _ _ _ _ _ _ _ _ _ _ _ _ _ _"

3. "I'll be ever'where—wherever
   you look. Wherever there's a
   fight so hungry people can
   eat, I'll be there. Wherever
   there's a cop beatin' up a
   guy, I'll be there . . ."

   "_ _ _ _ _ _ _ _ _ _

   _ _ _ _ _ _ _"

174

4. "Let's give 'em the gunsel—he
   actually did shoot Thursby
   and Jacoby, didn't he?
   Anyway, he's made to order
   for the part—look at 'im.
   Let's give 'im to them."

   "___ _____ ___
   ___ _____"

5. "I don't pray. Kneeling bags
   my nylons."

   "___ __ ___ ____"

6. "That's what it's all about—
   either be a victim or a thug.
   But suppose . . . suppose
   you don't want to be
   neither . . . not the 'are an'
   not the 'ound. Then what?"

   "____ ___ ___
   _____ _____"

7. "Ach—so-o-o-o . . ."

   "_____ __"

8. "I picked you for the job, not
   because I think you're so
   darned smart, but because I
   thought maybe you were a
   shade less dumb than the
   rest of the outfit. I guess I
   was all wet. You're not
   smarter, Walter—you're just
   a little taller."

   "_____
   _____"

9. "The Monte Carlo Ballet
   steenks!"

   "___ ___' _ ____
   __ ____ ___"

10. "It's a problem, isn't it? That
    nice young man that drinks,
    and the high-class young
    lady, and how did she ever
    get mixed up with him, and
    why does he drink, and why
    doesn't he stop. That's my
    novel, Nat."

    "___ ____ _____"

11. "Hi ya, Father—whaddya
    hear, whaddya say?"

    "_____ ____
    _____ _____"

12. "I'd just like to keep that
    particular piece of paper
    myself. I've got a hunch it
    might turn out to be
    something pretty
    important . . . a document,
    like the Declaration of

Independence, and the
Constitution . . . and my
first report card in school." "___ ___ ___ ___ ___ ___ ___ ___"

13. "Live fast, die young—and
have a good-looking corpse." "___ ___ ___ ___ ___ ___ ___ ___ ___ ___"

14. "Will I go? What a question!
Of course I'll go—any time,
any day. I only been waitin'
fer one or two guys to ask
me. Hunt for gold? Always "___ ___ ___ ___ ___ ___ ___ ___ ___ ___
at yer service." ___ ___ ___ ___ ___ ___ ___ ___ ___"

15. "Paramount? Ha! Let 'em wait. "___ ___ ___ ___ ___
I've waited long enough!" ___ ___ ___ ___ ___ ___"

___points

(Answers on page 330)

MORE QUOTABLES—DUFFERS' TEE

Again we present some lines of dialogue which are some of the more
memorable to have come from the screen. The motion pictures from
which the dialogue examples are taken are listed, out of order, in
Column Two. Select the title which included the line of dialogue. For
each correct matching, you receive 10 points.

1. "Of all the gin joints in all the towns in all
   the world, she walks into mine."
   a. "Sunset
      Boulevard"

2. "Well, nobody's perfect."
   b. "Double
      Indemnity"

3. "I'll be ever'where—wherever you look.
   Wherever there's a fight so hungry
   people can eat, I'll be there. Wherever
   there's a cop beatin' up a guy, I'll be
   there . . ."
   c. "The Lost
      Weekend"

4. "Let's give 'em the gunsel—he actually
   did shoot Thursby and Jacoby, didn't
   he? Anyway, he's made to order for
   the part—look at 'im. Let's give 'im
   to them."
   d. "Ace in the Hole"

5. "I don't pray. Kneeling bags my nylons."

6. "That's what it's all about—either be a victim or a thug. But suppose . . . suppose you don't want to be neither . . . not the 'are an' not the 'ound. Then what?"

7. "Ach—so-o-o-o . . ."

8. "I picked you for the job, not because I think you're so darned smart, but because I thought maybe you were a shade less dumb than the rest of the outfit. I guess I was all wet. You're not smarter, Walter—you're just a little taller."

9. "The Monte Carlo Ballet steenks!"

10. "It's a problem, isn't it? That nice young man that drinks, and the high-class young lady, and how did she ever get mixed up with him, and why does he drink, and why doesn't he stop. That's my novel, Nat."

11. "Hi ya, Father—whaddya hear, whaddya say?"

12. "I'd just like to keep that particular piece of paper myself. I've got a hunch it might turn out to be something pretty important . . . a document, like the Declaration of Independence, and the Constitution . . . and my first report card in school."

13. "Live fast, die young—and have a good-looking corpse."

14. "Will I go? What a question! Of course I'll go—any time, any day. I only been waitin' fer one or two guys to ask me. Hunt for gold? Always at yer service."

e. "Angels with Dirty Faces"

f. "Knock on Any Door"

g. "Some Like It Hot"

h. "The Treasure of the Sierra Madre"

i. "The Maltese Falcon"

j. "You Can't Take It with You"

k. "Stalag 17"

l. "None But the Lonely Heart"

m. "Casablanca"

n. "The Grapes of Wrath"

15. "Paramount? Ha! Let 'em wait. *I've*
    waited long enough!"

                                              o. "Citizen Kane"

                                                    _____points

(*Answers on page 330*)

LA RONDE ET LA RONDE

This exercise is based on the same premise as the earlier LA
RONDE. In it, we ask you to complete the wheel below by supplying the titles for the symbols we supply. For A, supply the title of
a film in which Cary Grant and Sophia Loren appeared—then for

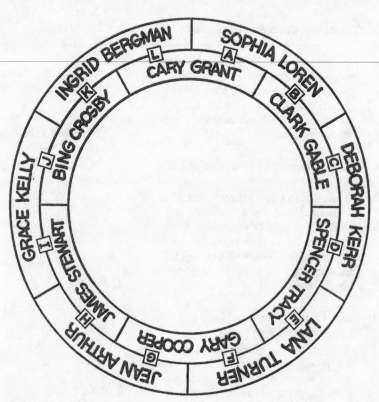

B, a film with Sophia Loren and Clark Gable, and on around until the wheel is completed. No score for an incomplete wheel, and no title may be used more than once. But get all titles, completing the wheel, and take 100 points. One clue to save you grief: All the players were not necessarily the stars in the films we're seeking.

A. Cary Grant and Sophia Loren "_____"

B. Sophia Loren and Clark Gable "_____"

C. Clark Gable and Deborah Kerr "_____"

D. Deborah Kerr and Spencer
   Tracy "_____"

E. Spencer Tracy and Lana Turner "_____"

F. Lana Turner and Gary Cooper "_____"

G. Gary Cooper and Jean Arthur "_____"

H. Jean Arthur and James Stewart "_____"

I. James Stewart and Grace Kelly "_____"

J. Grace Kelly and Bing Crosby "_____"

K. Bing Crosby and Ingrid
   Bergman "_____"

L. Ingrid Bergman and Cary Grant "_____"

_____points

(*Answers on page 330*)

LA RONDE ET LA RONDE—DUFFERS' TEE

This exercise is based on the same premise as the earlier LA RONDE. To complete the wheel on the preceding page, you are asked to substitute titles for the symbols A, B, etc. which we've provided. For A obviously, we're seeking the title of a film in which Cary Grant and Sophia Loren appeared. And the title of the film in which Sophia Loren appeared with Clark Gable would be represented by B, and so on around until the wheel is completed. For the Duffers, we've supplied a list of titles which will complete the wheel, but—as usual—the titles are out of order. Put them in order, completing the wheel, and take 50 points. No score for an incomplete wheel, but we'll give you a clue: Not all of the players were necessarily the stars of the films we've provided.

179

A. Cary Grant and Sophia Loren	1. "Rear Window"
B. Sophia Loren and Clark Gable	2. "Cass Timberlane"
C. Clark Gable and Deborah Kerr	3. "The Hucksters"
D. Deborah Kerr and Spencer Tracy	4. "The Plainsman"
E. Spencer Tracy and Lana Turner	5. "Edward, My Son"
F. Lana Turner and Gary Cooper	6. "The Adventures of Marco Polo"
G. Gary Cooper and Jean Arthur	7. "You Can't Take It with You"
H. Jean Arthur and James Stewart	8. "Houseboat"
I. James Stewart and Grace Kelly	9. "Notorious"
J. Grace Kelly and Bing Crosby	10. "It Started in Naples"
K. Bing Crosby and Ingrid Bergman	11. "The Country Girl"
L. Ingrid Bergman and Cary Grant	12. "The Bells of St. Mary's"

_____points

(*Answers on page 330*)

MORE WILD CARDS—BUFFS AND DUFFERS

Here are some more random questions—for Buffs and Duffers alike. You may ignore these if they're *too* obscure—or maybe we're dealing with an old film which was shown on your television screen only last night. If you choose to play this exercise, and you've been playing the Buffs' versions—and you're on your honor—take 15 points for each correct answer. But if you've been playing as a Duffer right along, you may have 30 points for each correct answer. Now—no fudging . . .

1. Much of the hero's drinking in the film "The Lost Weekend" was done in a particular New York City bar. Identify the actor who portrayed the proprietor-bartender.

2. Now that you've done that, give us the first names of the two characters mentioned in Question One.

3. You're having a party and you've invited these Hollywood names: John Shepperd, Julie Bishop, Herman Brix, Dorothy McNulty, Byron Barr, Bruce Bennett, Penny Singleton, Shepperd Strudwick, Gig

180

Young, and Jacqueline Wells. Including yourself, how many guests do you advise the caterer to prepare for?

4. What was the name of the gem that was stolen in the Gary Cooper version of "Beau Geste"?

5. In "All the King's Men," John Derek ends up in a wheelchair. How did he get that way?

6. What was the name of the theatrical award presented to Eve Harrington in "All About Eve"?—and *who* portrayed Eve Harrington?

7. What was the name or title of the newsreel in "Citizen Kane"?

8. Who portrayed each of these characters:
   a. Sam Grunion
   b. J. Chever Loophole
   c. Otis B. Driftwood
   d. Gordon Miller
   e. Ronald Kornblow
   f. Rufus T. Firefly
   g. S. Quentin Quale
   h. Dr. Hugo Z. Hackenbush
   i. Prof. Quincy Adams Wagstaff

9. Everyone remembers Margaret Hamilton as the Wicked Witch in "The Wizard of Oz"—but what was the name of the mean character she played in the *non-dream* portions of the film?

10. An important character in "State Fair" was the family's prize-winning hog. Was the hog's name: (a) Emily, (b) Goliath, or (c) Blue Boy?

_____points

(*Answers on page 331*)

AND EVEN MORE DOUBLE DUTY

And here are even more films which have been remade into films with different titles. Once more we're asking you to come up with the title of the remake, and we're supplying you with just a tiny hint of help. You may have 18 points (yes, that's right, 18! Our scoring process is very scientific—*very* scientific!) for each correct answer. And when you come up with the title of the remake, think of the stars. That will help you when you get to AND EVEN MORE DOUBLE DUTY: CASTING, which is coming right along.

1. "I Wake Up Screaming"   "V_____"
2. "When Tomorrow Comes"   "I_____"

181

3. "The Glass Slipper"　　　"C_____"
4. "The Asphalt Jungle"　　"C_____"
5. "Brother Rat"　　　　　　"A_____ F_____"
6. "The Champ"　　　　　　"T_____ C_____"
7. "If I Were King"　　　　"T_____ V_____ K_____"
8. "Nothing Sacred"　　　　"L_____ I__ U__"
9. "Mother Carey's Chickens"　"S_____ M_____"
10. "Topaze"　　　　　　　"I L_____ M_____"
11. "Mystey of the Wax Museum"　"H_____ o__ W_____"
12. "Marked Men"　　　　　"T_____ G_____"
13. "This Gun for Hire"　　　"S_____ C_____ t__ H_____"
14. "Murders in the Rue Morgue"　"P_____ o__ t_____ R_____ M_____"
15. "The Male Animal"　　　"S_____ W_____ H__ W__ T_____ C_____"

_____points

(*Answers on page 332*)

AND EVEN MORE DOUBLE DUTY—DUFFERS' TEE

And here are even more films which have been remade into films with different titles. Again, your task is to select from Column Two the proper title which is the remake title of the earlier film listed in Column One. Do it correctly, and take 12 points for each correct answer.

1. "I Wake Up Screaming"　　a. "Living It Up"
2. "When Tomorrow Comes"　　b. "She's Working Her Way Through College"
3. "The Glass Slipper"　　　　c. "House of Wax"

182

4. "The Asphalt Jungle"	d. "Short Cut to Hell"
5. "Brother Rat"	e. "Cinderfella"
6. "The Champ"	f. "The Clown"
7. "If I Were King"	g. "Vicki"
8. "Nothing Sacred"	h. "Phantom of the Rue Morgue"
9. "Mother Carey's Chickens"	i. "Three Godfathers"
10. "Topaze"	j. "Interlude"
11. "Mystery of the Wax Museum"	k. "Cairo"
12. "Marked Men"	l. "Summer Magic"
13. "This Gun for Hire"	m. "The Vagabond King"
14. "Murders in the Rue Morgue"	n. "I Like Money"
15. "The Male Animal"	o. "About Face"

_____points

(*Answers on page 332*)

AND EVEN MORE DOUBLE DUTY: CASTING

How did you do on the last set of remake titles? We told you, you'll recall, to be thinking of the stars of the earlier film and the remake version. As before, Columns One and Two list the earlier title and one of the stars of that film. Complete Column Three by telling us the name of the player who portrayed the same part in the remake. As before, take 15 points for each identification.

1. "I Wake Up Screaming"	Laird Cregar	R_____ _____e
2. "When Tomorrow Comes"	Charles Boyer	R_____ _____i
3. "The Glass Slipper"	Leslie Caron	J_____ _____s
4. "The Asphalt Jungle"	Sam Jaffe	G_____ _____s
5. "Brother Rat"	Eddie Albert	E_____ _____n
6. "The Champ"	Wallace Beery	R_____ _____n
7. "If I Were King"	Ronald Colman	O_____e

8. "Nothing Sacred"	Carole Lombard	J_____ _____s
9. "Mother Carey's Chickens"	Walter Brennan	B_____ _____s
10. "Topaze"	John Barrymore	P_____ _____s
11. "Mystery of the Wax Museum"	Lionel Atwill	V_____ _____e
12. "Marked Men"	Harry Carey, Sr.	H_____ ____y, Jr.
13. "This Gun for Hire"	Laird Cregar	J_____ _____n
14. "Murders in the Rue Morgue"	Lionel Atwill	K_____ _____n
15. "The Male Animal"	Henry Fonda	R_____ _____n

_____points

(*Answers on page 333*)

AND EVEN MORE DOUBLE DUTY:
CASTING—DUFFERS' TEE

We're sure you have the whole bag of remakes mastered now, particularly in that last set—so we know you'll do well in this exercise concerned with the casting of those remakes. As before, Columns One and Two list the title of the earlier version and one of the stars of that film. Column Three—again out of order, lists the actors or actresses who played the same part in the remake. You must match the player from Column Three with the appropriate title and star from Columns One and Two. Take 12 points for each correct answer.

1. "I Wake Up Screaming"	Laird Cregar	a. Jerry Lewis
2. "When Tomorrow Comes"	Charles Boyer	b. Ronald Reagan
3. "The Glass Slipper"	Leslie Caron	c. Jacques Aubuchon

4. "The Asphalt Jungle"	Sam Jaffe	d. Richard Boone
5. "Brother Rat"	Eddie Albert	e. Peter Sellers
6. "The Champ"	Wallace Beery	f. Burl Ives
7. "If I Were King"	Ronald Colman	g. Jerry Lewis
8. "Nothing Sacred"	Carole Lombard	h. Red Skelton
9. "Mother Carey's Chickens"	Walter Brennan	i. George Sanders
10. "Topaze"	John Barrymore	j. Karl Malden
11. "Mystery of the Wax Museum"	Lionel Atwill	k. Oreste
12. "Marked Men"	Harry Carey, Sr.	l. Rossano Brazzi
13. "This Gun for Hire"	Laird Cregar	m. Eddie Bracken
14. "Murders in the Rue Morgue"	Lionel Atwill	n. Harry Carey, Jr.
15. "The Male Animal"	Henry Fonda	o. Vincent Price

_____points

(*Answers on page 333*)

FROM SHUBERT ALLEY TO THE SUNSET STRIP #2

As before, we have listed Broadway shows which were later filmed.
We have also listed two stars or featured players of those Broadway
productions, one of whom was used in the filmization of that work.
Your job is to ascertain which one of the two members of the Broadway cast listed in Column Two was *not* used in the film version, and
to give the Hollywood name who served as the cinematic replacement. Take 10 points if you get both parts of each question correct.

| 1. "What a Life" | Betty Field
Ezra Stone | _____ |
| 2. "The Philadelphia Story" | Katharine Hepburn
Van Heflin | _____ |

3. "Watch on the Rhine"	Mady Christians Paul Lukas	_____
4. "Arsenic and Old Lace"	Josephine Hull Boris Karloff	_____
5. "Best Foot Forward"	Rosemary Lane Kenny Bowers	_____
6. "The Petrified Forest"	Peggy Conklin Leslie Howard	_____
7. "Death of a Salesman"	Mildred Dunnock Lee J. Cobb	_____
8. "Tomorrow the World"	Skip Homeier Ralph Bellamy	_____
9. "The Odd Couple"	Art Carney Walter Matthau	_____
10. "The King and I"	Gertrude Lawrence Yul Brynner	_____

_____points

(*Answers on page 334*)

FROM SHUBERT ALLEY TO THE SUNSET STRIP #2—DUFFERS' TEE

As before, we have listed a number of Broadway shows which were later filmed. In Column Two we provide a star from the Broadway version, and in Column Three we provide a multiple choice of the Hollywood actor or actress who portrayed the same part in the screen version. Take 10 points for each correct selection.

1. "What a Life"	Ezra Stone	a. Jackie Cooper b. Mickey Rooney c. Jimmy Lydon
2. "The Philadelphia Story"	Van Heflin	a. Van Johnson b. James Stewart c. John Howard
3. "Watch on the Rhine"	Mady Christians	a. Kaaren Verne b. Bette Davis c. Faye Emerson

186

4. "Arsenic and   Boris Karloff
   Old Lace"

   a. Lon Chaney, Jr.
   b. Bela Lugosi
   c. Raymond Massey

5. "Best Foot   Rosemary Lane
   Forward"

   a. Lucille Ball
   b. June Preisser
   c. Nancy Walker

6. "The Petrified   Peggy Conklin
   Forest"

   a. Lee Patrick
   b. Genevieve Tobin
   c. Bette Davis

7. "Death of a   Lee J. Cobb
   Salesman"

   a. Royal Beal
   b. Fredric March
   c. Luther Adler

8. "Tomorrow   Ralph Bellamy
   the World"

   a. Fredric March
   b. Paul Lukas
   c. George Coulouris

9. "The Odd   Art Carney
   Couple"

   a. Jackie Gleason
   b. Cliff Osmond
   c. Jack Lemmon

10. "The King and   Gertrude Lawrence
    I"

    a. Irene Dunne
    b. Deborah Kerr
    c. Dana Wynter

_____points

(*Answers on page 334*)

YES, MY DARLING DAUGHTER

Here is another exercise dealing with relationships in motion pictures. In each of the films below, a "daughter" relationship was part of the plot. We have provided a film title, and the actor or actress who played the parent. You must tell us the name of the actress who played the daughter in question. Take 10 points for each correct answer.

1. "Sabrina"	John Williams	_____
2. "To Catch a Thief"	Jessie Royce Landis	_____
3. "Butterfield 8"	Mildred Dunnock	_____
4. "Some Came Running	Larry Gates	_____
5. "State Fair"	Fay Bainter	_____
6. "The Desperate Hours"	Fredric March	_____
7. "A Place in the Sun"	Shepperd Strudwick	_____
8. "Bye Bye Birdie"	Paul Lynde	_____
9. "Watch on the Rhine"	Lucile Watson	_____
10. "A Christmas Carol"	Gene Lockhart	_____

_____points

(*Answers on page 334*)

YES, MY DARLING DAUGHTER—DUFFERS' TEE

In each of the films below, there was a "daughter" relationship included as part of the plot. We have provided the actor or actress who portrayed the parent. From the multiple choice in Column Three, select the actress who played the daughter, and take 5 points for each correct answer!

1. "Sabrina"	John Williams	a. Margaret Sullavan b. Audrey Hepburn c. Martha Hyer
2. "To Catch a Thief"	Jessie Royce Landis	a. Suzanne Pleshette b. Carole Landis c. Grace Kelly
3. "Butterfield 8"	Mildred Dunnock	a. Elizabeth Taylor b. Carroll Baker c. Elizabeth Montgomery

4. "Some Came Running"	Larry Gates	a. Shirley MacLaine b. Bethel Leslie c. Martha Hyer
5. "State Fair"	Fay Bainter	a. Vivian Blaine b. Jeanne Crain c. Ann-Margret
6. "The Desperate Hours"	Fredric March	a. Natalie Wood b. Gloria Talbot c. Mary Murphy
7. "A Place in the Sun"	Shepperd Strudwick	a. Joanne Dru b. Elizabeth Allen c. Elizabeth Taylor
8. "Bye Bye Birdie"	Paul Lynde	a. Tuesday Weld b. Jill St. John c. Ann-Margret
9. "Watch on the Rhine"	Lucile Watson	a. Bette Davis b. Olympe Bradna c. Signe Hasso
10. "A Christmas Carol"	Gene Lockhart	a. June Lockhart b. Donna Reed c. Lynne Carver

_____points

(*Answers on page 334*)

THE WRONG SIDE OF THE LAW

Below we list a number of real-life personages who were, according to their film biographical treatments, on "the wrong side of the law." We ask you to tell us who portrayed them in motion pictures about them. Take 10 points for each correct answer.

1. Clyde Barrow   W _ _ _ _ _   B _ _ _ _ _

2. Machine Gun Kelly   C _ _ _ _ _ _   B _ _ _ _ _ _

3. Legs Diamond   R _ _   D _ _ _ _ _

189

4. Pretty Boy Floyd	J _ _ _ E _ _ _ _ _ _ _
5. Roger Touhy	P _ _ _ _ _ _ _ F _ _ _ _ _
6. Owl Banghart	V _ _ _ _ _ M _ _ _ _ _ _ _
7. Bugs Moran	R _ _ _ _ _ M _ _ _ _ _
8. Barbara Graham	S _ _ _ _ H _ _ _ _ _ _ _
9. Abe Reles	P _ _ _ _ F _ _ _
10. Caryl Chessman	W _ _ _ _ _ _ C _ _ _ _ _ _ _
11. Ma Barker	S _ _ _ _ _ _ _ W _ _ _ _ _ _
12. Dutch Schultz	V _ _ M _ _ _ _ _
13. Baby Face Nelson	M _ _ _ _ _ _ R _ _ _ _ _ _
14. Lucky Luciano	C _ _ _ _ _ R _ _ _ _ _ _
15. Bonnie Parker	F _ _ _ D _ _ _ _ _ _

_____points

(*Answers on page 335*)

THE WRONG SIDE OF THE LAW—DUFFERS' TEE

Below we list a number of real-life personages who were, according to their film biographical treatments, on "the wrong side of the law." In Column Two, we supply, out of order, those film players who portrayed them. Match the real-life character to his screen counterpart, and take 10 points for each correct answer.

1. Clyde Barrow	a. William Campbell
2. Machine Gun Kelly	b. Ralph Meeker
3. Legs Diamond	c. Warren Beatty
4. Pretty Boy Floyd	d. Preston Foster
5. Roger Touhy	e. Cesar Romero
6. Owl Banghart	f. Mickey Rooney
7. Bugs Moran	g. John Ericson
8. Barbara Graham	h. Faye Dunaway
9. Abe Reles	i. Victor McLaglen
10. Caryl Chessman	j. Ray Danton
11. Ma Barker	k. Susan Hayward

12. Dutch Schultz   l. Charles Bronson
13. Baby Face Nelson   m. Peter Falk
14. Lucky Luciano   n. Vic Morrow
15. Bonnie Parker   o. Shelley Winters

_____points

(Answers on page 335)

OSCAR SHUFFLE #3—WILD CARD

Here's another wild card—an exercise for Buffs and Duffers. Below, we've scrambled the names of several Oscar winners, and ask you to unscramble them. Following this successful venture—we presume—you may then use the indicated letters to unscramble a hidden Oscar winner. As before, all of the Oscar winners are from the same category. Take 5 points for each name you correctly unscramble, and 10 more points for unearthing the hidden name . . . 25 points in all.

1. N W E J A Y M N A
   (_) (_) (_) (_) _ (_) _ (_) (_)
2. G R A S E N O R E R G
   _ _ _ _ (_) (_) _ _ _ (_) _
3. V A B E T I T E D S
   _ _ (_) _ _ _ _ _ _ _
         Hidden name:

   _ _ _ _   _ _ _ _ _

_____points

(Answers on page 335)

TELL US WHO #3

The third version of TELL US WHO is played in the same fashion as the earlier TELL US WHO exercises. We list two incidents, or plot points, from two films in which the same player appeared. From these clues, we ask you to identify the player—and for each correct identification, you receive 15 points. But if you identify *both* of the films we have suggested, you may add an additional 10 points. That's a possible 25 points for each of the ten questions . . . or 250 points possible on this one!

1. He related the secrets of Shangri-La to Ronald Colman, and was arrested for a safecracking job because he delayed his getaway in order to watch a young girl dance.

2. He gave a sedative to his wife, Doris Day, before telling her of the disappearance of their son, and pulled Kim Novak out of San Francisco Bay.

3. He was beaten severely by Ernest Borgnine in a prison stockade, and was shot by Nazis as he ran after a train which offered escape to freedom.

4. He met Judy Garland under a large clock, and watched Farley Granger compete in a tennis match.

5. She returned to New Orleans with Flora Robson and Jerry Austin, and as a missionary, led a band of children across the countryside away from invading Japanese armies.

6. A British pilot, he was shot down and wounded on D-day, and was appointed archbishop by his friend and drinking companion, Peter O'Toole.

7. He reluctantly invited his parents to a dinner party in San Francisco, and, along with Rod Steiger, battled a group of bigots.

8. She visited Montgomery Clift in Death Row, and left a note telling her husband she was flying to America with Louis Jourdan.

9. He sold a lottery ticket to Humphrey Bogart, and—with Scott Wilson—murdered the entire Clutter family in rural Kansas.

10. Lyle Bettger was jealous of her attentions to Charlton Heston, and she was scalded by hot coffee thrown on her by Lee Marvin.

———points

(*Answers on page 336*)

TELL US WHO #3—DUFFERS' TEE

This exercise is the same as earlier TELL US WHO quizzes. We list two incidents, or plot points, from two films in which the player appeared. You are to tell us, from these clues, which of the players in the misarranged Column Two we are suggesting. For each correct matching, you'll receive 15 points. If you can also name *both* of the films we have suggested for each player—and it must be *both*—you'll get an additional 15 points. There's a potential 300 points riding on this quiz, so sharpen your wits, and fatten your score.

1. He related the secrets of Shangri-La to Ronald Colman, and was arrested for a safecracking job because he delayed his getaway in order to watch a young girl dance.

   a. Robert Walker

2. He gave a sedative to his wife, Doris Day, before telling her of the disappearance of their son, and pulled Kim Novak out of San Francisco Bay.

   b. Sidney Poitier

3. He was beaten severely by Ernest Borgnine in a prison stockade, and was shot by Nazis as he ran after a train which offered escape to freedom.

   c. Ingrid Bergman

4. He met Judy Garland under a large clock, and watched Farley Granger compete in a tennis match.

   d. Sam Jaffe

5. She returned to New Orleans with Flora Robson and Jerry Austin, and as a missionary, led a band of children across the countryside away from the invading Japanese armies.

   e. Gloria Grahame

6. A British pilot, he was shot down and wounded on D-day, and was appointed archbishop by his friend and drinking companion, Peter O'Toole.

   f. Robert Blake

7. He reluctantly invited his parents to a dinner party in San Francisco, and, along with Rod Steiger, battled a group of bigots.

   g. Frank Sinatra

8. She visited Montgomery Clift in Death Row, and left a note telling her

husband she was flying to America with
Louis Jourdan.   h. James Stewart

9. He sold a lottery ticket to Humphrey
Bogart, and—with Scott Wilson—
murdered the entire Clutter family in
rural Kansas.   i. Richard Burton

10. Lyle Bettger was jealous of her attentions
to Charlton Heston, and she was scalded
by hot coffee thrown on her by Lee
Marvin.   j. Elizabeth Taylor

_____points

(*Answers on page 336*)

MY HOME TOWN

This one asks you to fill in the blank with the proper city, and thus
complete the movie title. If your movie memory and your geography
aren't the best, better move on to the Duffers' Tee following. But
these are really quite easy—so easy we're allowing only 8 points for
each correct answer.

1. "Mission to _____"
2. "_____ Joe"
3. "The _____ Gesture"
4. "_____ and Rio Grande"
5. "Meet me in __ _____"
6. "Five Graves to _____"
7. "_____ Melodrama"
8. "____ ____ Confidential"
9. "Two Guys from _____"
10. "The Flame of ___ _____"
11. "Stella _____"
12. "The _____ Strangler"
13. "_____ Deadline"
14. "_____ Holiday"

194

15. "Hotel _ _ _ _ _ _ _"

16. "The _ _ _ _ _ _ _ _ _ _ Kid"

17. "_ _ _ _ _ Adventure"

18. "_ _ _ _ _ _ _ _ _ _ _ Rifle"

19. "The Werewolf of _ _ _ _ _ _ _"

20. "A Night in _ _ _ _ _ _ _ _ _ _ _"

21. "It Started in _ _ _ _ _ _ _"

22. "The _ _ _ _ _ _ _ _ _ _ _ Story"

23. "Flying Down to _ _ _"

24. "Miss Grant Takes _ _ _ _ _ _ _ _ _"

25. "Our Man in _ _ _ _ _ _ _"

_____points

(Answers on page 336)

MY HOME TOWN—DUFFERS' TEE

Here we have some clues for you—in Column Two—to assist you in selecting the proper city, and thus complete each presently incomplete film title in Column One. These are quite easy, so we can only allow you 5 points for each correct answer. (What the hell! 125 points is not to be sneezed at!)

1. "Mission to _____"   a. Milwaukee

2. "_____ Joe"   b. Cincinnati

3. "The _____ Gesture"   c. Casablanca

4. "_____ and Rio
    Grande"   d. Springfield

5. "Meet Me in _____"   e. Manhattan

6. "Five Graves to _____"   f. Philadelphia

7. "_____ Melodrama"   g. Shanghai

8. "_____ Confidential"   h. Richmond

9. "Two Guys from
    _____"   i. New Orleans

195

10. "The Flame of _____"	j. Hong Kong
11. "Stella _____"	k. St. Louis
12. "The _____ Strangler"	l. Naples
13. "_____ Deadline"	m. London
14. "_____ Holiday"	n. Berlin
15. "Hotel _____"	o. Denver
16. "The _____ Kid"	p. Moscow
17. "_____ Adventure"	q. Havana
18. "_____ Rifle"	r. Dallas
19. "The Werewolf of _____"	s. Chicago
20. "A Night in _____"	t. Boston
21. "It Started in _____"	u. Tokyo
22. "The _____ Story"	v. Cairo
23. "Flying Down to _____"	w. Paris
24. "Miss Grant Takes _____"	x. Rome
25. "Our Man in _____"	y. Rio

_____points

(*Answers on page 336*)

MORE THREE OF A KIND

We're playing THREE OF A KIND again, and the rules are the same as before. Each question has three parts, and to get a question correct, you must answer *all three* parts. But we're allowing 20 points for each question answered correctly—and completely.

1. In "The High and the Mighty," there were three other male flight personnel in the cockpit of the airliner along with John Wayne. Name them.

2. Name the three films—to date—in which Doris Day has sung "Que Será Será."

3. Name the three actresses who portrayed "Three Smart Girls."

4. One Western series centered on the derring-do of "The Three Mesquiteers." Name the three cowboy stars who played the *original* trio in this series.

5. Name the three actors who portrayed the title roles in the film "Three Guys Named Mike."

6. Frank Miller and three of his buddies came gunning for Gary Cooper at "High Noon." Name three of the four actors who made up this menacing quartet.

7. Give us the titles of three films in which Greer Garson and Walter Pidgeon co-starred.

8. The "bridge table" scene in "Sunset Boulevard" used four old-timers from the Hollywood scene. In this film, the quartet was referred to as "the waxworks." Name three of the four players who comprised the "waxworks."

9. Name three biographical roles portrayed by Spencer Tracy.

10. The three actors who portrayed the Tin Woodman, the Scarecrow, and the Cowardly Lion in "The Wizard of Oz" also portrayed Kansas farm hands in the non-dream portions of the film. Give us the character names of the three farm hands.

_____points

(*Answers on page 337*)

MORE THREE OF A KIND—DUFFERS' TEE

You've played THREE OF A KIND before, and you'll remember that there are three answers to each question. We supply five possible answers, and your task is to eliminate the two incorrect answers. For each question on which you are correct in your solution, you may have 20 points—provided you have eliminated *both* incorrect answers.

1. In "The High and the Mighty" there were three other male flight personnel, along with John Wayne, in the cockpit of the airliner. They were:
    a. John Ridgely; b. Robert Stack; c. William Campbell; d. Stanley Ridges; e. Wally Brown.

2. Name the three films—to date—in which Doris Day has sung "Que Será Será":

a. "Julie"; b. "Please Don't Eat the Daisies"; c. "Love Me or Leave Me"; d. "The Man Who Knew Too Much"; e. "The Glass Bottom Boat."

3. Name the three actresses who portrayed "Three Smart Girls":

a. Nan Grey; b. Virginia Weidler; c. Barbara Read; d. Deanna Durbin; e. Dorothea Kent.

4. Name the three actors who portrayed the original "Three Mesquiteers":

a. Ray Corrigan; b. Robert Livingston; c. Robert Lowery; d. Donald "Red" Barry; e. Max Terhune.

5. Name the three actors who portrayed the title roles in "Three Guys Named Mike":

a. Van Johnson; b. Robert Mitchum; c. Barry Sullivan; d. Barry Nelson; e. Howard Keel.

6. Frank Miller and three of his buddies came gunning for Gary Cooper at "High Noon." Name three of the four actors who made up this menacing quartet:

a. Lee Van Cleef; b. Sheb Wooley; c. Ian MacDonald; d. Robert Lansing; e. Clint Eastwood.

7. Give us the titles of three films in which Greer Garson and Walter Pidgeon co-starred:

a. "Random Harvest"; b. "Madame Curie"; c. "Julia Misbehaves"; d. "Valley of Decision"; e. "Blossoms in the Dust."

8. Four Hollywood old-timers appeared as "the waxworks" in the bridge table scene in "Sunset Boulevard." Name three of them:

a. Anna Q. Nilsson; b. Hedda Hopper; c. Francis X. Bushman; d. Ramon Novarro; e. Buster Keaton.

9. Name three biographical roles played by Spencer Tracy:

a. Henry M. Stanley; b. Cardinal Spellman; c. Wendell Willkie; d. Thomas Edison; e. Maj. Jimmy Doolittle.

10. Give us the character names of the three farm hands in the nondream portions of "The Wizard of Oz"—played by Jack Haley, Ray Bolger, and Bert Lahr:

a. Zeke; b. Lem; c. Hunk; d. Moon; e. Hickory.

———points

(*Answers on page 337*)

AND STILL EVEN MORE "NAME THE STAR"

Once again we've listed two names of characters portrayed by the same star. From these you are to tell us the name of the star we're seeking. Of course, if things are too rough here, you *can* go on to the Duffers' Tee. But try these, and you may have 10 points for each correct answer.

1.	Chris Flanders	Paul Andros
2.	Freddy Benson	Harrison Carter MacWhite
3.	Groetschele	Willie Gingrich
4.	Kerry Bradford	Maj. Geoffrey Vickers
5.	Dan Disko	Ulysses MacAuley
6.	J. D. Sheldrake	Professor Ned Brainerd
7.	Trudy Evans	Stella Kirby
8.	Judy Barton	Polly the Pistol
9.	Virgil Smith	Buzz Blackwell
10.	Anne Dempster	Julia O. Tredway

_____points

(*Answers on page 338*)

AND STILL EVEN MORE "NAME THE STAR"— DUFFERS' TEE

For those of you who are here by virtue of skipping the Buffs' version of this exercise, you know that these clues provided to assist you to name the star are much more obvious. The rest of you will remember that we're looking for the star who played the two characters listed in each question below. From the character names—both of which were played by the same player—it should be a simple matter for you to name the talent in question, and thus take 5 points for each correct answer.

1.	The Reverend T. Lawrence Shannon	Thomas Becket
2.	Terry Molloy	Stanley Kowalski
3.	Oscar Madison	Horace Van Der Gelder
4.	Robin of Locksley	Capt. Peter Blood
5.	Whitey Marsh	Andy Hardy

6. Walter Neff   Anthony J. Drexel Biddle
7. Belle Fawcett   Lillian Russell
8. Lylah Clare   Moll Flanders
9. Frank Elgin   C. K. Dexter Haven
10. Phyllis Dietrichson   Martha Ivers

_____points

(*Answers on page 339*)

AND MORE CAREERS IN COMMON

As before in this exercise, CAREERS IN COMMON, we have listed in Column One two players and films in which they pursued the same occupation or career. In Column Two, we list another player who, in one of his or her roles, pursued the same vocation. We ask you to tell us the career in question and the film in which the player of Column Two pursued the same calling. Answers are in two parts and you receive 10 points for each part you get correct. That's a possible 200 points for this quiz!

1. Doris Day—"Calamity
   Jane"
   Andy Devine—
   "Stagecoach"   Slim Pickens _____ _____

2. Jill Haworth—"In
   Harm's Way"
   Mary Wickes—"The
   Man Who Came to
   Dinner"   Olivia de Havilland _____ _____

3. Kirk Douglas—"Young
   Man with a Horn"
   George Montgomery—
   "Orchestra Wives"   Jack Webb _____ _____

4. Spencer Tracy—"Broken
   Lance"
   John Wayne—"Red
   River"   Rock Hudson _____ _____

5. Jeffrey Lynn—"It All
     Came True"
   Marius Goring—"The
     Red Shoes"   Arthur Kennedy _____ _____

6. Clark Gable—
     "Manhattan
     Melodrama"
   Elliott Gould—
     "California Split"   Tyrone Power _____ _____

7. Edmond O'Brien—
     "Seven Days in May"
   Claude Rains—"Mr.
     Smith Goes to
     Washington"   William Powell _____ _____

8. Bob Hope—"Son of
     Paleface"
   Joel McCrea—"The
     Great Moment"   Walter Matthau _____ _____

9. Lana Turner—"The Bad
     and the Beautiful"
   Bette Davis—"The Star"   Jean Hagen _____ _____

10. Kirk Douglas—"The
      Story of Three Loves"
    Anne Baxter—"The
      Carnival Story"   Tony Curtis _____ _____

                                    _____points

(*Answers on page 339*)

AND MORE CAREERS IN COMMON—DUFFERS' TEE

In the first column, we have again listed pairs of players and given
the titles of films in which they pursued the same occupation or career. In the second and third columns, we list *three* players and films
in which *they* appeared. One of these had the same occupation as
the stars in Column One. Your task is to select which player in
Column Two matches the pair in Column One. You get 10 points for
each correct answer.

1. Doris Day—
   "Calamity Jane"
   Andy Devine—
   "Stagecoach"

   a. Walter Brennan
   b. Kurt Kasznar

   c. Slim Pickens

   "Red River"
   "A Farewell to
   Arms"
   "Stagecoach"

2. Jill Haworth—"In
   Harm's Way"
   Mary Wickes—
   "The Man Who
   Came To
   Dinner"

   a. Bette Davis
   b. Olivia de Havilland

   c. Hazel Brooks

   "Marked Woman"
   "Not As a
   Stranger"
   "Body and Soul"

3. Kirk Douglas—
   "Young Man
   with a Horn"
   George Montgomery
   —"Orchestra
   Wives"

   a. Jack Webb
   b. Milton Berle

   c. Harvey Korman

   "Pete Kelly's Blues"
   "Sun Valley
   Serenade"
   "Gypsy"

4. Spencer Tracy—
   "Broken Lance"
   John Wayne—
   "Red River"

   a. Edward G.
      Robinson
   b. James Stewart
   c. Rock Hudson

   "House of
   Strangers"
   "Broken Arrow"
   "Giant"

5. Jeffrey Lynn—
   "It All Came
   True"
   Marius Goring—
   "The Red Shoes"

   a. Albert Basserman
   b. Arthur Kennedy
   c. Danny Thomas

   "The Red Shoes"
   "City for Conquest"
   "Big City"

6. Clark Gable—
   "Manhattan
   Melodrama"
   Elliott Gould—
   "California Split"

   a. Tyrone Power

   b. Yves Montand
   c. Cliff Robertson

   "Mississippi
   Gambler"
   "Grand Prix"
   "The Best Man"

7. Claude Rains—
   "Mr. Smith Goes
   to Washington"
   Edmond O'Brien—
   "Seven Days in
   May"

   a. William Powell

   b. Stuart Erwin
   c. James Gleason

   "The Senator Was
   Indiscreet"
   "Our Town"
   "Meet John Doe"

8. Bob Hope—"Son
   of Paleface"
   Joel McCrea—"The
   Great Moment"

   a. Richard Kiley

   b. Walter Matthau
   c. Michael Chekhov

   "The Blackboard
   Jungle"
   "Cactus Flower"
   "Spellbound"

9. Lana Turner—"The	a. Jean Hagen	"Singin' in the
Bad and the		Rain"
Beautiful"	b. Joan Crawford	"Mildred Pierce"
Bette Davis—"The	c. Joanne Woodward	"Rachel, Rachel"
Star"		
10. Kirk Douglas—"The	a. Tony Curtis	"Trapeze"
Story of Three	b. Debra Paget	"Titanic"
Loves"	c. Gloria Grahame	"The Greatest Show
Anne Baxter—"The		on Earth"
Carnival Story"		

_____points

(Answers on page 339)

THE TEENY-TINY MARQUEE ✕4

We're playing TEENY-TINY MARQUEE again—and we have to admit that this one is a really far-out version with *combinations* yet! On these you have to insert two (and sometimes *three*) name substitutions to correct the title we're going after. But because it's tricky, we suggest you go back and check out the earlier versions of TEENY-TINY MARQUEE before you start on this one. And because it's a weirdo, we're allowing 20 points for each correct title you get. So, lotsa luck, and remember: Our clues in this version represent complete titles. No filling in blanks, merely substitution of the italicized names. Got it?

1. "Love Finds *Devine Kruger*"
2. "*Magnani* and the *Andrea* of Siam"
3. "The Adventures of *Neal Joe*"
4. "The *Arden* of *Eva Marie Stevens*"
5. "The Guilt of *Gaynor Leon*"
6. "The *Frances* in the *Gabriel*"
7. "The Story of *Wally* and *Ryan Peggie*"
8. "*Penner* and *Merman* Turp Call on the President"
9. "Mighty *Pevney Robert*"
10. "The Badge of *E. G. Walter*"

11. *"McCallum* and *Gaye"*
   . . . and are you ready for this one?
12. "The *Ruth Byington* of Mrs. *Lewis"*

_____points

(*Answers on page 340*)

THE TEENY-TINY MARQUEE ※4—DUFFERS' TEE

Again, it's TEENY-TINY MARQUEE time. But this time we're playing it a bit differently. First, we're playing *combinations,* and you no longer have to fill in the blanks. Look at the titles in Column One. The titles are incorrect, as indicated by the italicized names. If the name is a first name, look for the appropriate surname in Column Two, and substitute it. Conversely, if the Column One name is a surname, turn to Column Two for the first name. Do your substitutions correctly, and you'll end up with twelve complete (and correct) film titles. By *combination,* we mean that each question requires two substitutions—except Questions Four, Seven, and Twelve, which require three! Take 20 points for each correct title.

1. "Love Finds *Devine Kruger"*

2. *"Magnani* and the *Andrea* of Siam"

3. "The Adventures of *Neal Joe"*

4. "The *Arden* of *Eva Marie Stevens"*

5. "The Guilt of *Gaynor Leon"*

6. "The *Frances* in the *Gabriel"*

7. "The Story of *Wally* and *Ryan Peggie"*

8. *"Penner* and *Merman* Turp Call on the President"

9. "Mighty *Pevney Robert"*

aa. Ames
a. Anna
b. Brennan
c. Castle
d. Andy
e. Dell
f. Joe
g. Roman
h. Marshall
i. Sawyer
j. Farmer
k. Lisa
l. Hardy
m. Spring

n. King
o. David
p. Stone
q. Saint

10. "The Badge of *E. G. Walter*"

11. "*McCallum* and *Gaye*"

   . . . and are you ready for . . .

12. "The *Ruth Byington* of Mrs. *Lewis*"

r. Janet
s. Ethel
t. Young
u. Vernon
v. Joe
w. Tom
x. Eve
y. Irene
z. Mark

_____points

(*Answers on page 340*)

MY SON, MY SON

Relationships, again! In each of the films below, there was a "son"—and this fact was an important point to the plot in each case. We have provided the film title and the name of the actor or actress who portrayed one of the parents to the son. Tell us who played the son, and receive 10 points for each correct answer.

1. "To Each His Own"	Olivia de Havilland	_____
2. "Friendly Persuasion"	Gary Cooper	_____
3. "David Copperfield"	Elizabeth Allen	_____
4. "North by Northwest"	Jessie Royce Landis	_____
5. "Rebel Without a Cause"	Jim Backus	_____
6. "None But the Lonely Heart"	Ethel Barrymore	_____
7. "Treasure Island"	Dorothy Peterson	_____
8. "Sergeant York"	Margaret Wycherly	_____
9. "Marty"	Esther Minciotti	_____
10. "You Can't Take It with You"	Edward Arnold	_____

_____points

(*Answers on page 340*)

MY SON, MY SON—DUFFERS' TEE

Relationships, again! This time we're looking for the "son." The picture and player who portrayed the parent are listed in Columns One and Two. From the multiple possibilities in Column Three, identify the actor who played the son—and take 5 points for each correct answer.

1. "To Each His Own"   Olivia de Havilland
   a. Richard Basehart
   b. John Lund
   c. Richard Todd

2. "Friendly Persuasion"   Gary Cooper
   a. Tony Perkins
   b. John Smith
   c. Claude Jarman, Jr.

3. "David Copperfield"   Elizabeth Allen
   a. Freddie Bartholomew
   b. Jackie Searle
   c. David Holt

4. "North by Northwest"   Jessie Royce Landis
   a. James Mason
   b. Cary Grant
   c. Martin Landau

5. "Rebel Without a Cause"   Jim Backus
   a. Sal Mineo
   b. James MacArthur
   c. James Dean

6. "None But the Lonely Heart"   Ethel Barrymore
   a. Rex Harrison
   b. Gavin Muir
   c. Cary Grant

7. "Treasure Island"   Dorothy Peterson
   a. Jackie Cooper
   b. Georgie Winslow
   c. Tim Considine

8. "Sergeant York"   Margaret Wycherly
   a. Darren McGavin
   b. George Tobias
   c. Gary Cooper

9. "Marty"   Esther Minciotti
   a. Ernest Borgnine
   b. Joe Mantell
   c. Ralph Meeker

10. "You Can't
    Take It with   Edward Arnold
    You"

a. James Stewart
b. Stewart Granger
c. Farley Granger

_____points

(*Answers on page 340*)

NUMBER, PLEASE

All we're asking for here is one single answer—get it, and you may
have 250 points! What is required here is movie memory and a
knack for mathematics. To arrive at the answer, merely complete the
incomplete titles listed below, all of which can be completed by the
insertion of a number, or a word connoting a number. Then, when
you've completed all of the titles, merely add up the numbers to arrive at a grand total, which is the number we're seeking. Remember,
it's worth 250 points.

1. "_ _ _ for the Road"   _____
                                              +
2. "Shack Out on _ _ _"   _____
                                              +
3. "Anne of the _ _ _ _ _ _ _ _ Days"   _____
                                              +
4. "_ _ _ _ _ Daughters"   _____
                                              +
5. "_ _ _ _ _ Fingers"   _____
                                              +
6. "_ _ _ _ _ Hours to Rama"   _____
                                              +
7. "_ _ _ _ _ _ _ _ _ Hours"   _____
                                              +
8. "_ _ , _ _ _ Leagues Under the Sea"   _____
                                              +
9. "Over _ _"   _____
                                              +
10. "_ _ _ _ _ Iron Men"   _____
                                              +
11. "_ _ _ Life to Live"   _____

207

12. "_ _ _ _ _ _ Seconds over Tokyo"

         +   _____

13. "_ , _ _ _ Nights"

         +   _____

14. "_ _ Rue Madeleine"

         +   _____

15. "_ _ _ _ _ Little Words"

         +   _____

16. "_ _ _ _ _ _ _ _ _ _ Men and a Girl"

         +   _____

17. "The Magnificent _ _ _ _ _"

         +   _____

18. "Pilot Number _ _ _ _"

         +   _____

19. "_ , _ _ _ , _ _ _ B.C."

         +   _____

20. "_ _ _ _ _ Little Mothers"

               _____

Grand Total:

_____points

(*Answers on page 341*)

NUMBER, PLEASE—DUFFERS' TEE

All of the incomplete film titles in Column One may be completed by selecting the proper number—or words representing numbers—from Column Two. You may have 10 points for each title you complete correctly.

1. "_____ for the Road"   a. Seven
2. "Shack Out on _____"   b. Eight
3. "Anne of the _____ Days"   c. Nine
4. "_____ Daughters"   d. Thirty
5. "_____ Fingers"   e. Forty

6. "_____ Hours to Rama"   f. Five
7. "_____ Hours"   g. Three
8. "_____ Leagues Under the Sea"   h. 13
9. "Over _____"   i. Fourteen
10. "_____ Iron Men"   j. Four
11. "_____ Life to Live"   k. Five
12. "_____ Seconds over Tokyo"   l. 21
13. "_____ Nights"   m. 20,000
14. "_____ Rue Madeleine"   n. Two
15. "_____ Little Words"   o. One Hundred
16. "_____ Men and a Girl"   p. 101
17. "The Magnificent _____"   q. 1,000,000
18. "Pilot Number _____"   r. 1,001
19. "_____ B.C."   s. Thousand
20. "_____ Little Mothers"   t. One

_____points

(*Answers on page 341*)

AND AGAIN, MORE DOUBLE DUTY

Here, once again, are some films which have had at least two versions. Yet, when the earlier film was remade, the title (and frequently a great deal more) was changed. In Column One are the earlier titles, and in Column Two, you are to tell us the title of the remake. (Be thinking about the stars—you know what follows!) Take 18 points for each title you complete correctly.

1. "The Ghost Breakers"   "S_____ S_____"
2. "Five Came Back"   "B_____ f_____ E_____"
3. "Dark Victory"   "S_____ H_____"
4. "Craig's Wife"   "H_____ C_____"
5. "Ball of Fire"   "A S_____ L_ B_____"
6. "Bachelor Mother"   "B_____ o__ J_____"
7. "Algiers"   "C_____"
8. "And Then There Were
      None"   "T____ L_____ I_____"

209

9. "Anna and the King of
     Siam"   "T__ K_____ a_____ _____"
10. "The Shop Around the
     Corner"   "I__ t__ G_____ O_____ S_____"
11. "A Lady to Love"   "T_____ K_____ W_____ T_____ W_____"
12. "Lady for a Day"   "P_____ o__ M_____"
13. "The Lady Eve"   "T__ B_____ a__ t__ B_____"
14. "High Sierra"   "I D_____ a T_____ T_____"
15. "Grand Hotel"   "W_____ a__ t_____ W_____"

_____points

(*Answers on page 341*)

AND AGAIN, MORE DOUBLE DUTY—DUFFERS' TEE

One more time! Here are some more films from which double duty
was realized. All of the films in Column One were remade, under
different titles. The later versions of the films are listed in Column
Two, out of order. Select the correct title from Column Two, matching it with the proper title of Column One, and take 12 points for
each correct pairing. (And recall the stars—you know what's coming!)

1. "The Ghost Breakers"   a. "In the Good Old Summertime"
2. "Five Came Back"   b. "Weekend at the Waldorf"
3. "Dark Victory"   c. "A Song Is Born"
4. "Craig's Wife"   d. "Scared Stiff"
5. "Ball of Fire"   e. "Pocketful of Miracles"
6. "Bachelor Mother"   f. "Ten Little Indians"
7. "Algiers"   g. "Stolen Hours"
8. "And Then There Were
     None"   h. "I Died a Thousand Times"
9. "Anna and the King of
     Siam"   i. "Bundle of Joy"
10. "The Shop Around the
     Corner"   j. "Back from Eternity"
11. "A Lady to Love"   k. "They Knew What They Wanted"
12. "Lady for a Day"   l. "Harriet Craig"

210

13. "The Lady Eve"		m. "The King and I"
14. "High Sierra"		n. "Casbah"
15. "Grand Hotel"		o. "The Birds and the Bees"

_____points

(*Answers on page 341*)

AND AGAIN, MORE DOUBLE DUTY: CASTING

Once again, we're concerned with the casting aspect of the remake films you just encountered. As before, we've listed the earlier title and one of the stars from that version in Columns One and Two. Give us the name of the *actress* who played the same part in the remake version by completing the blanks of Column Three. You may have 15 points for each correct name.

1. "The Ghost Breakers"	Paulette Goddard	__za____ ___o__
2. "Five Came Back"	Lucille Ball	__it_ _k_____
3. "Dark Victory"	Bette Davis	_us___ ___y_____
4. "Craig's Wife"	Rosalind Russell	_o___ ____wf____
5. "Ball of Fire"	Barbara Stanwyck	__rg_____ ___y_
6. "Bachelor Mother"	Ginger Rogers	__bb___ ___yn_____
7. "Algiers"	Hedy Lamarr	__rt_ _or___
8. "And Then There Were None"	June Duprez	_____rl___ _at___
9. "Anna and the King of Siam"	Linda Darnell	_it_ ___re___
10. "The Shop Around the Corner"	Margaret Sullavan	_ud_ ___rl____
11. "Lady for a Day"	May Robson	_et___ ___vi_
12. "A Lady to Love"	Vilma Banky	__ro___ ___mb____
13. "The Lady Eve"	Barbara Stanwyck	___tz_ ___yn___
14. "High Sierra"	Ida Lupino	_he_____ ___nt____
15. "Grand Hotel"	Greta Garbo	___ng___ ___ge___

_____points

(*Answers on page 342*)

AND AGAIN, MORE DOUBLE DUTY:
CASTING—DUFFERS' TEE

One more time! We're concerned with the casting aspect of the remake films you just encountered. The earlier film and one of its stars are listed in Columns One and Two. Out of order in Column Three are the *actresses* who played the *same* part in the remake version. Select the appropriate actress from Column Three to match with the title and actress of Columns One and Two—and take 12 points for each correct answer.

1.	"The Ghost Breakers"	Paulette Goddard	a. Mitzi Gaynor
2.	"Five Came Back"	Lucille Ball	b. Bette Davis
3.	"Dark Victory"	Bette Davis	c. Lizabeth Scott
4.	"Craig's Wife"	Rosalind Russell	d. Marta Toren
5.	"Ball of Fire"	Barbara Stanwyck	e. Shelley Winters
6.	"Bachelor Mother"	Ginger Rogers	f. Ginger Rogers
7.	"Algiers"	Hedy Lamarr	g. Rita Moreno
8.	"And Then There Were None"	June Duprez	h. Susan Hayward
9.	"Anna and the King of Siam"	Linda Darnell	i. Virginia Mayo
10.	"The Shop Around the Corner"	Margaret Sullavan	j. Anita Ekberg
11.	"Lady for a Day"	May Robson	k. Shirley Eaton
12.	"A Lady to Love"	Vilma Banky	l. Joan Crawford
13.	"The Lady Eve"	Barbara Stanwyck	m. Debbie Reynolds
14.	"High Sierra"	Ida Lupino	n. Carole Lombard
15.	"Grand Hotel"	Greta Garbo	o. Judy Garland

_____points

(*Answers on page 342*)

AND EVEN MORE LINK-UPS—BUFFS AND DUFFERS

Here are the last of the link-ups, and this one is for Buffs and Duffers. As before, insert the missing name. The name will serve as a surname for the player suggested in Column One, and will also serve as the first name for the player suggested in Column Two. Take 10 points for each correct answer on this one.

1. Benita	_____	Cronyn
2. James	_____	Peck
3. Jan	_____	Holloway
4. Bob	_____	Lange
5. Norman	_____	Nolan
6. Robert	_____	Clift
7. Eddie	_____	Basserman
8. Anne	_____	MacLaine
9. George C.	_____	Brady
10. Lee	_____	Kaplan

_____points

(*Answers on page 343*)

SPOT THE BIO: SPORTS

Each of the players below portrayed a real-life sports figure in a motion picture. Tell us the name of the sports luminary portrayed by each player, and it's worth 5 points. Tell us the name of the film in which the portrayal was included and take 10 points if you have it correct. Get *both* parts correct and you may have 20 points for that question. So, here's a chance to fatten your score by 300 points as you head into the homestretch, or over the goal line, or whatever.

	SPORTS FIGURE	FILM TITLE
1. Tony Perkins	_____	_____
2. Ronald Reagan (football)	_____	_____
3. Dan Dailey	_____	_____
4. William Bendix	_____	_____
5. Ronald Reagan (baseball)	_____	_____

213

	SPORTS FIGURE	FILM TITLE
6. James Stewart	_____	_____
7. Glenn Ford	_____	_____
8. Thomas Gomez	_____	_____
9. Coley Wallace	_____	_____
10. Errol Flynn	_____	_____
11. Ward Bond	_____	_____
12. Gary Cooper	_____	_____
13. Frank Lovejoy	_____	_____
14. Richard Crenna	_____	_____
15. Paul Newman	_____	_____

_____points

(Answers on page 343)

SPOT THE BIO: SPORTS—DUFFERS' TEE

Each of the players below portrayed a real-life sports figure in a motion picture. In Column Two, we have listed, out of order, the sports figures portrayed by each of the actors listed in Column One. For each correct matching, you get 5 points. In Column Three, we have listed—again, out of order—those films in which the portrayals were included. Match the correct film title to your other pairing, and you get 10 points—PLUS a 5-point bonus for getting *both* parts correct. There are fifteen chances, then, for you to pull down 20 points, for a possible 300-point score! Gloryosky!

1. Tony Perkins	A. George Gipp	a. "Pride of the Yankees"
2. Ronald Reagan	B. John L. Sullivan	b. "Somebody Up There Likes Me"
3. Dan Dailey	C. Joe Louis	c. "The Pride of St. Louis"
4. William Bendix	D. Rogers Hornsby	d. "Gentleman Jim"
5. Ronald Reagan	E. Rocky Graziano	e. "Gentleman Jim"
6. James Stewart	F. Jimmy Piersall	f. "The Harlem Globetrotters"

214

7. Glenn Ford	G. Lou Gehrig	g. "The Winning Team"
8. Thomas Gomez	H. Grover Cleveland Alexander	h. "The Pride of St. Louis"
9. Coley Wallace	I. Daffy Dean	i. "Follow the Sun"
10. Errol Flynn	J. Dizzy Dean	j. "The Babe Ruth Story"
11. Ward Bond	K. Ben Hogan	k. "The Winning Team"
12. Gary Cooper	L. Jim Corbett	l. "The Joe Louis Story"
13. Frank Lovejoy	M. Babe Ruth	m. "The Stratton Story"
14. Richard Crenna	N. Monty Stratton	n. "Fear Strikes Out"
15. Paul Newman	O. Abe Saperstein	o. "Knute Rockne—All-American"

_____points

(*Answers on page 343*)

TRUE OR FALSE, WILD CARD— BUFFS AND DUFFERS

If you've learned to tie your shoes and feed yourself, you're undoubtedly aware of how a true-false quiz works. Don't ask us to explain—just go along with us. This is a true-false quiz, and since it's for Buffs and Duffers, your honor plays a part in this quiz. If you've been shooting the Buff side of the course, take 15 points for each question you answer correctly on this quiz. If you've been playing as a Duffer, however, you may have 30 points for each question answered correctly. Now, be honest!

	T	*F*
1. Abbott and Costello made their film debut in "Buck Privates."	( )	( )
2. The first all-talking film was "The Jazz Singer."	( )	( )

		T	F

3. The first Andy Hardy film had Lewis Stone and Fay Holden as the Judge and Mrs. Hardy. ( ) ( )

4. The film in which Walter Huston played Mr. Scratch and Edward Arnold played Daniel Webster—its official title was "The Devil and Daniel Webster." ( ) ( )

5. There has never been an instance in films where a real-life brother and sister played brother and sister in the film. ( ) ( )

6. Geraldine Page's first film appearance won her an Oscar nomination. The role was that of a woman of the plains in "Hondo," with John Wayne. ( ) ( )

7. The making of "King Kong" marked the first filmmaking expedition to the African continent by a film company. ( ) ( )

8. Alfred Hitchcock never made an American film which excluded the familiar "thriller" or suspense elements for which he is famous. ( ) ( )

9. "The first all-talking feature filmed outdoors" was the billing for "In Old Arizona." It was also the first sound motion picture which was actually filmed in its *true* location. ( ) ( )

10. John Wayne's first starring role was as the Ringo Kid in John Ford's "Stagecoach." ( ) ( )

_____points

(*Answers on page 344*)

GREAT SUPPORT CRISSCROSS

The GREAT SUPPORT CRISSCROSS deals with outstanding supporting players of the film world. The diagram following can be completed—and 400 points earned—by filling in the blanks with the correct surname (and a surname of the correct length!). Again, we've sneakily overlooked giving you the names to use, but rather we've supplied you with the clues below. Some of these, you might argue, went on to become stars, but we think that—by and large—they were at their best when playing in support of someone else. We've started you off with a three-letter name—that of our beloved Oriental villain, Philip AHN. But from here AHN, you're AHN your AHN. (Boo—hiss!)

Four-Letter Names

A balding, mustachioed fuss-budget, he was Charles A _ _ _ .
As the gunsel, Wilmer, this Junior sniveled.
His first name is Benson, and he's on the list when the call is for Orientals.
Number One Son.
He was the nervous whiskey-drummer, and his last name was appropriate.
Regrettably, his personal life got him more press coverage than his film work. And his first name was Tom.

Five-Letter Names

His southern accent got him a lot of work as the hero's buddy in the thirties—Eddie.
Vera Vague.
A long-time character woman, she is Beulah B _ _ _ _ .
He was a villain, or a comedian, or sometimes both. His name was Fred.
This Marcel was once described as "the French Peter Lorre."
Her name is Ann, and she went from the heroine's chum to the hero's mother.
This stiff-upper-lipped Britisher named Rex confirmed that "Gentlemen Prefer Blondes."
Joel Cairo.
Age took this Lloyd from a coldhearted gangster to the softhearted doctor.
This Tito was Italian, rather than Yugoslavian.
He caused trouble aboard Laughton's *Bounty*. His first name was Ian.

Six-Letter Names

Say old-timer, and this Clem springs to mind.
Long the proper butler, he found a home with the Sycamore family.
This Una had a real knock-down donnybrook with Marlene.
He was the screen father to some real-life quintuplets.
Usually a European villain, his first name was Konstantin.

Seven-Letter Names

A funny, lovable Italian, this Henry walked with a list to the larboard.
She got an Oscar for being a good but poverty-stricken ma.

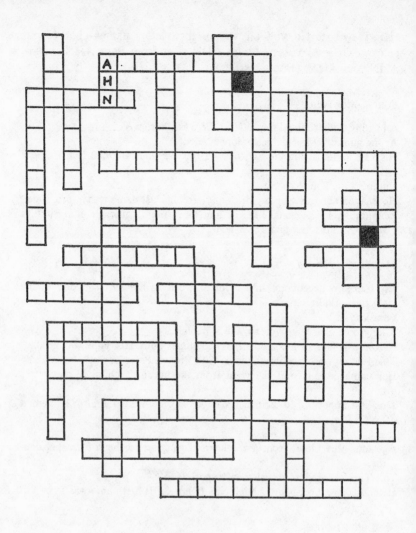

This Bess was usually in the background, but she was the best-dressed extra in films.

Fat and mustachioed, this Howard specialized in fuddy-duddy roles.

In his first role of prominence, his billing was simply: "The Monster Was Played by ?"

This Una was usually a persnickety Irish maid, but in one Oscar-winning film, she was Frankie's ma.

This Eddie was the husband of Rosasharn.

Eight-Letter Names

This George was a rough-and-tough one.
This Ted played Indians and gangsters—and frequently got bumped off.
This Frank plays ranchers and storekeepers.
Cecil was his name, and he was probably the closest any human came to being a leprechaun.
He was the law officer who finally locked up "the psycho."
This Vladimir also played Mexicans and Spaniards.

Nine-Letter Names

He was in charge of bringing back this giant gorilla, see?
The shyster lawyer or the conniver was this Douglas' forte.

Eleven-Letter Names

He was Hollywood's fattest and smoothest villain.
This Maria worried about vampires, full moons, wolfbane, and occasionally torrential rainstorms.

_____points

(*Answers on page 345*)

GREAT SUPPORT CRISSCROSS—DUFFERS' TEE

The GREAT SUPPORT CRISSCROSS diagram on the preceding page can be completed by filling in the last names of the supporting players from the film world. Complete the diagram, and add 300 points to your score, by inserting the correct name (of the appropriate length) so that the entire diagram interlocks. These supporting players, many of whom became stars in their own right, can be used to fill in the diagram merely by use of logic, deduction, and a pencil with a large eraser. There are no three-letter names required, so that explains why we've started you off with that beloved Oriental villain, Philip AHN. As we told the Buffs, from now AHN, you're AHN your AHN. (The Buffs didn't like it, either.)

Four-Letter Names	Five-Letter Names	Seven-Letter Names
Arnt, Charles	Acuff, Eddie	Armetta, Henry
Cook, Elisha (Jr.)	Allen, Barbara Jo	Darwell, Jane
Fong, Benson	Bondi, Beulah	Flowers, Bess
Luke, Keye	Clark, Fred	Freeman, Howard
Meek, Donald	Dalio, Marcel	Karloff, Boris
Neal, Tom	Doran, Ann	O'Connor, Una
	Evans, Rex	Quillan, Eddie
Six-Letter Names	Lorre, Peter	
Bevans, Clem	Nolan, Lloyd	**Eight-Letter Names**
Hobbes, Halliwell	Vuolo, Tito	Bancroft, George
Merkel, Una	Wolfe, Ian	De Corsia, Ted
Qualen, John		Ferguson, Frank
Shayne, Konstantin		Kellaway, Cecil
		McIntire, John
		Sokoloff, Vladimir

Nine-Letter Names	Eleven-Letter Names
Armstrong, Robert	Greenstreet, Sydney
Dumbrille, Douglas	Ouspenskaya, Maria

_____points

(*Answers on page 346*)

HISTORY IS MADE IN THE MOVIES

The following pairs of players all enacted portrayals of real-life historical characters, though *not* in the same film. It's reasonable to assume the historical characters we had in mind below either *knew* each other, *dealt* with each other, or *exerted some kind of influence* on each other. From the pairings we've provided, you are to name the characters each player portrayed who might've had some historical interaction on each other, and you are also to give the film titles in which the portrayals were included.

To give you an example, had we named William Powell and Barbra Streisand, you would remember that she portrayed Fanny Brice in "Funny Girl" and he played Florenz Ziegfeld, in "The Great Ziegfeld" and "Ziegfeld Follies." Knowing that the real-life Ziegfeld was once Fanny Brice's producer, you have the historical interaction. We're giving 10 points for each answer—and since each question has four parts, you have a chance at 40 points a question. Tricky, but profitable.

	HISTORICAL CHARACTER	FILM TITLE
1. Jeffrey Hunter Basil Rathbone		
2. Elizabeth Taylor Warren William		
3. Victor Mature Errol Flynn		
4. Ingrid Bergman Richard Widmark		
5. Paul Scofield Charles Laughton		
6. John Derek Henry Fonda		
7. Ralph Bellamy Karl Malden		
8. Betty Hutton Joel McCrea		
9. George Arliss Irene Dunne		
10. Orson Welles Richard Burton		

_____points

(*Answers on page 346*)

HISTORY IS MADE IN THE MOVIES—
DUFFERS' TEE

Many movies have re-created characters from history. If you know a little history *and* your movies, you should do well with this exercise. In Column One we list a player, and in Column Two we list a character from history the player portrayed as well as the film in which the portrayal was included. Column Three lists another player who portrayed another historical character. And we think there was a historical relationship between the real-life characters. Perhaps they knew each other, dealt with each other, or exerted some sort of influence on each other . . . or at least our history books would have us so believe. From the multiple choice provided in Column Four, select the character portrayed by the player in Column Three—and bear in mind that the character must have had *some* relationship with or influence on the historical character in Column Two. Take 20 points for each correct answer.

1. Basil Rathbone	Pontius Pilate "The Last Days of Pompeii"	Jeffrey Hunter	a. Barabbas b. Simon Peter c. Jesus Christ
2. Elizabeth Taylor	Cleopatra "Cleopatra"	Warren William	a. Pompey b. Caesar c. Ovid
3. Victor Mature	Crazy Horse "Chief Crazy Horse"	Errol Flynn	a. Gen. Custer b. Maj. Reno c. Gen. Phil Sheridan
4. Ingrid Bergman	Joan "Joan of Arc"	Richard Widmark	a. The Dauphin b. Bishop Stogumber c. Earl of Warwick
5. Charles Laughton	Henry VIII "Young Bess"	Paul Scofield	a. Thomas More b. Thomas Becket c. Tom Paine
6. Henry Fonda	Abraham Lincoln "Young Mr. Lincoln"	John Derek	a. Andrew Johnson b. Paul Stark c. John Wilkes Booth

7. Karl Malden	Omar Bradley "Patton"	Ralph Bellamy	a. Cordell Hull b. Henry Stimson c. Franklin Roosevelt
8. Betty Hutton	Annie Oakley "Annie Get Your Gun"	Joel McCrea	a. Wild Bill Hickok b. Buffalo Bill Cody c. Kit Carson
9. Irene Dunne	Queen Victoria "The Mudlark"	George Arliss	a. Disraeli b. Parnell c. Pitt
10. Richard Burton	Henry VIII "Anne of the Thousand Days"	Orson Welles	a. Cardinal Wolsey b. Cardinal Syn c. Cardinal Richelieu

_____points

(Answers on page 346)

HISTORY IS MADE IN THE MOVIES PART II

You must have done sensationally on that first version of HISTORY IS MADE IN THE MOVIES—so let's whip right into another version. Besides, if you didn't, they say that when you're thrown from a horse, it's best to get back on immediately and give it another go! These are a mite more difficult, so we're upping the ante, and giving 15 points per answer, or a possible 60 points per question. It's played exactly the same as Part I, so knock 'em dead!!

	HISTORICAL CHARACTER	FILM TITLE
1. Wallace Beery John Garfield	_____ _____	_____ _____
2. Erich Von Stroheim Richard Basehart	_____ _____	_____ _____

	HISTORICAL CHARACTER	FILM TITLE
3. Monty Woolley Jason Robards, Jr.	_____ _____	_____ _____
4. George Arliss David Niven	_____ _____	_____ _____
5. Deborah Kerr Larry Parks	_____ _____	_____ _____
6. Robert Donat Genevieve Bujold	_____ _____	_____ _____
7. George C. Scott Harry Carey, Jr.	_____ _____	_____ _____
8. Lionel Barrymore Michael Jayston	_____ _____	_____ _____
9. Julie Andrews George Hamilton	_____ _____	_____ _____
10. Katharine Hepburn Glenda Jackson	_____ _____	_____ _____

_____points

(*Answers on page 347*)

HISTORY IS MADE IN THE MOVIES
PART II—DUFFERS' TEE

You played the Duffers' Tee of HISTORY IS MADE IN THE MOVIES, so you know how to play this Part II version. The only difference is: We're giving you 20 points for making the proper selection from the multiple choice in Column Four. *But,* if you can *also* give the title of the film in which the portrayal suggested by Columns Three and Four was included, you may have 20 *more* points. That's a possible 40 points per question.

1. Wallace
   Beery   Pancho Villa   John Garfield   a. Emiliano
                                                         Zapata
           "Viva Villa!"   b. Simon
                                                         Bolivar
                                                         c. Porfirio
                                                         Díaz

2. Richard
   Basehart   Adolf Hitler   Erich Von
                                        Stroheim   a. Franz von
                                                          Papen
           "Hitler"   b. Hjalmar
                                                            Schacht
                                                         c. Erwin
                                                         Rommel

3. Jason
   Robards,
   Jr.   George Kaufman   Monty Woolley   a. Monty
                                                          Woolley
           "Act One"   b. Sheridan
                                                            Whiteside
                                                         c. Noel Coward

4. George
   Arliss   Alexander
                  Hamilton   David Niven   a. John Adams
           "Alexander
                  Hamilton"   b. Lafayette
                                                         c. Aaron Burr

5. Larry Parks   Al Jolson   Deborah Kerr   a. Ruby Keeler
           "The Jolson
                  Story"   b. Norma
                                                         Shearer
                                                        c. Sheilah
                                                        Graham

6. Genevieve
   Bujold   Anne Boleyn   Robert Donat   a. Henry VIII
           "Anne of the
                  Thousand
                  Days"   b. Thomas
                                                         Culpepper
                                                        c. Thomas
                                                        More

7. George C. Scott	Genl. George Patton	Harry Carey, Jr.	a. Douglas MacArthur
	"Patton"		b. Dwight Eisenhower
			c. Harry Truman

8. Michael Jayston	Czar Nicholas	Lionel Barrymore	a. Kaiser Wilhelm
	"Nicholas and Alexandra"		b. Rasputin
			c. Alexander Kerensky

9. Julie Andrews	Gertrude Lawrence "Star!"	George Hamilton	a. Moss Hart
			b. Noel Coward
			c. Jack Donohue

10. Katharine Hepburn	Mary Stuart	Glenda Jackson	a. Queen Elizabeth I
	"Mary of Scotland"		b. Queen Victoria
			c. Queen Elizabeth II

_____points

(*Answers on page 347*)

SOME DIRECTION, PLEASE

There are only four possible answers—for the most part—in these questions, so give us *some* direction, please, and take 10 points for each correct answer.

1. "Song of the _____"
2. "Walk _____ on Beacon"

226

3. "_____ of St. Louis"
4. "_____ side 1-1000"
5. "_____ Passage"
6. "_____ Side of Heaven"
7. "Call _____ side 777"
8. "Spawn of the _____"
9. "Mr. and Mrs. _____"
10. "The Ghost Goes _____"

_____ points

(*Answers on page 348*)

SOME DIRECTION, PLEASE—DUFFERS' TEE

There are only four possible answers—for the most part—in this quiz. Complete the following titles by giving us some direction, and take 10 points for each correct answer.

1. "How the _____ Was Won"
2. "_____ Mounted Police"
3. "_____ to Alaska"
4. "_____ Sea Sinner"
5. "_____ of Eden"
6. "_____ of the Border"
7. "The _____ Point Story"
8. "_____ ward the Women"
9. "Four Flags _____"
10. "_____ by Northwest"

_____ points

(*Answers on page 348*)

MORE OF "THE VIOLENT END"

Once again, we're concerned with how characters in various films met their death. Below, we've listed a group of players and the films in which the characters they portrayed suffered other than a natural

227

demise. Tell us how each of the following met their deaths in the films designated, and take 15 points for each correct answer.

1. C. Henry Gordon, in "The Charge of the Light Brigade" . . .
2. Edna May Oliver, in "Drums Along the Mohawk" . . .
3. Judith Anderson, in "Rebecca" . . .
4. Brian Aherne, in "Juarez" . . .
5. Robert Taylor, in "The Last Hunt" . . .
6. Slim Pickens, in "Dr. Strangelove" . . .
7. Margo, in "Lost Horizon" . . .
8. Addison Richards, in "Northwest Passage" . . .
9. Ronald Colman, in "A Tale of Two Cities" . . .
10. Kirk Douglas, in "Spartacus" . . .
11. Eduardo Ciannelli, in "Gunga Din" . . .
12. Luther Adler, in "The Brotherhood" . . .
13. Robert Walker, in "Strangers on a Train" . . .
14. Stephen Boyd, in "Ben-Hur" . . .
15. Marlon Brando, in "Viva Zapata!" . . .

———————points

(*Answers on page 349*)

MORE OF "THE VIOLENT END"—DUFFERS' TEE

Again we're concerned as to how characters in various films met their violent deaths. Below, in Column One, we've listed some players and films. In Column Two, out of order, we have listed the modi operandi of these several untimely ends. You are to match the manner of death, from Column Two, with the appropriate film and player combinations of Column One. You may have 10 points for each correct answer.

1. C. Henry Gordon, in "The Charge of the Light Brigade" . . .

    a. Ran amok and plunged off a cliff.

2. Edna May Oliver, in "Drums Along the Mohawk" . . .

    b. By firing squad.

228

3. Judith Anderson, in
   "Rebecca" . . .

   c. Slow strangulation by garroting.

4. Brian Aherne, in
   "Juarez" . . .

   d. By an Indian arrow.

5. Robert Taylor, in "The
   Last Hunt" . . .

   e. Dragged to his death behind his chariot.

6. Slim Pickens, in
   "Dr. Strangelove" . . .

   f. By crucifixion.

7. Margo, in "Lost
   Horizon" . . .

   g. By gunfire in an ambush.

8. Addison Richards, in
   "Northwest
   Passage" . . .

   h. Impaled on the lances of the charging British soldiers.

9. Ronald Colman, in "A
   Tale of Two Cities" . . .

   i. Trapped in a burning mansion.

10. Kirk Douglas, in
    "Spartacus" . . .

    j. Crushed by a runaway merry-go-round.

11. Eduardo Ciannelli, in
    "Gunga Din" . . .

    k. Rode to his death on a falling A-bomb.

12. Luther Adler, in "The
    Brotherhood" . . .

    l. Frozen to death.

13. Robert Walker, in
    "Strangers on a
    Train" . . .

    m. Jumped into a pit of poisonous snakes.

14. Stephen Boyd, in
    "Ben-Hur" . . .

    n. By guillotining.

15. Marlon Brando, in
    "Viva Zapata!" . . .

    o. By sudden aging on leaving Shangri-La.

_____points

(*Answers on page 349*)

AND YET STILL MORE "NAME THE STAR"

Once again we come to another NAME THE STAR quiz. As before, we have listed two characters played by the same star. You are asked to identify the star in question. For each correct identification, you make 10 points. But these are toughies, so if you find them too tough, you shouldn't be embarrassed by going to the Duffers' Tee.

1.	Connie Milligan	Clarissa Saunders
2.	Grandpa Bower	Jeff Slocum
3.	Ginny Moorehead	Fran Kubelik
4.	Bushrod Gentry	Roy Cronin
5.	Hubbell Gardiner	Jeremiah Johnson
6.	Lew Harper	Juan Carrasco
7.	Emily Barham	Sarah Sherman
8.	The General	Julian Northrup
9.	Georgi Gragore	Dolores "Sweets" Ramirez
10.	Patty Marlow	Jinny Marshland

————points

(*Answers on page 350*)

AND YET STILL MORE "NAME THE STAR" —DUFFERS' TEE

It's time to NAME THE STAR again. From the two characters we've provided, identify the star who played these parts. If you're here from the Buffs' version, you know that these are the same stars—and that the clues are better-known. For this reason, each correct answer receives only 5 points.

1.	Phoebe Frost	Alice Sycamore
2.	Doc Velie	Hunk Marriner
3.	Princess Aouda	Irma La Douce
4.	Marcus Vinicius	Armand Duval
5.	Jay Gatsby	The Sundance Kid
6.	Chance Wayne	Fast Eddie Felson
7.	Jerusha Bromley	Mary Poppins

    8. Martin Vanderhof   Dr. Leonard Gillespie

    9. Karen Vanmeer   Joan of Arc

   10. Beatrix Emery   Georgia Lorrison

_____points

(Answers on page 350)

OSCAR SHUFFLE #4—WILD CARD

Here's another wild card exercise for Duffer and Buff. As before, we've taken the names of some Oscar winners of the past and scrambled them to a fare-thee-well. Unscramble them, and you receive 5 points for each correct name you come up with. Then, use the key letters to unscramble a *fourth* hidden Oscar winner, and receive another 10 points. As before, all of the Oscar winners, including the hidden one, are from the same Oscar category.

   1. M E G A S J C Y N E A

       (_) _ (_) _ (_)   _ _ (_) (_) _ _

   2. D A R N Y L I L A M

       _ (_) _   _ (_) _ (_) _ (_) _

   3. T R I E S D I N Y I O P E

       _ (_) _ (_) _ _   _ _ _ _ _ (_) _

      And the hidden Oscar winner is:

     — — — — — — — — — — — —

_____points

(Answers on page 351)

THE ETERNAL TRIANGLE

The Eternal Triangle has been a plot staple since movies began. In this exercise, we supply two thirds of the triangle. For completing the triangle—that is, giving us the name of the actor or actress who was "the other man" or "the other woman," you earn 10 points. If you can also supply the name of the film in question, you may have another 10 points. Get *both* parts of *all* fifteen questions, and you'll earn not only the 300 basic points, but we'll add a bonus for a total potential of 400 points!

	ACTOR OR ACTRESS	FILM TITLE
1. Dick Powell, Gloria Grahame		
2. Deborah Kerr, Philip Ober		
3. Joan Bennett, Robert Preston		
4. Doris Day, James Cagney		
5. Carole Lombard, Charles Laughton		
6. Olivia de Havilland, Patric Knowles		
7. Shirley MacLaine, George C. Scott		
8. Orson Welles, Ruth Warrick		
9. Judy Holliday, Broderick Crawford		
10. Rita Hayworth, Everett Sloane		
11. Dana Andrews, Virginia Mayo		
12. Carroll Baker, Karl Malden		
13. Joseph Cotten, Bette Davis		
14. Joan Crawford, Bruce Bennett		
15. Gary Cooper, Geraldine Fitzgerald		

_____points
_____bonus?
_____total points

(*Answers on page 351*)

THE ETERNAL TRIANGLE—DUFFERS' TEE

Now we're concerned with that plot staple, the Eternal Triangle. Column One lists pairs of players who formed two thirds of the romantic triangle. Column Two lists the films in which these triangles were included, though the list is out of order. You must select the title which matches the pairing in Column One, and for each matching you get right, you get 10 points. Column Three lists the actors or actresses who played "the other man" or "the other woman" in these triangles. Match these with the correct pairings and titles of Columns One and Two, and you get 10 more points. Get *both* parts of *each* question, for a basic 300 points, and we'll toss in a bonus of 100 *more* points—a possible 400!

1. Dick Powell Gloria Grahame	A. "The Yellow Rolls-Royce"	a. Lee Patrick
2. Deborah Kerr Philip Ober	B. "The Best Years of Our Lives"	b. Orson Welles
3. Joan Bennett Robert Preston	C. "Mildred Pierce"	c. Gilbert Roland
4. Doris Day James Cagney	D. "Citizen Kane"	d. Eli Wallach
5. Carole Lombard Charles Laughton	E. "Beyond the Forest"	e. Gregory Peck
6. Olivia de Havilland Patric Knowles	F. "Ten North Frederick"	f. Burt Lancaster
7. Shirley MacLaine George C. Scott	G. "The Bad and the Beautiful"	g. Dorothy Comingore
8. Orson Welles Ruth Warrick	H. "Baby Doll"	h. Alain Delon
9. Judy Holliday Broderick Crawford	I. "From Here to Eternity"	i. Cameron Mitchell

233

10. Rita Hayworth Everett Sloane	J. "The Charge of the Light Brigade"	j. Suzy Parker
11. Dana Andrews Virginia Mayo	K. "The Macomber Affair"	k. William Holden
12. Carroll Baker Karl Malden	L. "The Lady from Shanghai"	l. Errol Flynn
13. Joseph Cotten Bette Davis	M. "They Knew What They Wanted"	m. Steve Cochran
14. Joan Crawford Bruce Bennett	N. "Born Yesterday"	n. William Gargan
15. Gary Cooper Geraldine Fitzgerald	O. "Love Me or Leave Me"	o. David Brian

————points

(Answers on page 351)

OH, JOHNNY!

The number of film characters who have been known as Johnny probably reaches into the thousands. However, some of these have also been the title of the film as well. We list ten films below with a "Johnny . . ." title, and ask you to identify the actor most closely identified with the film's Johnny. Take 10 points for each correct answer.

1. "Johnny Come Lately" _ _ _ _ _ _ _ _ _ _ _
2. "Johnny Allegro" _ _ _ _ _ _ _ _ _ _
3. "Johnny Concho" _ _ _ _ _ _ _ _ _ _ _
4. "Johnny Cool" _ _ _ _ _ _ _ _ _ _
5. "Johnny Apollo" _ _ _ _ _ _ _ _ _ _ _
6. "Johnny Eager" _ _ _ _ _ _ _ _ _ _ _ _
7. "Johnny Dark" _ _ _ _ _ _ _ _ _ _

8. "Johnny Rocco"   _____   _____
9. "Johnny O'Clock" ____   _____
10. "Johnny Yuma"   ____   _____

_____**points**

(*Answers on page 352*)

OH, JOHNNY!—DUFFERS' TEE

The number of film characters who have been known as Johnny probably reaches into the thousands. However, some of these have also been the title of the film as well. We list ten films below (though "Johnny Belinda" is *not* one of them, in case you were hoping) and in Column Two, out of order, are those actors who are most closely identified with the various Johnnys. Your task is to match the player with the appropriate title. And take 10 points for each correct answer.

1. "Johnny Come Lately"	a. Stephen McNally
2. "Johnny Allegro"	b. Henry Silva
3. "Johnny Concho"	c. Tony Curtis
4. "Johnny Cool"	d. Mark Damon
5. "Johnny Apollo"	e. Dick Powell
6. "Johnny Eager"	f. James Cagney
7. "Johnny Dark"	g. George Raft
8. "Johnny Rocco"	h. Tyrone Power
9. "Johnny O'Clock"	i. Robert Taylor
10. "Johnny Yuma"	j. Frank Sinatra

_____**points**

(*Answers on page 352*)

OUT OF THE LIMELIGHT

This exercise is concerned with those "out of the limelight"—not the performers or the personalities, but those backstage or out of the camera's range who make it all happen. The producers, the impresarios, the directors who have themselves been portrayed in films are our focus in this quiz. Below we list a number of theatrical and cinematic luminaries, and the actors who portrayed them (the latter are in Column One, the former in Column Two). We'll give you 10 points for each correct answer, and all you have to do is tell us the title of the film which included the portrayal.

1. Walter Pidgeon   Florenz Ziegfeld   "_ _ _ _ _ _ _ _ _"
2. Richard Whorf   Sam Harris   "_ _ _ _ _ _ _ _ _ _ _ _ _ _ _ _ _"
3. Robert Evans   Irving Thalberg   "_ _ _ _ _ _ _ _ _ _ _ _ _ _ _ _"
4. Leo Carrillo   Tony Pastor   "_ _ _ _ _ _ _ _ _ _ _ _ _ _"
5. Jason Robards,
       Jr.   George Kaufman   "_ _ _ _ _ _ _"
6. Walter Pidgeon   J. J. Shubert   "_ _ _ _ _ _ _ _ _ _ _ _ _"
7. Wallace Beery   P. T. Barnum   "_ _ _ _ _ _ _ _ _ _ _ _ _"
8. George
     Hamilton   Moss Hart   "_ _ _ _ _ _"
9. Ernest Borgnine   Boris Morros   "_ _ _ _ _ _ _ _ _ _ _"
10. David Wayne   Sol Hurok   "_ _ _ _ _ _ _ _ _ _ _ _ _ _"

_____ points

(*Answers on page 352*)

OUT OF THE LIMELIGHT—DUFFERS' TEE

This exercise is concerned with those "out of the limelight"—not the performers or the personalities, but those backstage or out of the camera's range who make it all happen. The producers, the impresarios, the playwrights, the directors—these are the ones we are looking at and specifically those who have been portrayed in motion pictures. Below, in Columns One and Two, we list a group of actors and the backstage luminaries they have portrayed. Column Three lists—out of order, of course—the films in which these portrayals were included. Select the appropriate film title from Column Three which matches with the player and the role. For each correct answer, take 10 points.

1.	Walter Pidgeon	Florenz Ziegfeld	a. "Rocket to the Moon"
2.	Richard Whorf	Sam Harris	b. "Lillian Russell"
3.	Wallace Beery	P. T. Barnum	c. "Tonight We Sing"
4.	Robert Evans	Irving Thalberg	d. "The Mighty Barnum"
5.	Leo Carrillo	Tony Pastor	e. "Deep in My Heart"
6.	Jason Robards, Jr.	George Kaufman	f. "Man on a String"
7.	Walter Pidgeon	J. J. Shubert	g. "Funny Girl"
8.	Burl Ives	P. T. Barnum	h. "Man of a Thousand Faces"
9.	Ernest Borgnine	Boris Morros	i. "Act One"
10.	David Wayne	Sol Hurok	j. "Yankee Doodle Dandy"

————points

(*Answers on page 353*)

PROTOCOL

In the questions below, we list a player and an incomplete film title. The missing word indicates the player's rank in the film. Supply the missing word or phrase and complete the film title. Take 5 points for each correct answer.

1. Yul Brynner   "The _____ and I"
2. Paul Robeson   "The _____ Jones"
3. Robert Wagner   "_____ Valiant"
4. Olivia de Havilland   "_____ O'Rourke"
5. Louis Hayward   "The _____ of West Point"
6. Vincent Price   "The _____ of Arizona"
7. Bette Davis   "The Virgin _____"
8. Ethel Barrymore   "Rasputin and the _____"
9. Akim Tamiroff   "The _____ Died at Dawn"

10. Robert Montgomery	"The _____ of Chicago"
11. Robert Donat	"The _____ of Monte Cristo"
12. Hedy Lamarr	"_____ _____ and the Bellboy"
13. Ava Gardner	"The Barefoot _____"
14. George Arliss	"_____ Richelieu"
15. Edmund Purdom	"The Student _____"

_____points

(*Answers on page 353*)

PROTOCOL—DUFFERS' TEE

Below we have listed some players and some partial titles of films in which they played members of nobility, or characters of some lofty stature. If you can supply the missing title-within-a-title, using properly selected words and phrases from Column Three, you will have completed the feature title we're seeking. You get 5 points for each correct selection.

1. Yul Brynner	"The _____ and I"	a. Queen
2. Paul Robeson	"The _____ Jones"	b. Contessa
3. Robert Wagner	"_____ Valiant"	c. Princess
4. Olivia de Havilland	"_____ O'Rourke"	d. Baron
5. Louis Hayward	"The _____ of West Point"	
6. Vincent Price	"The _____ of Arizona"	e. General
7. Bette Davis	"The Virgin _____"	f. Cardinal
8. Ethel Barrymore	"Rasputin and the _____"	g. Prince
9. Akim Tamiroff	"The _____ Died at Dawn"	h. Her Highness
10. Robert Montgomery	"The _____ of Chicago"	i. Emperor
11. Robert Donat	"The _____ of Monte Cristo"	j. Duke
		k. Earl

12. Hedy Lamarr	"_____ and the Bellboy"	l. Prince
13. Ava Gardner	"The Barefoot _____"	m. Empress
14. George Arliss	"_____ Richelieu"	n. Count
15. Edmund Purdom	"The Student _____"	o. King

_____**points**

(*Answers on page 353*)

HISTORY IS MADE IN THE MOVIES PART III

This exercise is played exactly as in Parts I and II of HISTORY IS MADE IN THE MOVIES—so if you can't remember the rules, refer back to the preceding quizzes with this title, and do something about your memory. We will venture that Part III is tougher than either Parts I or II—and some relatively more obscure casting assignments make it all the tougher. But we're increasing the score on each part of this quiz to 20 points per correct answer. Each question is therefore worth 80 points, so this is one of the biggies at a potential take of 800 points! So think, ponder, remember—and *guess* if you have to.

	HISTORICAL FIGURE	FILM TITLE
1. Alexander Knox Grant Mitchell	_____ _____	_____ _____
2. Jean Simmons Donald Crisp	_____ _____	_____ _____
3. Curt Jurgens Luther Adler	_____ _____	_____ _____
4. Cliff Robertson William Marshall	_____	_____
5. Alan Ladd Arthur Hunnicutt	_____	_____
6. Donald O'Connor Robert Evans	_____ _____	_____ _____

	HISTORICAL FIGURE	FILM TITLE
7. James Stewart Kenneth Tobey	_____ _____	_____ _____
8. Burgess Meredith Spring Byington	_____ _____	_____ _____
9. Howard Keel Porter Hall	_____ _____	_____ _____
10. Kirk Douglas Vladimir Sokoloff	_____ _____	_____ _____

_____points

(*Answers on page 354*)

HISTORY IS MADE IN THE MOVIES
PART III—DUFFERS' TEE

This exercise is played exactly as in Parts I and II of HISTORY IS MADE IN THE MOVIES—so if you can't remember what you're to do, refer back to the earlier parts, and do something about your memory. All we'll say about this Part III is that it's rougher than Parts I and II because we've picked some relatively more obscure casting assignments. For this one, we'll give 30 points for the correct selection of the multiple choice in Column Four—*plus another* 30 points if you can tell us the title of the film in which the portrayal suggested by Columns Three and Four was included. That's a possible 60 points per question, or a total potential of 600 points!

1. Grant Mitchell	Georges Clemenceau	Alexander Knox	a. Lloyd George
	"The Life of Emile Zola"		b. George V c. Woodrow Wilson
2. Donald Crisp	Sir Francis Bacon	Jean Simmons	a. Queen Elizabeth
	"The Private Lives of Elizabeth and Essex"		b. Lady Bothwell c. Doll Tearsheet

240

3. Curt Jurgens   Wernher von
               Braun   Luther Adler   a. Adolf Hitler
               "I Aim at the
               Stars"   b. Hermann
                                                         Goering
                                                         c. Robert
                                                         Goddard

4. William
     Marshall   Edward Brooke   Cliff Robertson   a. John F.
                                                         Kennedy
              "The Boston
              Strangler"   b. Estes
                                                       Kefauver
                                                     c. Albert
                                                     DeSalvo

5. Arthur
     Hunnicutt   Davy Crockett   Alan Ladd   a. Sam
                                                         Houston
              "The Last
              Command"   b. Jean Lafitte
                                                         c. Jim Bowie

6. Robert   Donald
     Evans   Irving Thalberg   O'Connor   a. Buster
                                                         Keaton
              "Man of a   b. Louis B.
              Thousand   Mayer
              Faces"   c. James
                                                         Cagney

7. Kenneth
     Tobey   Bat Masterson   James Stewart   a. Ike Clanton
              "Gunfight at the
                 O.K. Corral"   b. Sam Bass
                                                         c. Wyatt Earp

8. Spring   Burgess
     Byington   Dolly Madison   Meredith   a. Button
                                                         Gwinnett
              "The Buccaneer"   b. James
                                                         Madison
                                                         c. Dominique
                                                         You

9. Porter Hall   Jack McCall   Howard Keel   a. Grat Dalton
              "The Plainsman"   b. Wild Bill
                                                         Hickok
                                                         c. Kit Carson

10. Vladimir
    Sokoloff   Paul Cezanne   Kirk Douglas   a. Vincent van
                                                        Gogh
                 "The Life of   b. Paul
           Emile Zola"   Gauguin
                                              c. Rembrandt
                                              van Rijn

————points

(*Answers on page 354*)

HISTORY IS MADE IN THE MOVIES PART IV

This exercise is played exactly the same as in Parts I, II, and III—only we warn you that this version is a real killer. Refer back to Part I, if you must, to get the rules straight. But take heart in that we're offering 25 points for each correct answer. That's a possible 100 points per question. Take time with this one, get them all correct (heh-heh), and add 1,000 points to your score!

	HISTORICAL FIGURE	FILM TITLE
1. Van Heflin Edwin Maxwell		
2. James Cagney Dayton Lummis		
3. Robert Stack Richard Gaines		
4. Thomas Mitchell Moroni Olsen		
5. Raymond Massey Joseph Crehan		
6. Milburn Stone Alan Reed		
7. Peter Falk Phil Arnold		
8. Charles Laughton Brigid Bazlen		

242

	HISTORICAL FIGURE	FILM TITLE
9. William Bendix Ernie Adams	_____	_____
10. Ian Hunter Cornel Wilde	_____	_____

_____points

(Answers on page 355)

HISTORY IS MADE IN THE MOVIES
PART IV—DUFFERS' TEE

This exercise is played exactly the same as were Parts I, II, and III—only this one is a real killer. Refer back to Part I, Duffers' Tee, for a recap of the rules before you take the plunge. Because these are tougher, we're offering you 30 points if you can tell us the correct historical figure we're looking for from the choice provided in Column Four—plus (now, get this!) an *additional* 45 points if you can come up with the title of the film in which this portrayal (suggested by Columns Three and Four) was included. That's a possible 750 points to sweeten your total in the homestretch!

1. Edwin Maxwell	Secretary Stanton "The Plainsman"	Van Heflin	a. Horace Greeley b. Andrew Johnson c. U. S. Grant
2. Dayton Lummis	Douglas MacArthur "The Court-Martial of Billy Mitchell"	James Cagney	a. Adm. William Halsey b. Adm. Chester Nimitz c. Maj. Jimmy Doolittle
3. Richard Gaines	George Washington "Unconquered"	Robert Stack	a. John Hancock b. Nathan Hale c. John Paul Jones

4. Thomas Mitchell	Ned Buntline "Buffalo Bill"	Moroni Olsen	a. Richard Harding Davis b. W. Randolph Hearst c. William Cody
5. Joseph Crehan	U. S. Grant "Geronimo"	Raymond Massey	a. Jeb Stuart b. Abe Lincoln c. Stonewall Jackson
6. Alan Reed	Pancho Villa "Viva Zapata!"	Milburn Stone	a. President Juerta b. Richard Harding Davis c. John J. Pershing
7. Phil Arnold	Fiorello La Guardia "The Court-Martial of Billy Mitchell"	Peter Falk	a. Abe Reles b. Lucky Luciano c. Thomas Dewey
8. Brigid Bazlen	Salome "King of Kings"	Charles Laughton	a. Judas Iscariot b. John the Baptist c. King Herod
9. Ernie Adams	Miller Huggins "Pride of the Yankees"	William Bendix	a. Tex Rickard b. Babe Ruth c. Jimmy Foxx
10. Ian Hunter	Richard the Lion-Hearted "The Adventures of Robin Hood"	Cornel Wilde	a. Prince John b. Will Scarlet c. Robin Hood

————points

(*Answers on page 355*)

THE FINAL FADE-OUT

This quiz is concerned with the last films of some Hollywood greats. We ask you to give us the title of the last film in which they appeared. Take 25 points for each correct answer.

1. Clark Gable   _____
2. Spencer Tracy   _____
3. Humphrey Bogart   _____
4. Gary Cooper   _____
5. Errol Flynn   _____
6. Alan Ladd   _____
7. Tyrone Power   _____
8. Judy Garland   _____
9. Jean Harlow   _____
10. Carole Lombard   _____
11. Charles Laughton   _____
12. Robert Walker   _____
13. John Garfield   _____
14. Harold Lloyd   _____
15. Wallace Beery   _____
16. Lon Chaney, Sr.   _____
17. Constance Bennett   _____
18. Montgomery Clift   _____
19. ZaSu Pitts   _____
20. Ethel Barrymore   _____

_____points

(*Answers on page 356*)

THE FINAL FADE-OUT—DUFFERS' TEE

This quiz is concerned with the last films of some Hollywood greats. The list in Column Two gives the last films, out of order, in which the screen legends of Column One appeared prior to their death. You may have 25 points for each film you correctly match.

1. Clark Gable   a. "Saratoga"
2. Spencer Tracy   b. "Big Jack"

3.	Humphrey Bogart	c.	"Johnny Trouble"
4.	Gary Cooper	d.	"The Defector"
5.	Errol Flynn	e.	"He Ran All the Way"
6.	Alan Ladd	f.	"The Naked Edge"
7.	Tyrone Power	g.	"The Misfits"
8.	Judy Garland	h.	"It's a Mad, Mad, Mad, Mad World"
9.	Jean Harlow	i.	"Mad Wednesday"
10.	Carole Lombard	j.	"Witness for the Prosecution"
11.	Charles Laughton	k.	"The Unholy Three"
12.	Robert Walker	l.	"Guess Who's Coming to Dinner"
13.	John Garfield	m.	"Cuban Rebel Girls"
14.	Harold Lloyd	n.	"I Could Go On Singing"
15.	Wallace Beery	o.	"The Harder They Fall"
16.	Lon Chaney, Sr.	p.	"Advise and Consent"
17.	Constance Bennett	q.	"The Carpetbaggers"
18.	Montgomery Clift	r.	"My Son John"
19.	ZaSu Pitts	s.	"Madame X"
20.	Ethel Barrymore	t.	"To Be or Not to Be"

———points

(*Answers on page 356*)

HOMESTRETCH—BUFFS AND DUFFERS

This is the homestretch, with the same questions for Buffs and Duffers. And we warn you, *they are murder!* There are no concessions to the Duffers on this one, and everyone playing has to come up with the same answers. But in order that the Duffers might catch up in the stretch, each question has a different point value. So, if you've been playing the Duffers' Tees, here's your chance (a *slim* one, but a chance). And if you've been playing as a Buff, you must take the Buffs' point value for these questions—and you're on your honor.

246

1. **Buff Score, 375 points; Duffer Score, 700 points:**
   In the film "The Bad and the Beautiful," the movie actress (played by Lana Turner) had a father. The character of the father, however, was represented only by a voice on a recording. Name the character actor whose voice was used: _____.

2. **Buff Score, 430 points; Duffer Score, 1,200 points:**
   Occasionally, well-known stars were used by the studios to which they were under contract merely to narrate a film. The stars were not seen, and usually were *not* named in the credits. Name the stars (and you *must* name all three in order to claim the points promised) who narrated these three films:
   a. "The War of the Worlds," _____; b. "The Red Badge of Courage," _____; and c. "Mother Wore Tights," _____.

3. **Buff Score, 700 points; Duffer Score, 1,400 points:**
   In the film "West Side Story," a long-time Hollywood character actor appeared only as a picture on a political poster. The Jets and the Sharks raced by a long string of these posters in several scenes, but the actor's face was prominent and recognizable. Name him: _____.

4. **Buff Score, 950 points; Duffer Score, 1,835 points:**
   In the film which the Motion Picture Academy recognized as the Best Film of 1936, character actors A. A. Trimble and Buddy Doyle played brief supporting roles. However, they portrayed two superstars of the stage and screen. Name the two stars they portrayed: _____ and _____.

5. **Buff Score, 1,400 points; Duffer Score, 2,630 points:**
   In the film "The Bad and the Beautiful," the movie producer (played by Kirk Douglas) had a father. The character of the father, however, was represented only by a photograph. Name the character actor who posed for this photograph: _____.

————points

(*Answers on page 356*)

Whew!

ANSWERS

ANIMALS—BUFFS AND DUFFERS

1. ___ u.   "The BIRDman of Alcatraz"
2. ___ p.   "The Cat and the CANARY"
3. ___ t.   "OWL and the Pussycat"
4. ___ h.   "PONY Soldier"
5. ___ i.   "A Man Called HORSE"
6. ___ n.   "EAGLE Squadron"
7. ___ e.   "DUCK Soup"
8. ___ g. or o. "Track of the CAT"
9. ___ k.   "Lad, a DOG"
10. ___ o. or g. "Return of the CAT People"
11. ___ s.   "The Sea WOLF"
12. ___ b.   "The UnderPUP"
13. ___ v.   "The FLY"
14. ___ j.   "The FROGmen"
15. ___ c.   "ELEPHANT Walk"
16. ___ w.   "KITTEN with a Whip"
17. ___ f.   "Cult of the COBRA"
18. ___ l.   "20 MULE Team
19. ___ a.   "JACKASS Mail"
20. ___ y.   "The SHEEPman"
21. ___ d.   "The BIRDS"
22. ___ x.   "The MOUSE That Roared"
23. ___ m.   "King RAT"
24. ___ r.   "To Kill a MOCKINGBIRD"
25. ___ q.   "Night of the IGUANA"

NUMERICAL ORDER—BUFFS AND DUFFERS

h. "Ceiling ZERO"
e. "ONE, Two, Three"
f. "TWO Girls and a Sailor"

251

a. "THREE Godfathers"
j. "FOUR in a Jeep"
d. "FIVE Pennies"
k. "SIX Bridges to Cross"
b. "SEVEN Little Foys"
g. "EIGHT on the Lam"
c. "NINE Days a Queen"
i. "TEN North Frederick"

NAMES—BUFFS AND DUFFERS

1. Frank Cooper (GARY COOPER) and Audrey Hepburn-Ruston (AUDREY HEPBURN)

   g. "Love in the Afternoon"

2. Bernie Schwartz (TONY CURTIS) and Rosetta Jacobs (PIPER LAURIE)

   d. "The Prince Who Was a Thief"

3. Issur D. Demsky (KIRK DOUGLAS), Betty Jane Perske (LAUREN BACALL), and Doris von Kappelhoff (DORIS DAY)

   j. "Young Man with a Horn"

4. Sophia Sciccolone (SOPHIA LOREN) and Archibald Leach (CARY GRANT)

   h. "Houseboat"

5. Judy Tuvim (JUDY HOLLIDAY) and Dino Groccetti (DEAN MARTIN)

   k. "The Bells Are Ringing"

6. Reginald Truscott-Jones (RAY MILLAND) and Sarah Jane Fulks (JANE WYMAN)

   a. "The Lost Weekend"

7. Marion M. Morrison (JOHN WAYNE), Maureen Fitzsimmons (MAUREEN O'HARA), and William J. Shields, (BARRY FITZGERALD)

   i. "The Quiet Man"

8. Bill Gable (CLARK GABLE), Lucille Langhanke (MARY ASTOR), and Harlean Carpenter (JEAN HARLOW)

   f. "Red Dust"

9. Frederick Austerlitz (FRED ASTAIRE) and Susan Burce (JANE POWELL)   b. "Royal Wedding"

10. Zelma Hedrick (KATHRYN GRAYSON) and Alfred Arnold Cocozza (MARIO LANZA)   l. "Because You're Mine"

11. Spangler Arlington Brugh (ROBERT TAYLOR) and Vivien Mary Hartleigh (VIVIEN LEIGH)   e. "Waterloo Bridge"

12. Issur D. Demsky (KIRK DOUGLAS), Judy Turner (LANA TURNER), Patrick Barry (BARRY SULLIVAN), and Luis Antonio Damasco de Alonso (GILBERT ROLAND)   c. "The Bad and the Beautiful"

THE GREATEST!—BUFFS AND DUFFERS

1. "The Great Imposter"   f. Tony Curtis
2. "The Great John L."   g. Greg McClure
3. "The Great McGinty"   l. Brian Donlevy
4. "Catherine the Great"   b. Elisabeth Bergner
5. "Alexander the Great"   a. Richard Burton
6. "Patrick the Great"   h. Donald O'Connor
7. "The Great Dictator"   k. Charlie Chaplin
8. "The Great Ziegfeld"   j. William Powell
9. "The Great Gildersleeve"   o. Hal Peary
10. "The Great Gatsby"   n. or c. Alan Ladd or Robert Redford
11. "The Great Caruso"   i. Mario Lanza
12. "The Great Gatsby"   c. or n. Robert Redford or Alan Ladd
13. "The Great Profile"   e. or m. John Barrymore
14. "The Great Garrick"   d. Brian Aherne
15. "The Great Man Votes"   m. or e. John Barrymore

WHAT ARE THEY TRYING TO SAY?
PART I—BUFFS AND DUFFERS

1. From *The Garden of Allah,* by Sheilah Graham:
    (a) Paul Muni's real name was Muni Weisenfreund.
2. From *The Gangster Film,* by John Baxter:
    (c) The city in question was Chicago, not New York.
3. From *The Movies,* by Richard Griffith and Arthur Mayer, concerning "I Am a Fugitive from a Chain Gang":
    (c) It was not the Congressional Medal of Honor, but the Belgian Croix de Guerre.
4. From *Immortals of the Screen,* by Ray Stuart, concerning "Treasure Island":
    (c) Lionel Barrymore played Captain Billy Bones, while the role of Long John Silver was played by Wallace Beery.
5. From *The Name Above the Title,* by Frank Capra:
    (a) Tape recorders had not yet been invented in 1939.

CHARACTER SCRAMBLE—BUFFS AND DUFFERS

1. ALMA KRUGER
2. LARRY GATES
3. MINERVA URECAL
4. PERCY HELTON
5. WHIT BISSELL
6. JOHN MCGIVER
7. RAY TEAL
8. FRANK PUGLIA
9. STEVEN GERAY
10. MARY GORDON
11. NIGEL BRUCE
12. MARCEL DALIO
13. JOE SAWYER
14. JANE DARWELL
15. MONTAGU LOVE

254

WHO KILLED . . . ?—BUFFS AND DUFFERS

1. Janet Leigh, in "Psycho"?
2. Chuck Connors, in "The Big Country"?
3. Tyrone Power, in "Jesse James"?
4. Gregory Peck, in "The Gunfighter"?
5. Basil Rathbone, in "The Mark of Zorro"?
6. Steve Cochran, in "White Heat"?
7. Anne Francis, in "Bad Day at Black Rock"?
8. Zachary Scott, in "Mildred Pierce"?
9. Broderick Crawford, in "All the King's Men"?
10. Joseph Henabery, in "The Birth of a Nation"?
11. Bruce Cabot, in "The Last of the Mohicans"?
12. Edward G. Robinson, in "Little Caesar"?
13. Shelley Winters, in "A Double Life"?
14. Paul Hurst, in "Gone with the Wind"?
15. Leslie Howard, in "The Petrified Forest"?

d. Tony Perkins
h. Burl Ives
o. John Carradine
i. Skip Homeier
l. Tyrone Power
n. James Cagney

c. Robert Ryan
k. Ann Blyth

e. Shepperd Strudwick

a. Raoul Walsh

b. Robert Barrat
m. Thomas Jackson
f. Ronald Colman
g. Vivien Leigh
j. Humphrey Bogart

THE GORY DETAILS—BUFFS ONLY

1. Four: Janet Leigh, Basil Rathbone, Bruce Cabot, and Shelley Winters.
2. Tyrone Power, as Jesse James, in "Jesse James."
3. Tyrone Power, in "Jesse James"; Joseph Henabery, as Abraham Lincoln, in "The Birth of a Nation"; and Broderick Crawford, in "All the King's Men."
4. Broderick Crawford played Willie Stark in "All the King's Men," which had some parallel to the life of Huey Long, of Louisiana.
5. Bruce Cabot, in "The Last of the Mohicans."
6. Tyrone Power, as Jesse in "Jesse James," was shot in the back by "that dirty little coward—Bob Ford," played by John Carradine. The sequel: "The Return of Frank James."
7. Who can ever forget the shower slaying of Janet Leigh's character in "Psycho"—and Basil Rathbone was slain in a duel by Tyrone Power, as Zorro.

8. Only one—Broderick Crawford, in "All the King's Men."

9. Two: Ronald Colman, in "A Double Life," and Vivien Leigh, in "Gone with the Wind."

10. Four: Chuck Connors, in "The Big Country"; Paul Hurst, in "Gone with the Wind"; Anne Francis, in "Bad Day at Black Rock"; and Tyrone Power, in "Jesse James."

THE GORY DETAILS—DUFFERS' TEE

1. a. Janet Leigh, stabbed; b. Shelley Winters, strangled; c. Anne Francis, shot.

2. c. 6. "Western elements" is the key. "The Big Country," "Jesse James," "The Gunfighter," "Bad Day at Black Rock," "The Mark of Zorro," and "The Last of the Mohicans." Even though "Bad Day at Black Rock" was modern, we feel it qualifies with "Western elements"—ditto "Jesse James" and "The Last of the Mohicans," even though the former was laid in the Midwest, and the latter film was set in the Northeast section of the country.

3. d. 11. Those which were not: Janet Leigh, Basil Rathbone, Shelley Winters, and Bruce Cabot.

4. Janet Leigh, (c) secretary; Shelley Winters, (a) waitress; Anne Francis, (b) ran a service station.

5. c. 7. "The Big Country," "Jesse James," "The Gunfighter," "The Mark of Zorro," "The Birth of a Nation," "The Last of the Mohicans," and "Gone with the Wind."

6. a. None. "The Mark of Zorro" might've tripped you up, but that was in Los Angeles when it was still Old California.

7. Janet Leigh, (a) a sister; Shelley Winters, (c) no indication of any relatives at all; Anne Francis, (b) a brother.

8. b. 4. "The Big Country," "Jesse James," "Bad Day at Black Rock," "Gone with the Wind."

9. (b) Basil Rathbone.

10. (c) Edward G. Robinson.

TELL US WHEN—BUFFS ONLY

1. "Good MORNING, Miss Dove"
2. "London AFTER DARK"
3. "3:10 to Yuma"
4. "High NOON"
5. "Love in the AFTERNOON"
6. "SUNSET Boulevard"
7. "Marjorie MORNINGstar"
8. "Dinner at EIGHT"
9. "MIDNIGHT Lace"
10. "Tonight at 8:30"
11. "Cheyenne AUTUMN"
12. "Decision Before DAWN"
13. "WINTER Carnival"
14. "A MIDSUMMER Night's Dream"
15. "A SUMMER Place"
16. "Suddenly It's SPRING"
17. "Bugles in the AFTERNOON"
18. "History Is Made at NIGHT"
19. "Centennial SUMMER"
20. "Dead of NIGHT"

TELL US WHEN—DUFFERS' TEE

1. ___ j.   "Good MORNING, Miss Dove"
2. ___ l.   "London AFTER DARK"
3. ___ r.   "3:10 to Yuma"
4. ___ i.   "High NOON"
5. ___ c.   "Bugles in the AFTERNOON"
6. ___ s.   "SUNSET Boulevard"
7. ___ q.   "Violent SATURDAY"
8. ___ d.   "Dinner at EIGHT"
9. ___ t.   "MIDNIGHT Lace"
10. ___ m.   "Tonight at 8:30"
11. ___ a.   "Cheyenne AUTUMN"
12. ___ p.   "Decision Before DAWN"

13. __ g. "WINTER Carnival"
14. __ b. "A MIDSUMMER Night's Dream"
15. __ o. "A SUMMER Place"
16. __ e. "Suddenly It's SPRING"
17. __ h. "Hurry SUNDOWN"
18. __ k. "History Is Made at NIGHT"
19. __ f. "CHRISTMAS in Connecticut"
20. __ n. "DAYTIME Wife"

FIRST, THE WORD—BUFFS ONLY

1. Jack London | a. "The Adventures of Martin Eden"

2. Eugene O'Neill | c. "Summer Holiday"

3. James Jones | c. "Some Came Running"

4. Damon Runyon | b. "Little Miss Marker"

5. Rudyard Kipling | b. "Kim"

6. Tennessee Williams | a. "Boom!"

7. Ernest Hemingway | a. "To Have and Have Not"

8. H. G. Wells | a. "The Invisible Man"

9. Erich Maria Remarque | c. "The Road Back"

10. Edna Ferber | a. "So Big"

FIRST, THE WORD—DUFFERS' TEE

1. "Call of the Wild" "The Sea Wolf" | C. Jack London | d. "The Adventures of Martin Eden"

2. "Mourning Becomes Electra" "The Long Voyage Home" | G. Eugene O'Neill | h. "Summer Holiday"

3. "From Here to Eternity" "The Thin Red Line" | J. James Jones | j. "Some Came Running"

258

4. "Guys and
    Dolls"   H. Damon Runyon   i. "Little Miss Marker"
   "The Big
    Street"

5. "Captains
    Courageous"   A. Rudyard Kipling   g. "Kim"
   "Gunga Din"

6. "The Glass
    Menagerie"   D. Tennessee
   "Baby Doll"   Williams   a. "Boom!"

7. "The Old Man
    and the Sea" I. Ernest
   "The Killers"   Hemingway   b. "To Have and Have
                                            Not"

8. "The Time
    Machine"   F. H. G. Wells   f. "The Invisible Man"
   "Things to
    Come"

9. "All Quiet on
    the Western
    Front"   E. Erich Maria
   "Arch of   Remarque   c. "The Road Back"
    Triumph"

10. "Giant"   B. Edna Ferber   e. "So Big"
    "Ice Palace"

THE BETTER HALF—BUFFS ONLY

1. Grace Kelly: "The Country Girl"; "Dial M for Murder"; "Mogambo."

2. Barbara Stanwyck: "Double Indemnity"; "The Two Mrs. Carrolls"; "Titanic."

3. Bette Davis: "All About Eve"; "Mr. Skeffington"; and either "The Little Foxes" or "The Letter."

4. June Allyson: "The Stratton Story" (or "The Glenn Miller Story" or "Strategic Air Command"); "The McConnell Story"; "The Shrike."

5. Judy Garland: "I Could Go On Singing"; "For Me and My Gal"; "A Star Is Born."

6. Lauren Bacall: "Designing Woman"; "Written on the Wind" (or "A Gift of Love"); "Young Man with a Horn."

259

7. Dorothy McGuire: "A Summer Place"; "Friendly Persuasion"; "A Tree Grows in Brooklyn."

8. Elizabeth Taylor: "Giant"; "Father of the Bride" (or "Father's Little Dividend"); "Cat on a Hot Tin Roof."

9. Ginger Rogers: "Primrose Path"; "Black Widow"; "We're Not Married."

10. Doris Day: "Storm Warning"; "Midnight Lace"; "The Man Who Knew Too Much."

THE BETTER HALF—DUFFERS' TEE

1. Grace Kelly
2. Barbara Stanwyck
3. Bette Davis
4. June Allyson
5. Judy Garland
6. Lauren Bacall
7. Dorothy McGuire
8. Elizabeth Taylor
9. Ginger Rogers
10. Doris Day

LINK-UPS—BUFFS AND DUFFERS

1. Dean	MARTIN	Kosleck
2. Vera	MILES	Mander
3. Jessica	WALTER	Brennan
4. James	DONALD	O'Connor
5. William	CONRAD	Nagel
6. Dane	CLARK	Gable
7. James	STEWART	Granger
8. James	CRAIG	Stevens
9. Robert	KENT	Smith
10. Joan	LESLIE	Howard

SPOT THE BIO: MALES—BUFFS AND DUFFERS

Bob Hope	4. Eddie Foy	c. "The Seven Little Foys"
Tony Dexter	8. Rudolph Valentino	k. "Valentino"
Tony Curtis	14. Harry Houdini	f. "Houdini"
Donald O'Connor	13. Buster Keaton	i. "The Buster Keaton Story"
James Cagney	7. Lon Chaney	j. "Man of a Thousand Faces"
Larry Parks	12. Al Jolson	o. "The Jolson Story" (or the Buffs might've said "Jolson Sings Again")
Keefe Brasselle	15. Eddie Cantor	a. "The Eddie Cantor Story"
Errol Flynn	5. John Barrymore	l. "Too Much, Too Soon"
Mario Lanza	6. Enrico Caruso	d. "The Great Caruso"
Frank Sinatra	2. Joe E. Lewis	e. "The Joker Is Wild"
James Cagney	9. George M. Cohan	m. "Yankee Doodle Dandy" (or the Buffs might've suggested his cameo as Cohan in "The Seven Little Foys")
Will Rogers, Jr.	1. Will Rogers	n. "The Story of Will Rogers"
Ray Danton	11. George Raft	h. "The George Raft Story"
Fred Astaire	10. Vernon Castle	g. "The Story of Vernon and Irene Castle"
Richard Burton	3. Edwin Booth	b. "Prince of Players"

ODD MAN OUT—BUFFS AND DUFFERS

1. Sam Bass: Dan Duryea is out of place. Howard Duff played the outlaw in "Calamity Jane and Sam Bass"; Nestor Paiva, in "Badman's Territory"; and William Bishop, in "The Texas Rangers."

2. Billy the Kid: William Campbell should be excluded. Jack Buetel played William Bonney, or Billy the Kid, in "The Outlaw"; Audie Murphy, in "The Kid from Texas"; and Paul Newman was Billy in "The Left-Handed Gun."

3. Jim Bowie: Dewey Robinson is the ringer. The others: Macdonald Carey in "Comanche Territory"; Alan Ladd in "The Iron Mistress"; and Richard Widmark in "The Alamo."

4. Kit Carson: Scratch Rod Cameron from this line-up. The others were Jon Hall as "Kit Carson"; Bill Elliott in "Overland with Kit Carson"; and "Fighting Kit Carson" with Johnny Mack Brown.

5. The Cisco Kid: Pedro Armendariz seems appropriate but he never played the Cisco Kid. Warner Baxter was the first one, in "In Old Arizona"; Cesar Romero played the part several times, the first film in *his* series being "The Cisco Kid and the Lady"; Gilbert Roland played the part six times, the best-known one probably being "The Gay Cavalier."

6. Buffalo Bill: Steve Cochran doesn't belong. Joel McCrea played the title role in "Buffalo Bill"; James Ellison played him in "The Plainsman"; Moroni Olsen played him, as an older man, in "Annie Oakley."

7. Davy Crockett: Broderick Crawford never played Davy Crockett. Arthur Hunnicutt did, however, in "The Last Command"; Robert Barrat, in "Man of Conquest"; and, of course, John Wayne was Crockett in "The Alamo."

8. Crazy Horse: John Gavin is the odd Indian here. Victor Mature played Crazy Horse in "Chief Crazy Horse" (remember that, by the way); Anthony Quinn, in "They Died with Their Boots On"; and Iron Eyes Cody, in "The Great Sioux Massacre."

9. Genl. Custer: John Dehner should've, but never played Custer. The other casting was Robert Shaw in "Custer of the West"; Ronald Reagan in "Santa Fe Trail"; and Sheb Wooley in "Bugles in the Afternoon."

10. Wyatt Earp: Rex Reason is here for No Reason. Henry Fonda played Earp in "My Darling Clementine"; James Garner, in "Hour of the Gun"; and Will Geer (Grandpa Walton), in "Winchester 73."

NAME THE PLACE, BABY—BUFFS AND DUFFERS

1. ___ c. "Belle of the YUKON"
2. ___ d. "The Snows of KILIMANJARO"
3. ___ i. "WAIKIKI Wedding"
4. ___ g. "Springtime in the ROCKIES"
5. ___ h. "The White Cliffs of DOVER"
6. ___ e. "On the RIVIERA"
7. ___ j. "Hell on FRISCO BAY"
8. ___ a. "Wind Across the
        EVERGLADES"
9. ___ f. "NOB Hill"
10. ___ b. "SUN VALLEY Serenade"

WHO IS IT?—BUFFS AND DUFFERS

Judge Hardy	le **W** is stone
Nora Charles	myrn **A** loy
Alfalfa	car **L** switzer
Rochester	eddie an **D** erson
Mr. Dithers	j **O** nathan hale
Vera Vague	barbara jo a **L** len
Frog	smile **Y** burnette
Torchy Blane	glen **D** a farrell
Dr. Christian	jean h **E** rsholt
Pa Kettle	per **C** y kilbride
Number One Son	**K** eye luke
Boy	johnny sh **E** ffield
Maisie	ann sothe **R** n

And the name of the star is Clifton Webb, who played Waldo Lydecker in "Laura"!

TELL US WHO—BUFFS AND DUFFERS

1. ___ d. Basil Rathbone   "David Copperfield"
"Romeo and Juliet"

2. ___ j. Lon Chaney (Jr.)   "High Noon"
"Of Mice and Men"

3. ___ h. Lee Marvin   "The Wild One"
"Ship of Fools"

4. ___ i. Marjorie Main   "Dead End"
"Meet Me in St. Louis"

5. ___ f. Marlene Dietrich   "Destry Rides Again"
"Witness for the Prosecution"

6. ___ a. Melvyn Douglas   "Ninotchka"
"Hotel"

7. ___ g. Montgomery Clift   "Suddenly Last Summer"
"Raintree County"

8. ___ c. Brandon de Wilde   "Shane"
"In Harm's Way"

9. ___ e. Kirk Douglas   "The Vikings"
"Cast a Giant Shadow"

10. ___ b. Carole Lombard   "They Knew What They
Wanted"
"Nothing Sacred"

RE-DOS—BUFFS AND DUFFERS

1. "The Thirty-nine Steps"	Robert Donat Madeleine Carroll	i. Kenneth More Taina Elg
2. "Magnificent Obsession"	Robert Taylor Irene Dunne	h. Rock Hudson Jane Wyman
3. "The Ten Commandments"	Theodore Roberts Estelle Taylor	a. Charlton Heston Olive Deering
4. "Seventh Heaven"	Charles Farrell Janet Gaynor	g. James Stewart Simone Simon
5. "The Plainsman"	Gary Cooper Jean Arthur	f. Don Murray Abby Dalton
6. "A Tale of Two Cities"	Ronald Colman Elizabeth Allen	d. Dirk Bogarde Dorothy Tutin

7. "The Swan"	Adolphe Menjou Frances Howard	b. Alec Guinness Grace Kelly
8. "Cimarron"	Richard Dix Irene Dunne	j. Glenn Ford Maria Schell
9. "My Man Godfrey"	William Powell Carole Lombard	e. David Niven June Allyson
10. "My Sister Eileen"	Brian Aherne Rosalind Russell	c. Jack Lemmon Betty Garrett

TYPE-CASTING—BUFFS AND DUFFERS

1. ___ g. Robert Taylor: "Quo Vadis?"; "Knights of the Round Table" (or "Ivanhoe"); "Above and Beyond"; "Johnny Eager."

2. ___ h. Ginger Rogers: "Stage Door"; "I'll Be Seeing You"; "Kitty Foyle"; "Tender Comrade."

3. ___ l. Edward G. Robinson: "Cheyenne Autumn"; "The Cincinnati Kid"; "The Prize"; "Kid Galahad."

4. ___ o. Charlton Heston: "Khartoum"; "Pony Express"; "The Greatest Show on Earth"; "El Cid."

5. ___ n. Gregory Peck: "Twelve O'Clock High"; "Captain Newman, M.D."; "The Big Country"; "Moby Dick."

6. ___ b. Steve McQueen: "The Sand Pebbles"; "The Great Escape"; "The Cincinnati Kid"; "Bullitt."

7. ___ m. Marlon Brando: "The Ugly American"; "The Young Lions"; "Viva Zapata!"; "On the Waterfront."

8. ___ f. Rod Steiger: "The Sergeant"; "On the Waterfront"; "The Pawnbroker"; "Oklahoma!"

9. ___ c. Anthony Quinn: "Lust for Life"; "The Savage Innocents"; "The Shoes of the Fisherman"; "The Plainsman."

10. ___ j. James Stewart: "Mr. Smith Goes to Washington"; "The FBI Story"; "Carbine Williams"; "Call Northside 777."

11. ___ a. Rex Harrison: "Unfaithfully Yours"; "The Foxes of Harrow"; "Anna and the King of Siam"; "The Agony and the Ecstasy."

265

12. ___ i.   Marilyn Monroe: "The Asphalt Jungle"; "Don't Bother to Knock"; "Monkey Business"; "Some Like It Hot."

13. ___ e.   Clark Gable: "Command Decision"; "Too Hot to Handle"; "Mogambo"; "Key to the City."

14. ___ d.   Robert Mitchum: "Heaven Knows, Mr. Allison"; "The Grass Is Always Greener"; "Night of the Hunter"; "The Sundowners."

15. ___ k.   Olivia de Havilland: "The Adventures of Robin Hood" (or "The Private Lives of Elizabeth and Essex"); "They Died with Their Boots On"; "Dodge City"; "The Heiress."

QUOTABLES—BUFFS AND DUFFERS

1. "To think all this began in Brussels . . ."

    e. "Juarez"

2. "I make more money than Calvin Coolidge . . ."

    m. "Singin' in the Rain"

3. "I got vision . . ."

    h. "Butch Cassidy and the Sundance Kid"

4. "I am packing my belongings . . ."

    i. "How Green Was My Valley"

5. "I could'a been somebody, Charlie . . ."

    k. "On the Waterfront"

6. "Kill! Kill for the love of Kali!"

    d. "Gunga Din"

7. "What she needs is a guy . . ."

    l. "It Happened One Night"

8. ". . . et ceterah, et ceterah, et ceterah!"

    n. "The King and I"

9. "You can dish it out . . ."

    f. "Little Caesar"

10. "Where do the noses go?"

    g. "For Whom the Bell Tolls"

11. "Dames are no good . . ."

    o. "Kiss of Death"

12. "What'sa matter, Howard? . . ."

    c. "The Roaring Twenties"

13. "All aboard, folks! . . ."

    a. "Stagecoach"

14. "Gort Borada Nikto!"

    b. "The Day the Earth Stood Still"

15. "It is a war of the people . . ."

    j. "Mrs. Miniver"

CAREERS IN COMMON—BUFFS AND DUFFERS

1. Wayne Morris   "Kid Galahad"   Prize fighter.
2. Douglas Fowley   "Singin' in the Rain"   Motion picture director.
3. Eddie Albert   "Oklahoma!"   Traveling salesman.
4. Jack Kruschen   "The Apartment"   Doctor.
5. Fred Astaire   "Funny Face"   Photographer.
6. Ralph Richardson   "The Fallen Idol"   Butler.
7. Gary Merrill   "All About Eve"   Broadway theatrical director.
8. Humphrey Bogart   "Knock on Any Door"   Defense attorney.
9. Ray Milland   "Dial M for Murder"   Professional tennis player.
10. Kirk Douglas   "The Bad and the Beautiful"   Motion picture producer.

MORE RE-DOS—BUFFS AND DUFFERS

1. "Mutiny on the Bounty"   Clark Gable / Movita   d. Marlon Brando / Tarita
2. "The Blue Angel"   Emil Jannings / Marlene Dietrich   a. Curt Jurgens / May Britt
3. "Imitation of Life"   Warren William / Claudette Colbert   e. John Gavin / Lana Turner
4. "The Farmer Takes a Wife"   Henry Fonda / Janet Gaynor   f. Dale Robertson / Betty Grable
5. "The Four Horsemen of the Apocalypse"   Rudolph Valentino / Alice Terry   j. Glenn Ford / Ingrid Thulin
6. "Bird of Paradise"   Joel McCrea / Dolores Del Rio   c. Louis Jourdan / Debra Paget
7. "The Cabinet of Dr. Caligari"   Werner Krauss / Lil Dagover   h. Dan O'Herlihy / Glynis Johns
8. "Night Must Fall"   Robert Montgomery / Dame May Whitty   b. Albert Finney / Mona Washbourne
9. "The Barretts of Wimpole Street"   Fredric March / Norma Shearer   i. Bill Travers / Jennifer Jones

267

10. "A Farewell   Gary Cooper   g. Rock Hudson
     to Arms"   Helen Hayes   Jennifer Jones

THE TEENY-TINY MARQUEE—BUFFS ONLY

1. "The Longest (Laraine) *Day*"
2. "Along Came (Jennifer) *Jones*"
3. "Valiant Is the Word for *Carrie* (Snodgress)"
4. "Captain *Eddie* (Bracken)"
5. "My Man *Godfrey* (Cambridge)"
6. "(Pearl) *White* Cargo"
7. "(Marc) *Lawrence* of Arabia"
8. "Castle on the (Rock) *Hudson*"
9. "The (Michael) *Caine* Mutiny"
10. "Night of the (Tab) *Hunter*"
11. "The (Bert) *Wheeler* Dealers"
12. "(Tommy) *Sands* of Iwo Jima"

THE TEENY-TINY MARQUEE—DUFFERS' TEE

1. ___ g. "The Longest (Laraine) *Day*"
2. ___ j. "Along Came (Jennifer) *Jones*"
3. ___ k. "Valiant Is the Word for *Carrie* (Snodgress)"
4. ___ h. "Captain *Eddie* (Bracken)"
5. ___ c. "My Man *Godfrey* (Cambridge)"
6. ___ a. "(Pearl) *White* Cargo"
7. ___ e. "(Marc) *Lawrence* of Arabia"
8. ___ b. "Castle on the (Rock) *Hudson*"
9. ___ l. "The (Michael) *Caine* Mutiny"
10. ___ i. "Night of the (Tab) *Hunter*"
11. ___ f. "The (Bert) *Wheeler* Dealers"
12. ___ d. "(Tommy) *Sands* of Iwo Jima"

STRUCTURES—BUFFS ONLY

1. "The Big HOUSE"
2. "The HOUSE of Rothschild"
3. "CABIN in the Cotton"
4. "The Little HUT"
5. "CASTLE Keep"
6. "TOWER of London"
7. "Jamaica INN"
8. "Hollywood HOTEL"
9. "The Red BARN" *or* "The Red TENT"
10. "JAILHOUSE Rock"
11. "Green MANSIONS"
12. "The Old Dark HOUSE"

STRUCTURES—DUFFERS' TEE

1. ___ d. "Willy Wonka and the Chocolate FACTORY"
2. ___ c. "The Big HOUSE"
3. ___ g. "CABIN in the Cotton"
4. ___ b. "The Little HUT"
5. ___ i. "CASTLE Keep"
6. ___ l. "TOWER of London"
7. ___ e. "Jamaica INN"
8. ___ k. "Hollywood HOTEL"
9. ___ j. "The Red TENT"
10. ___ h. "JAILHOUSE Rock"
11. ___ a. "Green MANSIONS"
12. ___ f. "The Old Dark HOUSE"

MENTION MY NAME—BUFFS ONLY

1. Robert and Karen   MORLEY
2. Juanita and Porter   HALL

269

3.	Nigel and Virginia	BRUCE
4.	Charlie and Barrie	CHASE
5.	Glenn and Laurie	ANDERS
6.	James and Emma	DUNN
7.	Marilyn and Edwin	MAXWELL
8.	Rand and Phyllis	BROOKS
9.	Jon and Thurston	HALL
10.	K. T. and Mark	STEVENS
11.	Marie and Francis	MCDONALD
12.	Vic and Karen	MORROW
13.	Cliff and Dale	ROBERTSON
14.	Robert and Charles	MIDDLETON
15.	Alice and Scott	BRADY

MENTION MY NAME—DUFFERS' TEE

1.	Paul and Phyllis	NEWMAN
2.	Loretta and Gig	YOUNG
3.	James and Charles	COBURN
4.	James and Peggy Ann	GARNER
5.	Gene and Lawrence	TIERNEY
6.	James and Elaine	STEWART
7.	Jane and Dick	POWELL
8.	Dana and Julie	ANDREWS
9.	Joby and Carroll	BAKER
10.	Madeleine and Diahann	CARROLL
11.	Debbie and William	REYNOLDS
12.	Milo and Michael	O'SHEA
13.	Bette and Rufe	DAVIS
14.	Robert and Amanda	BLAKE
15.	Rock and Rochelle	HUDSON

WILD CARD—BUFFS AND DUFFERS:
THE LAST REEL

KAY MICHAELS was loaned out to the cheapie producer on Poverty Row.

MICHAEL BARTON was assigned to the private eye film.

BART COLLINS was assigned to the horror film.

COLIN MCKAY was assigned to the Western.

KAY's last name isn't BARTON or COLLINS (Clue b) and MCKAY is an actor (Clue e), therefore a male.

> CONCLUSION 1: *Thus, KAY's name is KAY MICHAELS.*

COLIN did not get assigned to the loan-out cheapie or the private eye film (Clue a), nor was he assigned to the horror film (Clue c), and MICHAELS got the loan-out assignment (Clue d);

> CONCLUSION 2: *KAY MICHAELS got the loan-out assignment.*

and

> CONCLUSION 3: *COLIN was assigned to the Western.*

If KAY MICHAELS was loaned out (Conclusion 2) and the actor MCKAY did not get the private eye film or the horror film (Clue e), then

> CONCLUSION 4: *The actor MCKAY was assigned to the Western.*

Combining Conclusions 3 and 4:

> CONCLUSION 5: *COLIN MCKAY was assigned to the Western.*

Since BART's last name isn't MCKAY (Conclusion 5) or MICHAELS (Conclusion 1), and since it is not BARTON (Clue d)

> CONCLUSION 6: *BART's last name is COLLINS.*

With the identification of KAY MICHAELS (Conclusion 1), COLIN MCKAY (Conclusion 5), and BART COLLINS (Conclusion 6)

> CONCLUSION 7: *MICHAEL's last name is BARTON.*

Now, if KAY MICHAELS was loaned out (Conclusion 2), COLIN MCKAY got the Western (Conclusion 5), and since MICHAEL BARTON did not get assigned to the horror film (Clue c), it must follow that . . .

CONCLUSION 8: *MICHAEL BARTON got the private eye assignment.*

This leaves only the assignment to the horror film, which would have to go to

> CONCLUSION 9: BART COLLINS!

C'mon, Nora—I need a martini, and Asta is scratching at the door.

NAME THE STAR—BUFFS ONLY

1. Greta Garbo — "Flesh and the Devil" — "Romance"
2. Van Johnson — "State of the Union" — "A Guy Named Joe"
3. Clark Gable — "The Hucksters" — "Boom Town"
4. Gary Cooper — "Love in the Afternoon" — "Peter Ibbetson"
5. Kirk Douglas — "Ace in the Hole"[1] — "20,000 Leagues Under the Sea"
6. Burt Lancaster — "Judgment at Nuremberg" — "Come Back, Little Sheba"
7. Sir Cedric Hardwicke — "Nicholas Nickleby" — "Helen of Troy"
8. Cary Grant — "North by Northwest" — "Arsenic and Old Lace"
9. Humphrey Bogart — "Knock on Any Door" — "It All Came True"
10. Marlene Dietrich — "The Blue Angel" — "A Foreign Affair"

NAME THE STAR—DUFFERS' TEE

1. Greta Garbo — "Conquest" — "Anna Karenina"
2. Van Johnson — "Thirty Seconds over Tokyo" — "The Caine Mutiny"
3. Clark Gable — "San Francisco" — "Gone with the Wind"
4. Gary Cooper — "High Noon" — "Mr. Deeds Goes to Town"
5. Kirk Douglas — "Ulysses" — "Lust for Life"
6. Burt Lancaster — "The Birdman of Alcatraz" — "Elmer Gantry"
7. Sir Cedric Hardwicke — "On Borrowed Time" — "Stanley and Livingstone"
8. Cary Grant — "His Girl Friday" — "None But the Lonely Heart"
9. Humphrey Bogart — "The Caine Mutiny" — "The Treasure of the Sierra Madre"
10. Marlene Dietrich — "Witness for the Prosecution" — "Judgment at Nuremberg"

1. Alternate title: "The Big Carnival."

THE DIRECTORS—BUFFS AND DUFFERS

HORIZONTAL

Line 1. (From the top) Jules DASSIN, 9; John FRANKENHEIMER, 20.

2. Raoul WALSH, 72; Billy WILDER, 75; Andrew STONE, 68.

3. David LEAN, 37; Edward LUDWIG, 45; Pietro GERMI, 22.

4. King VIDOR, 71; Carl FOREMAN, 19.

5. Sidney LUMET, 46.

9. Arthur PENN, 58; Gene SAKS, 64.

10. Stanley KRAMER, 32; Fred ZINNEMANN, 80.

11. Daniel MANN, 50.

12. Bud YORKIN, 78.

13. Mervyn LEROY, 39.

14. Andrew MCLAGLEN, 54.

15. Sam WOOD, 76.

18. Martin RITT, 62; Rowland V. LEE, 38.

19. Frank CAPRA, 5; William HOWARD, 26.

20. Sam PECKINPAH, 57; Richard Quine, 60; Elia KAZAN, 29.

VERTICAL

1. (From the left) Ralph NELSON, 56; Gene KELLY, 30; Henry HATHAWAY, 24.

2. John CROMWELL, 8; Dennis HOPPER, 25.

3. René CLAIR, 6; Stanley DONEN, 16.

4. Jerry LEWIS, 40; Robert WISE, 77; John FORD, 18.

5. Roger VADIM, 70; Jack SHER, 66.

6. William WELLMAN, 74; Delbert MANN, 51; Frank LLOYD, 41.

7. Richard BROOKS, 3; Vittorio DE SICA, 14.

8. Cecil B. DEMILLE, 13; Arthur LUBIN, 43; Norman TAUROG, 69.

9. Frank BORZAGE, 1; Anthony MANN, 49.

10. Robert DAY, 11; Blake EDWARDS, 17.

11. Andrew MARTON, 53; Anthony QUINN, 61.

12. D. W. GRIFFITH, 23; Walter LANG, 36; Sidney FURIE, 21.

13. Joshua LOGAN, 42; Paul LANDRES, 34; Douglas SIRK, 67.

14. Fritz LANG, 35; Edwin MARIN, 52; Clarence BROWN, 4.

15. Norman JEWISON, 28.

16. Basil DEAN, 12; Vincente MINNELLI, 55.

17. Muriel BOX, 2; Ernst LUBITSCH, 44.

18. Otto PREMINGER, 59; William DIETERLE, 15.

19. Mark ROBSON, 63; John HUSTON, 27; Delmer DAVES, 10.

20. Ernest SCHOEDSACK, 65; Henry KING, 31; Stanley KU-
    BRICK, 33.

DIAGONALS

a. Running to the left and downward from the "W" of *W*ILDER: Orson WELLES, 73.

b. Running to the right and upward from the "C" of M*C*LAGLEN:
   Henri-Georges CLOUZOT, 7.

c. Running to the left and upward from the "L" of MC*L*AGLEN: Francis LYON, 48.

d. Running to the right and upward from the "L" of *L*ANG: Ida LU-
   PINO, 47.

e. Running to the right and downward from the "Z" of *Z*INNEMANN:
   Franco ZEFFIRELLI, 79.

HUBBIES—BUFFS ONLY

1. Humphrey Bogart:	"The Harder They Fall"; "Beat the Devil"; "Action in the North Atlantic."
2. Robert Preston:	"The Macomber Affair"; "Face to Face"; "The Dark at the Top of the Stairs."
3. Charles Laughton:	"The Devil and the Deep"; "The Blue Veil"; "They Knew What They Wanted."
4. Robert Mitchum:	"Not As a Stranger"; "Desire Me"; "The Sundowners."
5. William Holden:	"Apartment for Peggy"; "Executive Suite"; "The Bridges at Toko-Ri."
6. Cary Grant:	"I Was a Male War Bride"; "Mr. Blandings Builds His Dream House"; "Crisis."
7. Spencer Tracy:	"Cass Timberlane"; "Edison the Man"; "Father of the Bride" (or "Father's Little Dividend").
8. Dick Powell:	"Mrs. Mike"; "Pitfall"; "The Bad and the Beautiful."
9. Gregory Peck:	"Cape Fear"; "The Paradine Case"; "The Yearling."
10. Rex Harrison:	"The Yellow Rolls-Royce"; "The Foxes of Harrow"; "The Four-Poster."

HUBBIES—DUFFERS' TEE

1. Humphrey Bogart
2. Robert Preston
3. Charles Laughton
4. Robert Mitchum
5. William Holden
6. Cary Grant
7. Spencer Tracy
8. Dick Powell
9. Gregory Peck
10. Rex Harrison

TRUSTY STEED—BUFFS AND DUFFERS

1. William S. Hart	c. Fritz
2. Tom Mix	j. Tony
3. Buck Jones	a. Silver
4. Ken Maynard	b. Tarzan
5. Hopalong Cassidy	i. Topper
6. Tex Ritter	l. White Flash
7. Rex Allen	d. Koko
8. Gene Autry	f. Champion
9. Allan "Rocky" Lane	e. Blackjack
10. Roy Rogers	k. Trigger
11. Smiley Burnette	h. Ringeye
12. Dale Evans	g. Buttermilk

SPOT THE BIO—BUFFS AND DUFFERS

Susan Hayward	5. Jane Froman	h. "With a Song in My Heart"
Kim Novak	11. Jeanne Eagels	j. "Jeanne Eagels"
Eleanor Parker	10. Marjorie Lawrence	o. "Interrupted Melody"

Ann Blyth	9. Helen Morgan	m. "The Helen Morgan Story"
Dorothy Malone	14. Diana Barrymore	k. "Too Much, Too Soon"
Luise Rainer	8. Anna Held	a. "The Great Ziegfeld"
Doris Day	1. Ruth Etting	d. "Love Me or Leave Me"
Barbra Streisand	13. Fanny Brice	e. "Funny Girl"
Carroll Baker	2. Jean Harlow	n. "Harlow"
Ginger Rogers	3. Irene Castle	b. "The Story of Vernon and Irene Castle"
Vanessa Redgrave	7. Isadora Duncan	l. "Isadora" (or "The Loves of Isadora")
Susan Hayward	15. Lillian Roth	g. "I'll Cry Tomorrow"
Maria Tallchief	6. Anna Pavlova	i. "Million Dollar Mermaid"
Julie Andrews	12. Gertrude Lawrence	c. "Star!" (or "Those Were the Days")
Alice Faye	4. Lillian Russell	f. "Lillian Russell"

OSCAR SHUFFLE—WILD CARD

1. D O N G U R T H O R
   (R) U T H (G) O R (D) (O) (N)

2. S E P L A L E R S T O N E S
   E (S) T E (L) L (E) P (A) R S O N S

3. A K A L I D R O V E L
   L I L (A) K (E) (D) (R) O V A

4. H A M E G A R L I A R G O
   G L O R I (A) (G) R A H A M E

And the hidden name:
G A L E S O N D E R G A A R D

276

EVEN MORE RE-DOS—BUFFS AND DUFFERS

1. "One Million B.C." — Victor Mature, Carole Landis — b. John Richardson, Raquel Welch

2. "The Man Who Knew Too Much" — Leslie Banks, Edna Best — a. James Stewart, Doris Day

3. "The Taming of the Shrew" — Douglas Fairbanks, Mary Pickford — g. Richard Burton, Elizabeth Taylor

4. "The Prisoner of Zenda" — Raymond Massey, Madeleine Carroll — h. James Mason, Deborah Kerr

5. "A Star Is Born" — Fredric March, Janet Gaynor — i. James Mason, Judy Garland

6. "Rose Marie" — Nelson Eddy, Jeanette MacDonald — d. Howard Keel, Ann Blyth

7. "King Solomon's Mines" — Cedric Hardwicke, Anna Lee — f. Stewart Granger, Deborah Kerr

8. "Anna Karenina" — Fredric March, Greta Garbo — e. Kieron Moore, Vivien Leigh

9. "Mayerling" — Charles Boyer, Danielle Darrieux — j. Omar Sharif, Catherine Deneuve

10. "Goodbye, Mr. Chips" — Robert Donat, Greer Garson — c. Peter O'Toole, Petula Clark

FEMALES' FIRST FILMS—BUFFS AND DUFFERS

1. Dorothy McGuire — e. "Claudia"
2. Jane Russell — g. "The Outlaw"
3. Jennifer Jones — i. "New Frontier"
4. Linda Darnell — k. "Daytime Wife"
5. Lauren Bacall — o. "To Have and Have Not"
6. Jane Fonda — t. "Tall Story"
7. Marie Dressler — b. "Tillie's Punctured Romance"
8. Leslie Caron — s. "An American in Paris"
9. Grace Kelly — a. "Fourteen Hours"
10. Greer Garson — r. "Goodbye, Mr. Chips"
11. Maureen O'Hara — f. "Jamaica Inn"

12. Julie Andrews	j. "Mary Poppins"
13. Ruby Keeler	q. "42nd Street"
14. Jean Seberg	p. "Saint Joan"
15. Kim Novak	d. "Pushover"
16. Carmen Miranda	h. "Down Argentine Way"
17. Eva Marie Saint	m. "On the Waterfront"
18. Katharine Hepburn	n. "A Bill of Divorcement"
19. Bette Davis	c. "Bad Sister"
20. Olivia de Havilland	l. "A Midsummer Night's Dream"

THREE OF A KIND—BUFFS AND DUFFERS

1. Name the three actors who portrayed "My Three Angels":
   a. Aldo Ray; c. Humphrey Bogart; d. Peter Ustinov. (Eliminate b. and e.)

2. Name the three actors who were victims of the lynch mob in "The Ox-Bow Incident":
   b. Francis Ford; d. Dana Andrews; e. Anthony Quinn. (Eliminate a. and c.)

3. Name the three actors who broke into the vault in "The Asphalt Jungle":
   a. Sam Jaffe; d. Sterling Hayden; e. Anthony Caruso. (Eliminate b. and c.)

4. Name at least three of the Dead End Kids, as they appeared in "Dead End":
   a. Bobby Jordan; c. Bernard Punsley; e. Huntz Hall. (Eliminate b. and d.) Also—for the Buffs—Leo Gorcey, Billy Halop, and Gabriel Dell.

5. Name the three films in which James Dean was featured:
   a. "East of Eden"; b. "Giant"; e. "Rebel Without a Cause." (Eliminate c. and d.)

6. Name at least three of the seven actors who were the original (American version) "Magnificent Seven":
   b. Brad Dexter; c. Robert Vaughn; d. Horst Buchholz. (Eliminate a. and e.) Also—for the Buffs—Steve McQueen, Yul Brynner, Charles Bronson, James Coburn.

7. Name three plays by Shakespeare which have been filmed:
   a. "Richard III"; c. "Henry V"; e. "Othello." (Eliminate b. and

d.) Also, the Buffs might've included: "A Midsummer Night's Dream"; "Romeo and Juliet"; "King Lear"; "Macbeth"; "The Taming of the Shrew"; "Hamlet"; "Julius Caesar"; "As You Like It"; "Measure for Measure"; "The Merry Wives of Windsor"; and "Twelfth Night." And from Buffs we'll even accept: "Forbidden Planet"; "Joe Macbeth"; and "West Side Story."

8. Give the first names of the three Ritz Brothers:
   a. Harry; d. Al; e. Jimmy. (Eliminate b. and c.)

9. Name at least three biographical roles played by Marlon Brando:
   a. Emiliano Zapata; c. Marc Antony; d. Napoleon. (Eliminate b. and e.) Buffs might also include Fletcher Christian.

10. Give us the first names of the three Lane sisters:
    a. Priscilla; c. Lola; d. Rosemary. (Eliminate b. and e.)

MORE LINK-UPS—BUFFS AND DUFFERS

1. Trevor	HOWARD	Duff
2. Doris	DUDLEY	Digges
3. Robert	VAUGHN	Taylor
4. Donna	REED	Hadley
5. Gladys	GEORGE	Brent
6. Gene	BARRY	Fitzgerald
7. Tony	BILL	Williams
8. Jean	ARTHUR	Lake
9. Robert	PRESTON	Foster
10. Robert	TAYLOR	Holmes

AND YET MORE LINK-UPS—BUFFS AND DUFFERS

1. Jessie	RALPH	Forbes
2. Edna May	OLIVER	Hardy
3. Warren	WILLIAM	Gargan
4. H. B.	WARNER	Oland
5. Billy	GILBERT	Roland
6. Kim	STANLEY	Ridges

7. Douglas	DICK	Powell
8. Mary	BRIAN	Aherne
9. Charlotte	HENRY	Wilcoxon
10. Alice	FAYE	Emerson

ODD MAN OUT #2—BUFFS AND DUFFERS

1. Marc Lawrence was the only one of the group *not* born in Iowa.
2. Lex Barker was the only one of the group who did *not* play D'Artagnan in a film version of "The Three Musketeers."
3. Spencer Tracy was the only one of the group who did *not* appear in silent films.
4. Douglas Shearer was a sound engineer, and does *not* belong in the group with the others, who gained their renown in the animated cartoon field.
5. Kirk Douglas is the only one of the group who did *not* have a brother also appearing in films at the same time, as did Dana Andrews (Steve Forrest), Barry Fitzgerald (Arthur Shields), George Sanders (Tom Conway), and Frank McHugh (Matt McHugh).
6. Cinerama does *not* belong in the same grouping with the other widescreen techniques, since it was the only system to require more than one projector.
7. "Crossfire" doesn't belong, even though all of the films may be categorized as having been "socially significant." This film was released by RKO; all of the others were 20th Century-Fox productions.
8. Humphrey Bogart was the only one of the group who *never* played a biographical role.
9. Walter Brennan doesn't belong since he's the only one of the group who was *not* a member of the Group Theatre in New York.
10. Joan Crawford doesn't belong, since the other ladies each won *two* Oscars, while Miss Crawford won only one.

MOVIE-MAKERS' CRISSCROSS—BUFFS

Three-Letter Names	Four-Letter Names	Five-Letter Names		Six-Letter Names	
Fox	Gish	Capra	Pathé	Disney	Porter
Mix	Hart	Hakim	Spoor	Fowler	Sidney
		Lasky	Vidor	Hughes	Zanuck
		Mayer	Zukor		

280

Seven-Letter Names
Chaplin
DeMille
Goldwyn
Laemmle
Schenck
Sennett
Skouras

Eight-Letter Names
Anderson
Griffith
Selznick
Thalberg

Nine-Letter Names
Schulberg

(See diagram following.)

MOVIE-MAKERS' CRISSCROSS—BUFFS AND DUFFERS

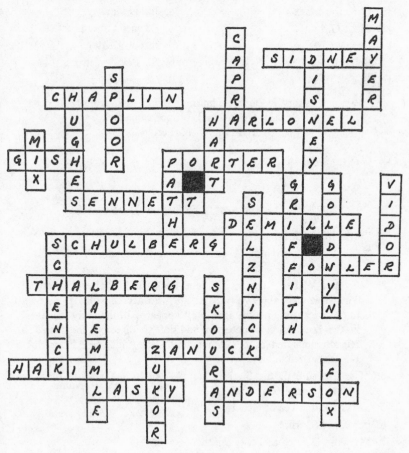

IMPROPER NAMES—BUFFS AND DUFFERS

1.	Bing Crosby	f.	Harry Crosby
2.	Gabby Hayes	i. (or o.)	George Hayes
3.	Slim Summerville	o. (or i.)	George Summerville
4.	Bud Abbott	k.	William Abbott
5.	Wild Bill Elliott	m.	Gordon Elliott
6.	Fuzzy Knight	d.	J. Forrest Knight
7.	Buddy Ebsen	n.	Christian Rudolf Ebsen
8.	Red Skelton	c.	Richard Skelton
9.	Fatty Arbuckle	e.	Roscoe Arbuckle
10.	Harpo Marx	p.	Adolph Marx
11.	Chico Marx	g.	Leonard Marx
12.	Groucho Marx	a.	Julius Marx
13.	Hoot Gibson	l.	Edward Gibson
14.	Buster Keaton	j.	Joseph Keaton
15.	Spike Jones	h.	Lindley Armstrong Jones
16.	Buck Jones	b.	Charles Jones

And for the Duffers who might triple their score,
Spanky McFarland's proper name is:
George Emmett McFarland!

WILD CARD—BUFFS AND DUFFERS

1. "Meet Me in St. Louis."
2. ". . . 5135 Kensington Avenue"—from the song. ("And I live at 5133 . . .")
3. John and Walter Huston; Tim and Jack Holt. Walter Huston and Tim Holt were the two prospectors who accompanied Bogart into the Mexican mountains. Jack Holt appeared in the early scenes laid in the Mexican flophouse. In addition to directing the film John Huston appeared as the American in the white suit from whom Bogart begged money.
4. "The Treasure of the Sierra Madre"—not "The Treasure of Sierra Madre." Sorry 'bout that!
5. a. "The Bitter Tea of General Yen."
6. b. "Becky Sharp."
7. Margaret O'Brien as Tooty Smith.

282

8. A dead monkey.
9. a. Bashful; c. Dopey; e. Doc; g. Happy; h. Sneezy; i. Grumpy;
   j. Sleepy.
10. Punchy, Stuffy, Wacky, Rusty and Pinky were all played by Harpo
    Marx.

HEY, DADDY!—BUFFS AND DUFFERS

1. "The Barretts of Wimpole Street"	Norma Shearer	b. Charles Laughton
2. "Death of a Salesman"	Kevin McCarthy	c. Fredric March
3. "Never Too Late"	Connie Stevens	a. Paul Ford
4. "Captains Courageous"	Freddie Bartholomew	a. Melvyn Douglas
5. "The Actress"	Jean Simmons	c. Spencer Tracy
6. "Prince of Players"	Richard Burton	c. Raymond Massey
7. "Captains Courageous"	Mickey Rooney	a. Lionel Barrymore
8. "Gone with the Wind"	Vivien Leigh	b. Thomas Mitchell
9. "Shane"	Brandon de Wilde	c. Van Heflin
10. "Hud"	Paul Newman	a. Melvyn Douglas

TELL US WHO ※2—BUFFS AND DUFFERS

1. ___ e. Gary Cooper	"Meet John Doe" "The Adventures of Marco Polo"
2. ___ j. Ernest Borgnine	"Marty" "Bad Day at Black Rock"
3. ___ g. Steve McQueen	"The Great Escape" "Bullitt"

4. ___ a. Errol Flynn	"The Adventures of Robin Hood"
	"The Private Lives of Elizabeth and Essex"
5. ___ i. William Holden	"Golden Boy"
	"The Bridges at Toko-Ri"
6. ___ h. Grace Kelly	"Fourteen Hours"
	"Rear Window"
7. ___ c. Burt Lancaster	"Mr. 880"
	"The Train"
8. ___ d. Carroll Baker	"Harlow"
	"How the West Was Won"
9. ___ b. Laurence Harvey	"The Alamo"
	"The Manchurian Candidate"
10. ___ f. Gene Kelly	"For Me and My Gal"
	"Anchors Aweigh"

ON THE SIDE OF THE LAW—BUFFS AND DUFFERS

1. Sam Spade	"The Maltese Falcon"	h. Humphrey Bogart
2. Mr. Wong	"Doomed to Die"	d. Boris Karloff
3. Mike Hammer	"Kiss Me Deadly"	r. Ralph Meeker
4. Boston Blackie	"Meet Boston Blackie"	k. Chester Morris
5. Philo Vance	"The Kennel Murder Case"	c. William Powell
6. Perry Mason	"The Case of the Howling Dog"	a. Warren William
7. Nick Carter	"Nick Carter, Master Detective"	q. Walter Pidgeon
8. Michael Shayne	"Michael Shayne, Private Detective"	o. Lloyd Nolan
9. Nero Wolfe	"Meet Nero Wolfe"	g. Edward Arnold
10. Father Brown	"Father Brown, Detective"	b. Walter Connolly
11. Inspector Maigret	"Man on the Eiffel Tower"	l. Charles Laughton
12. Hercule Poirot	"The Alphabet Murders"	s. Tony Randall
13. Nancy Drew	"Nancy Drew, Detective"	j. Bonita Granville

284

14. Miss Marple	"Murder, She Said"	f. Margaret Rutherford
15. Matt Helm	"The Silencers"	t. Dean Martin
16. The Lone Wolf	"The Lone Wolf Spy Hunt"	m. Warren William
17. Inspector Clouseau	"A Shot in the Dark"	i. Peter Sellers
18. Derek Flint	"Our Man Flint"	p. James Coburn
19. Nick Charles	"The Thin Man"	n. William Powell
20. Mr. Moto	"Thank You, Mr. Moto"	e. Peter Lorre

MORE "NAME THE STAR"—BUFFS ONLY

1. José Ferrer: "Joan of Arc"   "The Caine Mutiny"
2. Joan Crawford: "What Ever Happened to Baby Jane?"   "The Women"
3. Frank Sinatra: "Meet Danny Wilson"   "The Manchurian Candidate"
4. Sydney Greenstreet: "They Died with Their Boots On"   "Malaya"
5. Judy Garland: "Babes in Arms"   "Judgment at Nuremberg"
6. William Holden: "Sabrina"   "Golden Boy"
7. Henry Fonda: "The Trail of the Lonesome Pine"   "Jezebel"
8. Fredric March: "Desperate Hours"   "Seven Days in May"
9. Edward G. Robinson: "The Sea Wolf"   "Double Indemnity"
10. Jack Lemmon: "The Apartment"   "The Fortune Cookie"

MORE "NAME THE STAR"—DUFFERS' TEE

1. José Ferrer: "Moulin Rouge"   "Cyrano de Bergerac"
2. Joan Crawford: "Grand Hotel"   "Mildred Pierce"
3. Frank Sinatra: "Johnny Concho"   "From Here to Eternity"

4. Sydney Greenstreet:	"Casablanca"	"The Maltese Falcon"
5. Judy Garland:	"Presenting Lily Mars"	"A Star Is Born"
6. William Holden:	"Sunset Boulevard"	"Stalag 17"
7. Henry Fonda:	"Chad Hanna"	"The Grapes of Wrath"
8. Fredric March:	"Anna Karenina"	"The Barretts of Wimpole Street"
9. Edward G. Robinson:	"Key Largo"	"Dr. Ehrlich's Magic Bullet"
10. Jack Lemmon:	"The Odd Couple"	"Mr. Roberts"

FILMS IN COMMON—BUFFS ONLY

1. "Cast a Giant Shadow"	The three films focused on the formation of Israel as a state.
2. "Edison, the Man"	The two films listed focused on the inventions of the steamboat and the telephone, while this film dealt with the several inventions of Thomas Edison.
3. "Land of the Pharaohs"	This film focused on the construction of the Pyramids, while the other films dealt with the construction of the Suez Canal and the transcontinental railroad.
4. "Mildred Pierce"	In each of the three films, women committed murder.
5. "The Black Rose"	All three films dealt with exploration of the Orient.
6. "Dr. Ehrlich's Magic Bullet"	All three films were concerned with scientific discovery.
7. "Suddenly"	The three films were concerned with plots to assassinate heads of state.
8. "Here Comes Mr. Jordan"	The three films were concerned with heavenly emissaries returning to Earth to manipulate the lives of men.
9. "King Rat"	The three films were concerned with life in prisoner-of-war camps.
10. "San Francisco"	In each of the three films, natural disasters were pivotal to the plot.

286

FILMS IN COMMON—DUFFERS' TEE

1. _____ b. "Cast a Giant Shadow" — The three films dealt with the formation of Israel as a state.

2. _____ b. "The Magic Box" — The two films listed focused on the invention of the steamboat and the telephone, while this film dealt with the invention of the motion picture camera and color film.

3. _____ a. "Land of the Pharaohs" — The two films listed dealt with the construction of the Suez Canal and the trans-America railroad, while this film focused on the construction of the Pyramids.

4. _____ b. "Black Widow" — In the three films, women committed murder.

5. _____ c. "The Black Rose" — The three films were concerned with the exploration of the Orient.

6. _____ c. "Dr. Ehrlich's Magic Bullet" — The three films were concerned with scientific discovery.

7. _____ b. "Suddenly" — The three films were concerned with plots to assassinate heads of state.

8. _____ a. "Here Comes Mr. Jordan" — The three films were concerned with heavenly emissaries returning to Earth to manipulate the lives of men.

9. _____ c. "King Rat" — The three films were concerned with life in prisoner-of-war camps.

10. _____ a. "San Francisco" — In all three films, natural disasters were pivotal to the plot.

LA RONDE—BUFFS AND DUFFERS

A. Robert Taylor and Greta Garbo
B. Greta Garbo and Charles Boyer
C. Charles Boyer and Hedy Lamarr
D. Hedy Lamarr and Clark Gable
E. Clark Gable and Grace Kelly
F. Grace Kelly and Gary Cooper
G. Gary Cooper and Audrey Hepburn

H. Audrey Hepburn and Humphrey Bogart
I. Humphrey Bogart and June Allyson
J. June Allyson and William Holden
K. William Holden and Barbara Stanwyck
L. Barbara Stanwyck and Robert Taylor

7. "Camille"
6. "Conquest"
4. "Algiers"
3. "Boom Town"
8. "Mogambo"
9. "High Noon"
11. "Love in the
    Afternoon"
10. "Sabrina"
2. "Battle Circus"
12. "Executive Suite"
5. "Golden Boy"[1]
1. "This Is My Affair"[2]

MORE RE-DOS YET—BUFFS AND DUFFERS

1. "One Sunday
   Afternoon"

   Gary Cooper
   Fay Wray

   f. Dennis Morgan
      Dorothy Malone

2. "Swiss Family
   Robinson"

   Thomas Mitchell
   Edna Best

   i. John Mills
      Dorothy McGuire

3. "The Adven-
   tures of Tom
   Sawyer"

   Jack Pickford
   Edythe Chapman

   g. Tommy Kelly
      May Robson

4. "The Desert
   Song"

   Dennis Morgan
   Irene Manning

   j. John Boles
      Carlotta Kay

5. "Ben-Hur"

   Ramon Novarro
   May McAvoy

   b. Charlton Heston
      Haya Harareet

6. "Little Women"

   Peter Lawford
   Janet Leigh

   a. Paul Lukas
      Frances Dee

1. The Buffs might hold out for "Executive Suite," but in the rules we
   stated that no title may be used more than once. Sorry!
2. For the Buffs' version, the titles "His Brother's Wife," or "The Night
   Walker" would be acceptable.

288

7. "The Maltese Falcon"	Ricardo Cortez Bebe Daniels	h. Humphrey Bogart Mary Astor
8. "Dr. Jekyll and Mr. Hyde"	Spencer Tracy Ingrid Bergman	c. Fredric March Miriam Hopkins
9. "Raffles"	Ronald Colman Kay Francis	d. David Niven Olivia de Havilland
10. "Smilin' Through"	Brian Aherne Jeanette MacDonald	e. Leslie Howard Norma Shearer

ONCE MORE, WHO IS IT?—BUFFS AND DUFFERS

Scattergood Baines	guy ki	B	bee
Dr. Kildare	lew	A	yres
Dr. Watson	nigel	B	ruce
Dick Tracy	ralph b	Y	rd
Bomba	johnny she	F	field
Flash Gordon	larry cr	A	bbe
James Bond	sean	C	onnery
Inspector Lestrade	dennis ho	E	y
Baby Dumpling	larry si	M	ms'
Hopalong Cassidy	willi	A	m boyd
Mr. Moto	peter lo	R	re
Charlie Chan	sidney	T	oler
Ma Kettle	marjor	I	e main
Larry Talbot	lon cha	N	ey

And the name of the star, from "Dead End," is Humphrey Bogart!

CHARACTERS—BUFFS AND DUFFERS

1. President Merkin Muffley
2. John J. Macreedy
3. Cody Jarrett
4. Gold Hat

5. Gaylord Ravenal
6. Boss Jim Gettys
7. Henry Gondorff
8. Jett Rink
9. Addie Pray
10. Tommy Udo
11. J. J. Gittes
12. Max de Winter
13. Lina Lamont
14. Capt. Munsey
15. Hedley Lamarr

g. "Dr. Strangelove"
j. "Bad Day at Black Rock"
h. "White Heat"
n. "The Treasure of the Sierra Madre"
k. "Show Boat"
b. "Citizen Kane"
a. "The Sting"
l. "Giant"
o. "Paper Moon"
e. "Kiss of Death"
f. "Chinatown"
m. "Rebecca"
i. "Singin' in the Rain"
c. "Brute Force"
d. "Blazing Saddles"

AND MORE LINK-UPS—BUFFS AND DUFFERS

1. Gloria   JEAN   Muir
2. Edward   ARNOLD   Stang
3. Paul   HARVEY   Korman
4. Marion   MARSHALL   Thompson
5. Peggy   RYAN   O'Neal
6. June   VINCENT   Price
7. Glenn   FORD   Sterling
8. Claire   TREVOR   Howard
9. Melvyn   DOUGLAS   Fairbanks
10. Jean   PORTER   Hall

ORDER IN THE COURT—BUFFS AND DUFFERS

1. "A Place in the Sun"
2. "Witness for the Prosecution"
3. "The Caine Mutiny"
4. "The Paradine Case"
5. "Trial"
6. "Anatomy of a Murder"
7. "Knock on Any Door"
8. "The Court-Martial of Billy Mitchell"
9. "Inherit the Wind"
10. "They Won't Forget"
11. "The People Against O'Hara"
12. "Madame X"
13. "Cell 2455 Death Row"
14. "I Want to Live"
15. "Compulsion"

l. Montgomery Clift
j. Tyrone Power
k. Van Johnson
o. Alida Valli
d. Rafael Campos
i. Ben Gazzara
e. John Derek

c. Gary Cooper
n. Dick York
h. Edward Norris
a. James Arness
m. Lana Turner
b. William Campbell
g. Susan Hayward
f. Brad Dillman and Dean Stockwell

MUH-MUH-MUH-MUH-MOMMA—BUFFS AND DUFFERS

1. "Gentleman's Agreement" Gregory Peck c. Anne Revere
2. "Somebody Up There Likes Me" Paul Newman a. Eileen Heckart
3. "I Remember Mama" Barbara Bel Geddes a. Irene Dunne
4. "The Catered Affair" Debbie Reynolds c. Bette Davis
5. "The Best Years of Our Lives" Teresa Wright a. Myrna Loy
6. "Citizen Kane" Orson Welles b. Agnes Moorehead
7. "The Grapes of Wrath" Henry Fonda c. Jane Darwell
8. "Ben-Hur" Cathy O'Donnell and Charlton Heston c. Martha Scott

| 9. "The Glass
Menagerie" | Arthur Kennedy and
Jane Wyman | b. Gertrude Lawrence |
| 10. "King of Kings" | Jeffrey Hunter | a. Siobhan McKenna |

SPOT THE BIO: WRITERS—BUFFS AND DUFFERS

1. Burgess Meredith	"The Story of G.I. Joe"	j. Ernie Pyle
2. Gregory Peck	"Beloved Infidel"	h. F. Scott Fitzgerald
3. Sydney Greenstreet	"Devotion"	g. Wm. Makepeace Thackeray
4. Jack Lemmon	"Cowboy"	c. Frank Harris
5. Morris Carnovsky	"The Life of Emile Zola"	i. Anatole France
6. Merle Oberon	"A Song to Remember"	e. George Sand
7. John Carradine	"The Adventures of Mark Twain"	d. Bret Harte
8. Ida Lupino	"Devotion"	b. Emily Brontë
9. Jeffrey Lynn	"The Fighting 69th"	f. Joyce Kilmer
10. Elsa Lanchester	"The Bride of Frankenstein"	a. Mary Shelley

WHAT'S MY LINE?—BUFFS AND DUFFERS

1. __ m.	"The CAPTAIN's Paradise"
2. __ d.	"The Big FISHERMAN"
3. __ g.	"Death of a SALESMAN"
4. __ p.	"DETECTIVE Story"
5. __ t.	"The PRIZEFIGHTER and the Lady"
6. __ j.	"Diary of a CHAMBERMAID"
7. __ o.	"The AMBASSADOR's Daughter"
8. __ s.	"Test PILOT"
9. __ e.	"The Amazing DOCTOR Clitterhouse"
10. __ q.	"SOLDIER in the Rain"

SCRIPT DOCTOR—BUFFS AND DUFFERS

"It's like this, chief," said the writer. "First off, in Scene 105, we know that Cook and the Security Head are two different guys. And from the directions in Scene 106, we learn that Cook isn't the owner. And Scene 108 tells us that the sneaky Assistant and Jenkins are two different individuals."

"But I still ain't got the key to the scene," replied the baffled producer.

"It's all right here," said the writer, "in Scene 109. Look here where the shifty-eyed Night Watchman says: "Won't you believe me? I said it once and I'll say it again—Tobias was behind it all!"

"I still don't get it."

"Well, up to that point, Tobias hadn't been accused by name. So when, in Scene 109, the shifty-eyed Watchman says, 'I said it before,' he's obviously referring to the accusation he first brought up in Scene 106. So *Cook* has to be the shifty-eyed *Night Watchman*—and the crooked *Security Head* is *Tobias.*"

"Okay, wise guy," said the producer, "so who're Brophy, Jenkins, and Calleia?"

"You gave Pitman two instructions—the owner should not be accused, and he should not be given any lines. Well, Brophy has a line in Scene 111, and Jenkins is accused in 108—"

"So *Calleia* is the *owner!*" answered the producer.

"Right—making the shyster Lawyer either Brophy or Jenkins, and the sneaky Assistant either Jenkins or Brophy. Yet, looking back to Scene 108, the sneaky Assistant accuses Jenkins—"

"So *Brophy* must be the sneaky *Assistant!*"

"And that leaves *Jenkins* as the shyster *Lawyer!*"

"But who's the ringleader?" cried the producer.

"Remember," reminded the writer. "You told Pitman to accuse neither the owner nor the ringleader."

"Right!"

"Look back through the script. Nowhere is there an accusation leveled at either Brophy or the sneaky Assistant—"

"So! Brophy, the sneaky Assistant, is also the ringleader!"

"Right!" laughed the writer.

"There's only one thing that worries me," the producer went on.

"What's that?" asked the writer.

"Whaddya think Pitman's gonna charge me for this?"

ODD MAN OUT ※3—BUFFS ONLY

1. "Brigadoon" is the odd one. It was first a Broadway musical, and *then* a film. The other titles originated as films, and then were translated into Broadway musicals.

2. Van Nest Polglase is out of place. He was an art director, whereas the other gentlemen were all concerned with composing and scoring the musical tracks of films.

3. Jane Brian doesn't belong. The rest of the group all appeared in a summer theater together—along with director Josh Logan—following their college life and prior to entering films.

4. Warren Beatty is the only one who is not the offspring of an actor. Tony Perkins is the son of Osgood Perkins. Peter Fonda is the son of Henry Fonda. Robert Walker, Jr., is the son of Robert Walker, Sr. Jason Robards, Jr., is the son of Jason Robards, Sr.

5. "The Dirty Dozen" does not belong since it was taken from a novel while all of the other films were made from Broadway plays.

6. "Happy Land" is the only one of the group of films which does not have a member of the clergy as its central figure.

7. Ted (Healy) doesn't really belong. He appeared *with* the Three Stooges:
   Larry (Fine), Moe (Howard), and Curly (Howard). Later on, Joe (Besser), Shemp (Howard), and Joe (De Rita) appeared as replacement Stooges.

8. "South Pacific" is the only film of the group which was not originally photographed in the 3-D process.

9. "In Cold Blood" is the odd one. The other films all had, as a major plot point, the commission of the act of rape.

10. "The Green Berets" focused on Vietnamese hostilities. The other films were all concerned with the Korean conflict.

ODD MAN OUT ⅜3—DUFFERS' TEE

1. _ b. "Brigadoon"
2. _ c. Van Nest Polglase
3. _ e. Jane Brian
4. _ d. Warren Beatty
5. _ d. "The Dirty Dozen"
6. _ c. "Happy Land"
7. _ d. Ted (Healy)
8. _ b. "South Pacific"
9. _ b. "In Cold Blood"
10. _ d. "The Green Berets"

FROM SHUBERT ALLEY TO THE SUNSET STRIP—BUFFS AND DUFFERS

1.	"Our Town"	John Craven	b. William Holden
2.	"Night Must Fall"	Emlyn Williams	a. Robert Montgomery
3.	"The Farmer Takes a Wife"	June Walker	c. Janet Gaynor
4.	"The Gay Divorce"	Clare Luce	b. Ginger Rogers
5.	"Cabin in the Sky"	Dooley Wilson	c. Eddie "Rochester" Anderson
6.	"Claudia"	Donald Cook	a. Robert Young
7.	"The Man Who Came to Dinner"	Carol Goodner	a. Bette Davis
8.	"Louisiana Purchase"	William Gaxton	b. Bob Hope
9.	"The Little Foxes"	Tallulah Bankhead	b. Bette Davis
10.	"Harvey"	Frank Fay	a. James Stewart

SOME MORE "WHO KILLED . . . ?"— BUFFS AND DUFFERS

1. Cecil Kellaway . . .
2. Lionel Barrymore . . .
3. Sessue Hayakawa . . .
4. John Barrymore . . .
5. William Holden . . .
6. Kirk Douglas . . .
7. Howard Da Silva . . .
8. Elisha Cook, Jr. . . .
9. Suzanne Cloutier . . .
10. Rod Steiger . . .
11. Burt Lancaster . . .

12. Sam Levene . . .
13. Akim Tamiroff . . .
14. Charles McGraw . . .
15. Anthony Dawson . . .

f. John Garfield
g. John Barrymore
l. Geoffrey Horne
j. Basil Rathbone
o. Gloria Swanson
m. Alex Cord
n. Gary Cooper
b. Jack Palance
c. Orson Welles
e. Gordon Macrae
d. Charles McGraw and
   William Conrad
k. Robert Ryan
h. Orson Welles
i. Kirk Douglas
a. Grace Kelly

WHAT ARE THEY TRYING TO SAY? PART II—BUFFS AND DUFFERS

1. From *The New York Times Guide to Movies on TV*, regarding "Witness for the Prosecution":

    (c) Charles Laughton played the defense attorney.

2. From *The Garden of Allah*, by Sheilah Graham:

    (c) The correct title of the second film is "Yolanda and the Thief."

3. From *Billy Wilder*, by Axel Madsen, concerning "Sunset Boulevard":

    (a) DeMille did not do the phoning. This was done by a member of the staff. Swanson bumped into DeMille merely be accident.

4. From *The Movies*, by Richard Griffith and Arthur Mayer, concerning "G-Men":

    (b) William Harrigan was not a captured Fed, but a rival gang chieftain.

5. From *The Name Above the Title,* by Frank Capra:
   (c) In 1935, Ronald Reagan was not yet in motion pictures, but was still a radio announcer in Iowa.

RE-DOS, THE MALE SIDE—BUFFS AND DUFFERS

1. "A Christmas Carol" — Reginald Owen / Gene Lockhart — i. Alastair Sim / Mervyn Johns

2. "The Killers" — Charles McGraw / William Conrad — g. Lee Marvin / Clu Gulager

3. "King of Kings" — H. B. Warner / Victor Varconi — j. Jeffrey Hunter / Hurd Hatfield

4. "Kid Galahad" — Edward G. Robinson / Wayne Morris — h. Gig Young / Elvis Presley

5. "Les Miserables" — Fredric March / Charles Laughton — a. Michael Rennie / Robert Newton

6. "Oliver Twist" — Irving Pichel / Dickie Moore — d. Alec Guinness / John Howard Davies

7. "Romeo and Juliet" — Leslie Howard / Henry Kolker — e. Laurence Harvey / Mervyn Johns

8. "Julius Caesar" — Louis Calhern / John Gielgud — b. John Gielgud / Richard Johnson

9. "Stagecoach" — Donald Meek / Berton Churchill — f. Red Buttons / Robert Cummings

10. "Dawn Patrol" — Neil Hamilton / Douglas Fairbanks, Jr. — c. Basil Rathbone / David Niven

THE STATE OF THINGS—BUFFS AND DUFFERS

1.   c. _ "In Old CALIFORNIA"
2.   m. _ "OREGON Trail"
3.   r. _ "MISSISSIPPI Gambler"
4.   t. _ "COLORADO Territory"

5.	p. __ "TENNESSEE Johnson"
6.	i. __ "WYOMING Mail"
7.	d. __ "Little Old NEW YORK"
8.	b. __ "The TEXAS Rangers"
9.	g. __ "KANSAS Pacific"
10.	n. __ "Bad Men of MISSOURI"
11.	o. __ "NEVADA Smith"
12.	l. __ "Badlands of MONTANA"
13.	a. __ "The ARKANSAS Traveler"[1]
14.	q. __ "KENTUCKY Rifle"
15.	k. __ "VIRGINIA City"
16.	e. __ "The OKLAHOMA Kid"
17.	h. __ "North to ALASKA"
18.	s. __ "LOUISIANA Purchase"
19.	j. __ "The Baron of ARIZONA"
20.	f. __ "DAKOTA Lil"

MORE CAREERS IN COMMON—
BUFFS AND DUFFERS

1. Humphrey Bogart	"Chicago Deadline"	Newspaper editor.
2. George Sanders	"All About Eve"	Drama critic.
3. Polly Bergen	"Kisses for My President"	U.S. President.
4. Natalie Wood	"Gypsy"	Striptease artist.
5. Peter Lorre	"Mask of Dimitrios"	Novelist.
6. Edmond O'Brien	"A Double Life"[2]	Publicity agent.
7. Joseph Welch	"Anatomy of a Murder"	Judge.
8. Leo Genn	"The Snake Pit"	Psychiatrist.
9. Milton Berle	"Margin for Error"	New York City police patrolman.
10. Kirk Douglas	"Detective Story"	New York City police detective.

1. In the Buffs' version, "The MISSOURI Traveler" would also be acceptable.
2. For the Buffs' version, "The Barefoot Contessa" would also be acceptable.

THE LADIES—BUFFS AND DUFFERS

VERTICAL

Line 1. (From the left) Jean PETERS, 84; Marie WINDSOR, 106; Barbara RUICK, 92.

2. Jean MUIR, 78; Mabel NORMAND, 80.

3. Toby WING, 107; Jo Anne WORLEY, 109.

4. Patty DUKE, 30; Dorothy MALONE, 68; Celeste HOLM, 53.

5. Patricia NEAL, 79; Elizabeth TAYLOR, 100; Alida VALLI, 103.

6. Priscilla LANE, 57; Barbara RUSH, 93; Alice FAYE, 34.

7. Gloria SWANSON, 99.

8. Jane RUSSELL, 94; Gale STORM, 98.

9. Jean HARLOW, 46; Helen HAYES, 49; Anne SHIRLEY, 96.

10. Marilyn MONROE, 76; Hope LANGE, 59; June LANG, 58.

11. Jeanne CRAIN, 22; Jane FONDA, 35; Bette DAVIS, 24; Françoise ROSAY, 90.

12. Ingrid BERGMAN, 8; Samantha EGGAR, 32; Greta GARBO, 38.

13. Myrna LOY, 64; Yvonne DE CARLO, 27; Marilyn MAXWELL, 72.

14. Vivian BLAINE, 10; Jacqueline BISSET, 9.

15. Ann DVORAK, 31; Dorothea KENT, 55; Mona MARIS, 71.

16. Sidney FOX, 36; Mary BRIAN, 17; Adele MARA, 69.

17. Beverly TYLER, 102; Sue LYON, 66; Diane VARSI, 104.

18. Barbara READ, 86; Doris LLOYD, 61.

19. Sophia LOREN, 63.

20. Dolores DEL RIO, 29; Shirley BOOTH, 15.

HORIZONTAL

Line 1. (From the top) Jean HAGEN, 45; Frances DEE, 28; Doris DAY, 25; Claudette COLBERT, 21; Dolores HART, 47.

2. Diana LYNN, 65; Anne GWYNNE, 44; May WYNN, 112; Betty GRABLE, 40; Nan GREY, 43.

3. Marjorie MAIN, 67; Ruth ROMAN, 88; Mary BOLAND, 13.

4. Eleanor POWELL, 85; Jacqueline WELLS, 105; Laraine DAY, 26.

5. Constance MOORE, 77; Peggy RYAN, 95.

6. Lana TURNER, 101; Susan OLIVER, 82; Marjorie LORD, 62.

7. Sally EILERS, 33; Leslie CARON, 18; Dixie LEE, 60.

8. Deborah KERR, 56; Madeleine CARROLL, 19.

9. Fay BAINTER, 3.

10. Natalie WOOD, 108; Kim NOVAK, 81.

11. Louise BEAVERS, 6; Patricia DANE, 23.

12. Janis CARTER, 20; Rossana RORI, 89.

13. Lucille BALL, 4; Katharine ROSS, 91.

14. Janet GAYNOR, 39; Anne BAXTER, 5; Janet BLAIR, 11.

15. Ann BLYTH, 12; Teresa WRIGHT, 110; Jane WYMAN, 111.

16. June HAVER, 48; Bea BENADARET, 7.

17. Elaine MAY, 73; Virginia MAYO, 74; MARGO, 70.

18. Elizabeth ALLEN, 1; Georgia MOLL, 75; Marianna HILL, 52.

19. Simone SIGNORET, 97; Beulah BONDI, 14.

20. Aliza KASHI, 54; Kathryn GRAYSON, 41; Charlotte GREEN-WOOD, 42.

DIAGONALS

a. Running from the "D" of *DEE*, left and downward: Ruth RO-LAND, 87.

b. Running from the "O" of MAL*O*NE, left and downward, right and upward: Estelle PARSONS, 83.

c. Running from the "H" of BOOT*H*, left and downward: Eileen HERLIE, 51.

d. Running from the "B" of *B*ALL, upward and to the left: Alice BRADY, 16.

e. Running from the "N" of TUR*N*ER, right and downward: Katharine HEPBURN, 50.

f. Running from the "Y" of GW*Y*NNE, right and downward: Loretta YOUNG, 113.

g. Running from the "G" of *G*WYNNE, right and downward: Franceska GAAL, 37.

h. Running from the "B" of GRA*B*LE, right and downward: Lauren BACALL, 2.

FIRST FILMS, THE MEN—BUFFS AND DUFFERS

1. Spencer Tracy

2. Gregory Peck

3. Claude Rains

4. Paul Newman

d. "Up the River"

f. "Days of Glory"

p. "The Invisible Man"

i. "The Silver Chalice"

300

5.	James Stewart	s.	"Murder Man"
6.	Gene Kelly	q.	"For Me and My Gal"
7.	Steve McQueen	r.	"The Blob"
8.	Kirk Douglas	m.	"The Strange Love of Martha Ivers"
9.	Tony Curtis	o.	"City Across the River"
10.	Marlon Brando	b.	"The Men"
11.	Jack Lemmon	h.	"It Should Happen to You"
12.	Dean Martin	g.	"My Friend Irma"
13.	Lee J. Cobb	k.	"Golden Boy"
14.	José Ferrer	c.	"Joan of Arc"
15.	Richard Widmark	t.	"Kiss of Death"
16.	Walter Matthau	l.	"The Kentuckian"
17.	Eli Wallach	a.	"Baby Doll"
18.	Danny Kaye	j.	"Up in Arms"
19.	Van Johnson	e.	"Murder in the Big House"
20.	Burt Lancaster	n.	"The Killers"

SOME MORE "NAME THE STAR"—BUFFS ONLY

1.	James Stewart	"Rope"	"Vertigo"
2.	Basil Rathbone	"The Last Hurrah"	"Captain Blood"
3.	Spencer Tracy	"Edward, My Son"	"Fury"
4.	Lee Marvin	"Bad Day at Black Rock"	"Donovan's Reef"
5.	Ingrid Bergman	"Dr. Jekyll and Mr. Hyde"	"Notorious"
6.	Ava Gardner	"Knights of the Round Table"	"The Bible"
7.	Tony Curtis	"The Great Impostor"	"The Boston Strangler"
8.	James Cagney	"One, Two, Three"	"The Oklahoma Kid"
9.	Katharine Hepburn	"Little Women"	"Adam's Rib"
10.	Jane Fonda	"Sunday in New York"	"Hurry Sundown"

SOME MORE "NAME THE STAR"—DUFFERS' TEE

1. James Stewart   "Broken Arrow"   "Mr. Smith Goes to Washington"

2. Basil Rathbone   "David Copperfield"   "The Adventures of Robin Hood"

3. Spencer Tracy   "Guess Who's Coming to Dinner"   "Inherit the Wind"

4. Lee Marvin   "The Man Who Shot Liberty Valance"   "Cat Ballou"

5. Ingrid Bergman   "Saratoga Trunk"   "Casablanca"

6. Ava Gardner   "The Sun Also Rises"   "The Naked Maja"

7. Tony Curtis   "Sweet Smell of Success"   "Houdini"

8. James Cagney   "The Fighting 69th"   "The Roaring Twenties"

9. Katharine Hepburn   "The African Queen"   "The Philadelphia Story"

10. Jane Fonda   "Walk on the Wild Side"   "Barbarella"

THE TEENY-TINY MARQUEE
#2—BUFFS AND DUFFERS

1. _ e.   "Mrs. *Mike* (Mazurki)"

2. _ f.   "*Johnny* (Downs) Apollo"

3. _ l.   "The Tower of (Julie) *London*"

4. _ b.   "Champagne for (Sid) *Caesar*"

5. _ g.   "The Diary of Anne *Frank* (McHugh)"

6. _ i.   "The Private Life of *Henry* (Travers) VIII"

7. _ k.   "What Ever Happened to Baby *Jane* (Darwell)?"

8. _ j.   "Bonnie Prince *Charlie* (Butterworth)"

9. _ a.   "Harriet (James) *Craig*"

10. _ c. "Citizen *Kane* (Richmond)"
11. _ h. "*Sunset* (Carson) Boulevard"
12. _ d. "(Glenn) *Strange* Cargo"

MORE RE-DOS, THE MALE SIDE— BUFFS AND DUFFERS

1. "The Front
   Page"   Walter Matthau   j. Adolphe Menjou
        Jack Lemmon   Pat O'Brien

2. "The Prince and
   the Pauper"   William Sorrell   i. Errol Flynn
        William Barrons   Claude Rains

3. "The Adven-
   tures of
   Huckleberry
   Finn"   Eddie Hodges   b. Mickey Rooney
        Tony Randall   Walter Connolly

4. "M"   Peter Lorre   g. David Wayne
        Gustaf Grundgens   Martin Gabel

5. "Great
   Expectations"   Phillips Holmes   a. Alec Guinness
        Henry Hull   Finlay Currie

6. "The Virginian"   Joel McCrea   e. Gary Cooper
        Sonny Tufts   Richard Arlen

7. "Lost Horizon"   Peter Finch   h. Ronald Colman
        Charles Boyer   Sam Jaffe

8. "What Price
   Glory?"   James Cagney   f. Victor McLaglen
        Dan Dailey   Edmund Lowe

9. "The
   Buccaneer"   Fredric March   c. Yul Brynner
        Akim Tamiroff   Charles Boyer

10. "Billy the Kid"   Johnny Mack Brown   d. Robert Taylor
         Wallace Beery   Brian Donlevy

MULTIPLE RE-DOS—BUFFS AND DUFFERS

1. "Back Street" — Irene Dunne, John Boles — K. Margaret Sullavan, Charles Boyer — d. Susan Hayward, John Gavin

2. "Beau Geste" — Ronald Colman, Noah Beery, Sr. — F. Gary Cooper, Brian Donlevy — c. Guy Stockwell, Telly Savalas

3. "Madame X" — Ruth Chatterton, Raymond Hackett — B. Gladys George, John Beal — i. Lana Turner, Keir Dullea

4. "The Merry Widow" — Mae Murray, John Gilbert — A. Jeanette MacDonald, Maurice Chevalier — k. Lana Turner, Fernando Lamas

5. "The Phantom of the Opera" — Mary Philbin, Lon Chaney — G. Susanna Foster, Claude Rains — f. Heather Sears, Herbert Lom

6. "Show Boat" — Laura la Plante, Joseph Schildkraut — H. Irene Dunne, Allan Jones — a. Kathryn Grayson, Howard Keel

7. "State Fair" — Janet Gaynor, Will Rogers — I. Jeanne Crain, Charles Winninger — j. Pamela Tiffin, Tom Ewell

8. "Kidnapped" — Freddie Bartholomew, Warner Baxter — J. Roddy McDowall, Dan O'Herlihy — g. James MacArthur, Peter Finch

9. "Of Human Bondage" — Bette Davis, Leslie Howard — C. Eleanor Parker, Paul Henreid — e. Kim Novak, Laurence Harvey

10. "The Hunchback of Notre Dame" — Patsy Ruth Miller, Lon Chaney — E. Maureen O'Hara, Charles Laughton — b. Gina Lollobrigida, Anthony Quinn

11.	"Treasure Island"	Shirley Mason Charles Ogle	D. Jackie Cooper Wallace Beery	h. Bobby Driscoll Robert Newton

SISTERS, SISTERS—BUFFS AND DUFFERS

1. "The Hard Way"		c. Ida Lupino
2. "Psycho"		b. Janet Leigh
3. "Since You Went Away"		a. Jennifer Jones
4. "Picnic"		c. Kim Novak
5. "Love Finds Andy Hardy"		a. Cecilia Parker
6. "The Cardinal"		b. Carol Lynley[1]
7. "Dead End"		a. Sylvia Sidney
8. "The Diary of Anne Frank"		b. Millie Perkins
9. "White Christmas"		c. Rosemary Clooney
10. "A Tree Grows in Brooklyn"		a. Peggy Ann Garner

OSCAR SHUFFLE #2—WILD CARD

1. H I N Q U N T A N Y O N
   (A) (N) (T) H O N Y Q U I (N) (N)

2. N E W D U D E M N G N
   (E) D M U N D G (W) E N N

3. G Y A A D Z T I R B R F L E R
   (B) (A) R (R) Y F I T Z G (E) (R) A (L) D

Hidden name: W A L T E R B R E N N A N

1. For the Buffs' version, Maggie McNamara is also acceptable.

305

THREE OF A KIND, AGAIN—BUFFS ONLY

1. Name the three actors who played Cutter, MacChesney, and Ballantine in "Gunga Din":
   Cary Grant, Victor McLaglen, and Douglas Fairbanks, Jr.

2. Name the three actors who played Stone, Forsythe, and McGregor in "The Lives of a Bengal Lancer":
   Richard Cromwell, Franchot Tone, and Gary Cooper.

3. Name three of the four films which co-starred Jackie Cooper and Wallace Beery:
   "The Champ," "The Bowery," "Treasure Island," and "O'Shaughnessy's Boy."

4. Name the three actors who played the reporter with whom the family's daughter falls in love in the three versions of "State Fair":
   Lew Ayres, Dana Andrews, and Bobby Darin.

5. Give the first names of (three of) the Dalton Boys:
   Grat, Bob, Emmett, and Bill.

6. Name the three actress-daughters of actor Richard Bennett:
   Constance, Joan, and Barbara.

7. Name three biographical roles played by Gary Cooper:
   Sgt. Alvin York, Lou Gehrig, Marco Polo, "Wild Bill" Hickok, Genl. Billy Mitchell, and Dr. Corydon Wassell.

8. Name three of the actors or actresses interviewed by the newsreel reporter in "Citizen Kane":
   Paul Stewart, Dorothy Comingore, Joseph Cotten, Everett Sloane.

9. Who played the three wives in "A Letter to Three Wives":
   Linda Darnell, Ann Sothern, and Jeanne Crain.

10. Name at least three films in which Fred Astaire and Ginger Rogers appeared together:
    "Flying Down to Rio," "Roberta," "Top Hat," "The Gay Divorce," "Follow the Fleet," "Swing Time," "Shall We Dance?" "Carefree," "The Story of Vernon and Irene Castle," "The Barkleys of Broadway."

THREE OF A KIND, AGAIN—DUFFERS' TEE

1. Name the three actors who played the swashbuckling soldiers in "Gunga Din":
   b. Victor McLaglen; d. Cary Grant; e. Douglas Fairbanks, Jr.

2. Name the three actors who portrayed the swashbuckling soldiers in "The Lives of a Bengal Lancer":
   a. Franchot Tone; d. Richard Cromwell; e. Gary Cooper.

3. Name the three films which co-starred Jackie Cooper and Wallace Beery:
   a. "The Champ"; c. "The Bowery"; d. "Treasure Island."

4. There have been three versions of the film "State Fair." Name the three actors who played the reporter with whom the daughter falls in love:
   a. Lew Ayres; d. Dana Andrews; e. Bobby Darin.

5. As every Western fan knows, there were *four* Dalton Boys. Three of them were:
   c. Grat; d. Bob; e. Emmett.

6. Actor Richard Bennett had three daughters, all of whom appeared in films—though with varying degrees of success. Their names:
   b. Constance; c. Barbara; d. Joan.

7. A number of actors or actresses were interviewed by the newsreel reporter in "Citizen Kane." Three of them were:
   a. Paul Stewart; d. Everett Sloane; e. Joseph Cotten.

8. Name at least three biographical roles played by Gary Cooper:
   a. Dr. Corydon Wassell; c. Lou Gehrig; e. Billy Mitchell.

9. The film was "A Letter to Three Wives." The wives were played by:
   b. Linda Darnell; c. Jeanne Crain; e. Ann Sothern.

10. Choose the three films in which Fred Astaire and Ginger Rogers appeared together:
    a. "Carefree"; c. "Follow the Fleet"; e. "Swing Time."

DOUBLE DUTY—BUFFS AND DUFFERS

1. "Little Miss Marker"
2. "Charley's Aunt"
3. "Four Daughters"
4. "It Happened One Night"

5. "Outward Bound"
6. "These Three"
7. "The Front Page"
8. "Ruggles of Red Gap"

c. "Sorrowful Jones"[1]
j. "Where's Charley?"
k. "Young at Heart"
l. "You Can't Run Away from It"
m. "Between Two Worlds"
n. "The Children's Hour"
o. "His Girl Friday"
a. "Fancy Pants"

1. In the Buffs' version, the title "Forty Pounds of Trouble" is also acceptable.

9. "The Sea Beast"		b. "Moby Dick"
10. "The Matchmaker"		f. "Hello, Dolly!"
11. "The More the Merrier"		g. "Walk, Don't Run!"
12. "The Milky Way"		d. "The Kid from Brooklyn"
13. "An American Tragedy"		h. "A Place in the Sun"
14. "House of Strangers"		e. "Broken Lance"
15. "Broadway Bill"		i. "Ridin' High"

DOUBLE DUTY: CASTING—BUFFS AND DUFFERS

1. "Little Miss Marker"	Adolphe Menjou	b. Bob Hope
2. "Charley's Aunt"	Jack Benny	i. Ray Bolger
3. "Four Daughters"	John Garfield	l. Frank Sinatra
4. "It Happened One Night"	Clark Gable	n. Jack Lemmon
5. "Outward Bound"	Leslie Howard	f. John Garfield
6. "These Three"	Joel McCrea	e. James Garner
7. "The Front Page"	Pat O'Brien	k. Rosalind Russell
8. "Ruggles of Red Gap"	Charles Laughton	m. Bob Hope
9. "The Sea Beast"	John Barrymore	g. Gregory Peck
10. "The Match-maker"	Paul Ford	o. Walter Matthau
11. "The More the Merrier"	Charles Coburn	d. Cary Grant
12. "The Milky Way"	Harold Lloyd	a. Danny Kaye
13. "House of Strangers"	Edward G. Robinson	c. Spencer Tracy
14. "An American Tragedy"	Phillips Holmes	j. Montgomery Clift
15. "Broadway Bill"	Warner Baxter	h. Bing Crosby

MORE FIRST FILMS (TOUGHIES)—
BUFFS AND DUFFERS

1. Robert Mitchum
2. Marilyn Monroe
3. Ronald Reagan
4. Deborah Kerr
5. Yul Brynner
6. Teresa Wright
7. Bob Hope
8. Rita Hayworth
9. Rock Hudson
10. Betty Hutton

g. "Hoppy Serves a Writ"
f. "Dangerous Years"
e. "Love Is on the Air"
h. "Major Barbara"
i. "Port of New York"
d. "The Little Foxes"
j. "Big Broadcast of 1938"
c. "Dante's Inferno"
a. "Fighter Squadron"
b. "The Fleet's In"

FIRST, THE WORD ⚞2—BUFFS ONLY

1. George Bernard
   Shaw
2. William Faulkner
3. Booth Tarkington
4. James Michener
5. Jules Verne
6. Daphne du
   Maurier
7. Thornton Wilder
8. Robert Louis
   Stevenson
9. Mark Twain
10. Lillian Hellman

b. "The Devil's Disciple"

c. "The Story of Temple Drake"
a. "The Magnificent Ambersons"
a. "The Bridges at Toko-Ri"
c. "Journey to the Center of the Earth"

a. "The Birds"
c. "The Bridge of San Luis Rey"

c. "The Strange Door"
c. "Man with a Million"
b. "Toys in the Attic"

FIRST, THE WORD ⚞2—DUFFERS' TEE

1. "Major Barbara" F. George Bernard
   "Caesar and   Shaw   b. "The Devil's
   Cleopatra"   Disciple"

2. "The Long Hot Summer" J. William Faulkner g. "The Story of Temple Drake"
   "The Sound and the Fury"

3. "Penrod and Sam" G. Booth Tarkington e. "The Magnificent Ambersons"
   "Seventeen"

4. "South Pacific" A. James Michener f. "The Bridges at Toko-Ri"
   "Return to Paradise"

5. "Five Weeks in a Balloon" H. Jules Verne c. "Journey to the Center of the Earth"
   "20,000 Leagues Under the Sea"

6. "Frenchman's Creek" I. Daphne du Maurier j. "The Birds"
   "Rebecca"

7. "The Match-maker" B. Thornton Wilder i. "The Bridge of San Luis Rey"
   "Our Town"

8. "Kidnapped' D. Robert L. Stevenson a. "The Strange Door"
   "The Master of Ballantrae"

9. "The Adventures of Tom Sawyer" C. Mark Twain h. "Man with a Million"
   "A Connecticut Yankee in King Arthur's Court"

10. "The Little Foxes" E. Lillian Hellman d. "Toys in the Attic"
    "The Children's Hour"

READING THE CREDITS—BUFFS AND DUFFERS

The film:	d.	"Gone with the Wind."
The stars:	c.	Clark Gable;
	i.	Vivien Leigh.
The producer:	a.	David O. Selznick.

SOME MORE DOUBLE DUTY—BUFFS AND DUFFERS

1. "Blind Alley"
2. "The Sea Wolf"
3. "Roberta"
4. "Valley of the Giants"
5. "A Slight Case of Murder"
6. "Gunga Din"
7. "Ah, Wilderness"
8. "The Man Who Played God"
9. "The Paleface"
10. "The Petrified Forest"
11. "The Awful Truth"
12. "The Black Watch"
13. "The Major and the Minor"
14. "The Crowd Roars"
15. "One Way Passage"

j. "The Dark Past"
i. "Wolf Larsen"
f. "Lovely to Look At"
k. "The Big Trees"
l. "Stop, You're Killing Me"
b. "Sergeants Three"
c. "Summer Holiday"
d. "Sincerely Yours"
e. "The Shakiest Gun in the West"
m. "Escape in the Desert"
n. "Let's Do It Again"
o. "King of the Khyber Rifles"
g. "You're Never Too Young"
a. "Killer McCoy"
h. "Till We Meet Again"

SOME MORE DOUBLE DUTY:
CASTING—BUFFS ONLY

1. "Blind Alley"	Chester Morris	William Holden
2. "The Sea Wolf"	Edward G. Robinson	Barry Sullivan
3. "Roberta"	Fred Astaire	Howard Keel
4. "Valley of the Giants"	Wayne Morris	Kirk Douglas

5.	"A Slight Case of Murder"	Edward G. Robinson	Broderick Crawford
6.	"Gunga Din"	Robert Coote	Joey Bishop
7.	"Ah, Wilderness"	Lionel Barrymore	Walter Huston
8.	"The Man Who Played God"	George Arliss	Liberace
9.	"The Paleface"	Bob Hope	Don Knotts
10.	"The Petrified Forest"	Humphrey Bogart	Helmut Dantine
11.	"The Awful Truth"	Ralph Bellamy	Aldo Ray
12.	"The Black Watch"	Victor McLaglen	Tyrone Power
13.	"The Major and the Minor"	Ginger Rogers	Jerry Lewis
14.	"The Crowd Roars"	Frank Morgan	James Dunn
15.	"One Way Passage"	William Powell	George Brent

SOME MORE DOUBLE DUTY:
CASTING—DUFFERS' TEE

1.	"Blind Alley"	Chester Morris	f. William Holden
2.	"The Sea Wolf"	Edward G. Robinson	j. Barry Sullivan
3.	"Roberta"	Fred Astaire	l. Howard Keel
4.	"Valley of the Giants"	Wayne Morris	h. Kirk Douglas
5.	"A Slight Case of Murder"	Edward G. Robinson	c. Broderick Crawford
6.	"Gunga Din"	Sam Jaffe	n. Sammy Davis, Jr.
7.	"Ah, Wilderness"	Lionel Barrymore	o. Walter Huston
8.	"The Man Who Played God"	George Arliss	d. Liberace
9.	"The Paleface"	Bob Hope	e. Don Knotts
10.	"The Petrified Forest"	Humphrey Bogart	k. Helmut Dantine

11. "The Awful Truth"	Ralph Bellamy	m. Aldo Ray
12. "The Black Watch"	Victor McLaglen	a. Tyrone Power
13. "The Major and the Minor"	Ginger Rogers	b. Jerry Lewis
14. "The Crowd Roars"	Frank Morgan	i. James Dunn
15. "One Way Passage"	William Powell	g. George Brent

AND SOME MORE "NAME THE STAR"—BUFFS ONLY

1. Charles Laughton "Jamaica Inn" "Advise and Consent"
2. Peter Lorre "Casablanca" "M"
3. Bette Davis "Beyond the Forest" "The Man Who Came to Dinner"
4. John Wayne "Fort Apache" "The Long Voyage Home"
5. Elizabeth Taylor "Little Women" "Giant"
6. Tyrone Power "The Rains Came" "An American Guerrilla in the Philippines"
7. Rosalind Russell "The Guilt of Janet Ames" "The Women"
8. Will Rogers "Steamboat 'Round the Bend" "As Young As You Feel"
9. Gregory Peck "The Paradine Case" "The Gunfighter"
10. David Niven "The Prisoner of Zenda" "The Moon Is Blue"

AND SOME MORE "NAME THE STAR"— DUFFERS' TEE

1. Charles Laughton "Witness for the Prosecution" "Mutiny on the Bounty"

2. Peter Lorre	"Arsenic and Old Lace"	"The Maltese Falcon"
3. Bette Davis	"The Corn Is Green"	"All About Eve"
4. John Wayne	"The Wings of Eagles"	"Stagecoach"
5. Elizabeth Taylor	"Ivanhoe"	"Cat on a Hot Tin Roof"
6. Tyrone Power	"Blood and Sand"	"The Long Gray Line"
7. Rosalind Russell	"Mourning Becomes Electra"	"Sister Kenny"
8. Will Rogers	"Judge Priest"	"David Harum"
9. Gregory Peck	"To Kill a Mockingbird"	"Moby Dick"
10. David Niven	"Separate Tables"	"Around the World in 80 Days"

FUNNY FOLKS CRISSCROSS—BUFFS ONLY

Four-Letter Names	Five-Letter Names	Six-Letter Names	Seven-Letter Names
Arno, Sig	Allen, Gracie	Abbott, Bud	Conklin, Chester
Auer, Mischa	Askin, Leon	Dumont, Margaret	Fazenda, Louise
Best, Willie	Clute, Chester	Horton, Edw.	Flippen, Jay C.
Bing, Herman	Daley, Cass	Everett	Gilbert, Billy
Blue, Ben	Davis, Joan	Howard, Shemp	Herbert, Hugh
Dale, Charlie	Jenks, Frank	Kelton, Pert	Kennedy, Edgar
Dane, Karl	Kelly, Patsy	Kovacs, Ernie	Miranda, Carmen
Feld, Fritz	Moore, Victor	Morgan, Frank	Wheeler, Bert
Fung, Willy	Moran, Polly	Norton, Jack	Woolsey, Robert
Hope, Bob	Oakie, Jack	Oliver, Edna May	
Lamb, Gil	Olsen, Ole	Penner, Joe	
Main, Marjorie	Pitts, ZaSu	Robson, May	
Marx, Zeppo	Riano, Renie	Rogers, Will	
Orth, Frank	Semon, Larry	Rumann, Sig	
Raye, Martha	Tracy, William	Sutton, Grady	
Ritz, Harry		Turpin, Ben	
Todd, Thelma			
Yule, Joe			

Eight-Letter Names

Carrillo, Leo
Costello, Lou
Holloway, Sterling
Mayehoff, Eddie
Moreland, Mantan
Pangborn, Franklin

Nine-Letter Names

Finlayson, Jimmie
Pendleton, Nat
Skipworth, Alison

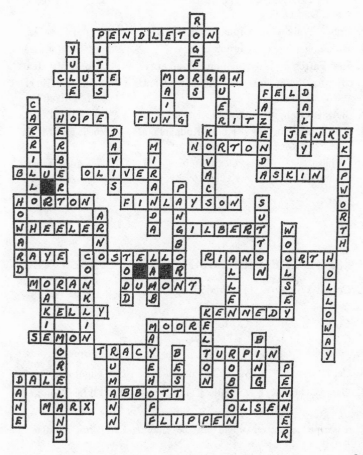

SPOT THE BIO: COMPOSERS—BUFFS ONLY

1. Cornel Wilde	Frédéric Chopin	"A Song to Remember"
2. Clifton Webb	John Philip Sousa	"Stars and Stripes Forever"
3. Cary Grant	Cole Porter	"Night and Day"
4. Danny Thomas	Gus Kahn	"I'll See You in My Dreams"
5. Red Skelton and Fred Astaire	Harry Ruby and Bert Kalmar	"Three Little Words"
6. Robert Alda	George Gershwin	"Rhapsody in Blue"
7. Don Ameche	Stephen Foster	"Swanee River"
8. Gordon Macrae, Ernest Borgnine, and Dan Dailey	De Sylva, Henderson, and Brown	"The Best Things in Life Are Free"
9. Robert Walker	Johannes Brahms[1]	"Song of Love"[1]
10. Dirk Bogarde	Franz Liszt	"Song Without End"
11. José Ferrer	Sigmund Romberg	"Deep in My Heart"
12. Maurice Evans and Robert Morley	Gilbert and Sullivan	"The Great Gilbert and Sullivan"
13. Stewart Granger	Niccolò Paganini	"The Magic Bow"
14. Tom Drake and Mickey Rooney	Richard Rodgers and Lorenz Hart	"Words and Music"
15. Richard Chamberlain	Peter Ilyitch Tchaikovsky	"The Music Lovers"

SPOT THE BIO: COMPOSERS—DUFFERS' TEE

1. Cornel Wilde	E. Frédéric Chopin	b. "A Song to Remember"
2. Clifton Webb	G. John Philip Sousa	n. "Stars and Stripes Forever"
3. Cary Grant	M. Cole Porter	o. "Night and Day"
4. Danny Thomas	O. Gus Kahn	k. "I'll See You in My Dreams"

1. An acceptable answer would also be "Jerome Kern" in "Till the Clouds Roll By."

5. Red Skelton and
   Fred Astaire   B. Harry Ruby and
          Bert Kalmar   g. "Three Little Words"

6. Robert Alda   I. George Gershwin   l. "Rhapsody in Blue"

7. Don Ameche   N. Stephen Foster   d. "Swanee River"

8. Walter
   Connolly   L. Victor Herbert   e. "The Great Victor
                                                  Herbert"

9. Robert Walker   F. Johannes Brahms   a. "Song of Love"

10. Dirk Bogarde   A. Franz Liszt   c. "Song Without End"

11. José Ferrer   C. Sigmund
                   Romberg   f. "Deep in My Heart"

12. Maurice Evans
   and Robert
   Morley   J. Gilbert and
                   Sullivan   h. "The Great Gilbert
                                                  and Sullivan"

13. Stewart Granger   K. Niccolò
                   Paganini   i. "The Magic Bow"

14. Tom Drake and
   Mickey
   Rooney   H. Richard Rodgers
                  and Lorenz
                  Hart   m. "Words and Music"

15. Richard
   Chamberlain   D. Peter Ilyitch
                  Tchaikovsky   j. "The Music Lovers"

THE TEENY-TINY MARQUEE
#3—BUFFS AND DUFFERS

1. __ e.   *Catherine* (McLeod) the Great"
2. __ g.   "After the (Sidney) *Fox*"
3. __ k.   "The (Ned) *Glass* Key"
4. __ b.   "East *Lynne* (Overman)"
5. __ l.   "The War Against Mrs. (Reed)
          Hadley"

6. _ j. "The Pied *Piper* (Laurie)"
7. _ a. "The (Mitzi) *Green* Years"
8. _ d. "(Colin) *Clive* of India"
9. _ f. "(Gail) *Patrick* the Great"
10. _ c. "Roxie (Dolores) *Hart*"
11. _ h. "Four Flags (Mae) *West*"
12. _ i. "Baby Face (Barry) *Nelson*"

MORE TYPE-CASTING—BUFFS AND DUFFERS

1. _ f. Eleanor Parker: "Detective Story"; "The Naked Jungle"; "Mission to Moscow"; "The Man with the Golden Arm."

2. _ j. Susan Hayward: "The President's Lady"; "White Witch Doctor"; "I Can Get It for You Wholesale"; "Valley of the Dolls."

3. _ m. James Mason: "The Marriage Go-Round"; "A Star Is Born"; "The Desert Fox" or "The Desert Rats"; "Odd Man Out."

4. _ g. Jennifer Jones: "Love Is a Many-Splendored Thing"; "A Farewell to Arms"; "We Were Strangers"; "Good Morning, Miss Dove."

5. _ l. Sophia Loren: "Boccaccio '70"; "The Pride and the Passion"; "Houseboat"; "The Condemned of Altona."

6. _ d. Charles Laughton: "The Big Clock"; "Spartacus"; "This Land Is Mine"; "Mutiny on the Bounty."

7. _ e. Barbara Stanwyck: "Walk on the Wild Side"; "Executive Suite"; "Lady of Burlesque" or "Ball of Fire"; "Annie Oakley."

8. _ k. Gene Kelly: "The Three Musketeers"; "Singin' in the Rain"; "Inherit the Wind"; "An American in Paris."

9. _ n. Lauren Bacall: "Designing Woman"; "Shock Treatment"; "Flame over India"; "Key Largo."

10. _ i. William Holden: "Golden Boy"; "Sunset Boulevard"; "The Bridges at Toko-Ri"; "Executive Suite."

11. __ b. Bette Davis: "The Man Who Came to Dinner";
            "The Corn Is Green"; "The Private Lives of
            Elizabeth and Essex" or "The Virgin Queen";
            "A Pocketful of Miracles."

12. __ o. Paul Newman: "The Hustler"; "Harper"; "Cool
            Hand Luke"; "The Young Philadelphians."

13. __ h. Shirley MacLaine: "The Apartment"; "The
            Children's Hour"; "The Yellow Rolls-Royce";
            "Irma La Douce."

14. __ a. Broderick Crawford: "Broadway"; "Not As a
            Stranger"; "All the King's Men"; "Born
            Yesterday."

15. __ c. Alec Guinness: "Lawrence of Arabia";
            "Cromwell"; "The Mudlark"; "The Captain's
            Paradise."

OH, BROTHER—BUFFS AND DUFFERS

1. "Sweet Bird of Youth"   c. Rip Torn
2. "A Thousand Clowns"   a. Martin Balsam
3. "Bonnie and Clyde"   c. Warren Beatty
4. "City for Conquest"   c. James Cagney
5. "The Glass Menagerie"   a. Arthur Kennedy
6. "A Hole in the Head"   c. Edward G. Robinson
7. "Royal Wedding"   a. Keenan Wynn[1]
8. "The Human Comedy"   c. Jackie "Butch" Jenkins[2]
9. "Public Enemy"   c. James Cagney
10. "Sunday in New York"   c. Cliff Robertson

WILD CARD—DEAR GOPHER

If you had the following career assignments and cities in this combination, you have yourself some more points, and you'd make some
producer a most efficient gopher[3]:

1. No, no mistake—Keenan Wynn portrayed twin brothers in this dual role.
2. In the Buffs' version, Van Johnson would also be acceptable.
3. In motion picture production, the "gopher" is indispensable, and very important to the film's success. His function is to "go fer" this and "go fer" that!

San Francisco	Rick Wraque	Swashbuckler
Chicago	Roland Stone	Western Hero
New York	Samuel Hill	Comedian
London	Les Dants	Character Actor
Rome	Loden Zoahn	Tragedian

Now, if you haven't been able to work out the deductions required, here's our line of reasoning. Slow-l-y n-o-w . . .

Initially, we must figure out which cities are involved, so your movie expertise tells you . . .

> The city in "Bullitt" is *San Francisco;*
>
> the city featured in "The St. Valentine's Day Massacre" is *Chicago;*
>
> the city in "Naked City" is *New York;*
>
> the city of "Three Coins in the Fountain" is *Rome;*
>
> and, of course, Basil Rathbone and Nigel Bruce were Sherlock Holmes and Dr. Watson, so the city in question is *London.*

1. *Loden Zoahn and the Character Actor now live in Europe.*

    This tells us that Loden Zoahn and the Character Actor are not the same person, and that the two men live in Rome and London.

2. *Samuel Hill has refused to work in films which require him to handle swords or horses.*

    From this we conclude that Samuel Hill is neither the Swashbuckler nor the Western Hero.

3. *Rick Wraque cannot abide, or even endure being around, character actors.*

    This would indicate that Rick Wraque is not the Character Actor.

4. *The actor now residing on the East Coast (i.e., New York) has the same prejudice against Mr. Wraque that Mr. Wraque has for character actors.*

    A. This would indicate that Rick and the New York actor are not the same person, and therefore Rick does not live in New York.

    B. Referring back to Clue 1 above, we know that Loden Zoahn and the Character Actor are the only two residing in Europe. Since this clue, and Clue 3, tells us that Rick is *not* the Character Actor—and certainly he is not Loden Zoahn—then Rick does not live in Europe.

    C. Since Rick lives neither in New York nor Europe, he must live in either Chicago or San Francisco.

5. *Roland Stone lives west of the Comedian.*

Aside from the geography revealed, we know also that Roland Stone is *not* the Comedian.

6. *The Western Hero lives east of Rick Wraque.*
   So we know that Rick is *not* the Western Hero.

7. *The actor now living in southern Europe (Rome) once made a film with the Character Actor.*
   A. We learned from Clue 1 that the Character Actor lives either in Rome or London.
   B. Since this Clue 7 indicates that the "actor living in Rome" and the Character Actor are two different people, we can conclude that THE CHARACTER ACTOR LIVES IN LONDON (CONCLUSION #1)!
   C. We also learned in Clue 1 that only the Character Actor (London) and Loden Zoahn live in Europe. Therefore, LODEN ZOAHN MUST BE A RESIDENT OF ROME (CONCLUSION #2).

8. *Mr. Dants once appeared in a film with the Tragedian.*
   So we know that Les Dants is *not* the Tragedian.

9. *Only if the Tragedian now lives in the city where Charles Laughton's first film was shot is Mr. Zoahn the Swashbuckler.*
   Your own movie expertise tells you that Charles Laughton's first film was shot in London. From Clue 7, we know that the Character Actor lives in London, and therefore the Tragedian can *not*. Therefore, Loden Zoahn is *not* the Swashbuckler!

10. *Samuel Hill never appeared in a film with any of the four actors.*
    A. Clue 7 tells us that the actor living in Rome (Loden Zoahn, Conclusion #2) and the Character Actor once made a film together. Therefore, Samuel Hill is *not* the Character Actor.
    B. Clue 8 tells us that Les Dants once appeared in a film with the Tragedian. Therefore, Samuel Hill is *not* the Tragedian.
    C. Clue 2 told us that Hill is neither the Western Hero nor the Swashbuckler.
    D. Therefore, the only category remaining indicates that SAMUEL HILL IS THE COMEDIAN (CONCLUSION #3).

11. *The actor now residing in Chicago once suffered a black eye in a barroom brawl with the Comedian.*
    Conclusion #3 told us that Samuel Hill is the Comedian, and this clue therefore confirms that Samuel Hill does *not* live in Chicago.

12. *Loden Zoahn has never worn a ten-gallon hat or handled a six-gun in his entire cinematic career.*
    A. Clue 1 told us that Zoahn is *not* the Character Actor.
    B. Clue 9 told us that Zoahn is *not* the Swashbuckler.

C. From Conclusion ☒3, we know that Hill is the Comedian; therefore, Zoahn is *not*.

D. From this clue, we know that Zoahn cannot be the Western Hero.

E. Therefore, LODEN ZOAHN HAS TO BE THE TRAGEDIAN (CONCLUSION ☒4).

At this point, our list is beginning to take shape, since we have the full picture on Loden Zoahn. We know that he lives in Rome (Conclusion ☒2), and that he is the Tragedian (Conclusion ☒4).

We have also established that the Character Actor lives in London (Conclusion ☒1) and that Samuel Hill is the Comedian (Conclusion ☒3). Let's zero in on Hill . . .

Samuel Hill, Comedian

A. Clue 5 told us that Roland Stone lives west of the Comedian (Hill). Conclusion ☒1 told us that the Character Actor lives in London, and Conclusion ☒2 told us that Zoahn, the Tragedian, lives in Rome. And Clue 11 told us that Samuel Hill doesn't live in Chicago.

B. Therefore, this leaves only New York and San Francisco as possible cities in which to locate Hill.

C. But if Hill lives in San Francisco, then Roland Stone could *not* live west of Hill, the Comedian, as we're told in Clue 5.

D. Therefore, SAMUEL HILL HAS TO LIVE IN NEW YORK (CONCLUSION ☒5).

Remaining Cities

With Loden Zoahn (the Tragedian) living in Rome, the Character Actor in London, and Samuel Hill (the Comedian) living in New York, we have yet to establish the actors living in San Francisco and Chicago.

Returning to Clue 6, we know that the Western Hero lives east of Rick Wraque. With Hill living in New York, and Zoahn living in Rome, and since Rick is *not* the Character Actor (Clue 3) living in London—then Rick and the Western Hero live in San Francisco and Chicago . . . but which?

Were Rick to live in Chicago, then the Western Hero in San Francisco would live *west* of Rick—not east, as in Clue 6. Therefore, RICK WRAQUE HAS TO LIVE IN SAN FRANCISCO (CONCLUSION ☒6), and THE WESTERN HERO HAS TO LIVE IN CHICAGO (CONCLUSION ☒7).

Rick Wraque, San Francisco

A. From Conclusion ☒3, since Samuel Hill is the Comedian, Rick is *not*.

B. From Conclusion ☒4, since Loden Zoahn is the Tragedian, Rick is *not*.

C. From Clue 6, we know that Rick is *not* the Western Hero.

D. From Clue 3, we know that Rick is *not* the Character Actor.

E. Therefore, Rick has to be the Swashbuckler (CONCLUSION #8).

So let's stand back for a moment, and see what we have:

San Francisco	Rick Wraque	Swashbuckler
Chicago	?	Western Hero
New York	Samuel Hill	Comedian
London	?	Character Actor
Rome	Loden Zoahn	Tragedian

We do not know, at this point, if Roland Stone or Les Dants is the Western Hero or the Character Actor. So let's look at Stone . . .

Roland Stone

A. Clue 5 tells us that Roland lives west of the Comedian, Samuel Hill. Since Hill lives in New York, the only two cities which would be *west* are Chicago and San Francisco.

B. But Rick Wraque lives in San Francisco, as we learned from Conclusion #6.

C. Therefore, ROLAND STONE COULD ONLY LIVE IN CHICAGO (CONCLUSION #9).

D. But Conclusion #7 told us that the Western Hero lives in Chicago.

E. Therefore, ROLAND STONE, OF CHICAGO, IS THE WESTERN HERO (CONCLUSION #10).

Les Dants

Since Les Dants is now the only one unaccounted for, and since we have not identified the Character Actor living in London, we must conclude that THIS WOULD BE LES DANTS (CONCLUSION #11).

Simple . . . ?

AND AGAIN, WHO IS IT?—BUFFS ONLY

Spats Colombo	geo**R**ge raft
Doc Boone	thomas m**I**tchell
Cody Jarrett	james **C**agney
Col. Clint Maroon	gary c**O**oper

Peter Warne	c l a r k g a **B**	l e
Doc Erwin Riedenschneider	s a m j **A**	f f e
Lina Lamont	j e a **N**	h a g e n
Diamond Jim Brady	e d w a r **D**	a r n o l d
Charlie Allnut	h u m p h r **E**	y b o g a r t
Boss Jim Gettys	r a y c o **L**	l i n s
Victor Laszlo	p a u **L**	h e n r e i d
Genl. Buck Turgidson	g e o r g e c s c **O**	t t

And the name of the star who played the character of Rico Bandello is Edward G. Robinson!

AND AGAIN, WHO IS IT?—DUFFERS' TEE

Rhett Butler	c l a r k g a (b) **L**	e
Willy Loman	f r (e) d r **I**	c m a r c h
Gerald O'Hara	t h o m a s m (i) **T**	c h e l l
Father Flanagan	(s) p e n c e r **T**	(r) a c y
Charles Foster Kane	o (r) s o n w e **L**	l e s
Minnesota Fats	j (a) c k i e g l **E**	a s o (n)
The Virginian	g a r y **C**	o (o) p e r
Capt. Bat Guano	k e e (n) **A**	n (w) y n n
Duke Mantee	h u m p h r **E**	y b o g a r t
Genl. George Patton	(g) e o r g e c **S**	c (o) t t
Mrs. Danvers	j u (d) i t h **A**	n (d) e r s o n
Willy Stark	b r o d e r i c k c **R**	a w f o r d

And the name of the star is Edward G. Robinson!

324

AND SOME MORE DOUBLE DUTY—
BUFFS AND DUFFERS

1. "Nights of Cabiria"
2. "The Women"
3. "Sentimental Journey"
4. "Red Dust"
5. "Rain"
6. "The Philadelphia Story"
7. "No, No, Nanette"
8. "The Informer"
9. "Waterloo Bridge"
10. "Destry Rides Again"
11. "Ninotchka"
12. "The Maltese Falcon"
13. "My Favorite Wife"
14. "Love Is News"
15. "Love Affair"

f. "Sweet Charity"
i. "The Opposite Sex"
d. "The Gift of Love"
o. "Congo Maisie"[1]
j. "Miss Sadie Thompson"
m. "High Society"
k. "Tea for Two"
b. "Up Tight"
e. "Gaby"
l. "Frenchie"
c. "Silk Stockings"
g. "Satan Met a Lady"
n. "Move Over, Darling"
a. "That Wonderful Urge"
h. "An Affair to Remember"

AND SOME MORE DOUBLE DUTY:
CASTING—BUFFS AND DUFFERS

1. "Nights of Cabiria"   Giulietta Masina   d. Shirley MacLaine
2. "The Women"   Joan Crawford   g. Joan Collins
3. "Sentimental Journey"   Maureen O'Hara   l. Lauren Bacall
4. "Red Dust"   Jean Harlow   n. Ann Sothern
5. "Rain"   Joan Crawford   i. Rita Hayworth
6. "The Philadelphia Story"   Ruth Hussey   j. Celeste Holm
7. "No, No, Nanette"   Anna Neagle   b. Doris Day
8. "The Informer"   Margot Grahame   c. Ruby Dee
9. "Waterloo Bridge"   Vivien Leigh   m. Leslie Caron

1. No, Buffs—we didn't forget "Mogambo"—just being tricky!

10. "Destry Rides
    Again"   Marlene Dietrich   a. Shelley Winters
11. "Ninotchka"   Greta Garbo   e. Cyd Charisse
12. "The Maltese
    Falcon"   Bebe Daniels   h. Bette Davis[1]
13. "My Favorite
    Wife"   Irene Dunne   o. Doris Day
14. "Love Is News"   Loretta Young   k. Gene Tierney
15. "Love Affair"   Irene Dunne   f. Deborah Kerr

SENSATIONAL COLOR!—BUFFS AND DUFFERS

1. "SCARLET Street"
2. "The LAVENDER Hill Mob"
3. "The Solid GOLD Cadillac"
4. "The Girl in the RED Velvet Swing"
5. "The PINK Panther"
6. "The Man in the GRAY Flannel Suit"
7. "The Man in the WHITE Suit"
8. "GREEN Hell"
9. "The SILVER Chalice"
10. "Forever AMBER"
11. "YELLOW Sky"
12. "RUBY Gentry"
13. "The BLUE Bird"
14. "BLACK Hand"
15. "The Long GRAY Line"
16. "The GREEN Man"
17. "Heller in PINK Tights"
18. "The PURPLE Plain"

1. We know there's bound to be confusion about "The Maltese Falcon," who played what, and when or if a version was a re-do or a remake. The film was first made, as "The Maltese Falcon," in 1931, with Bebe Daniels and Ricardo Cortez. A second version was produced five years later, under the title "Satan Met a Lady," with Bette Davis and Warren William. The classic version, under the original title "The Maltese Falcon," and starring Humphrey Bogart, Mary Astor, Sydney Greenstreet, Peter Lorre, which is best-remembered, came out in 1941.

19. "The ROSE Tattoo"

20. "Navy BLUE and GOLD"

ODD MAN OUT #4—BUFFS AND DUFFERS

1. ELLERY QUEEN: Dan Duryea is out of place. Eddie Quillan played the detective in "The Mandarin Mystery"; Ralph Bellamy in "Ellery Queen, Master Detective"; and William Gargan was Queen in "A Close Call for Ellery Queen."

2. CLEOPATRA: Lynn Redgrave never played Cleopatra. Elizabeth Taylor and Claudette Colbert had the title role in two different versions of "Cleopatra," while Vivien Leigh played the role in a film version of Shaw's "Caesar and Cleopatra."

3. THE FRANKENSTEIN MONSTER: Glenn Langan doesn't belong. Charles Ogle was the first Frankenstein Monster in a silent film entitled "Frankenstein," circa 1910. Glenn Strange played the part in "House of Frankenstein," while Boris Karloff originated the most popular version in the 1931 Universal release.

4. DOC HOLLIDAY: Burt Lancaster is the odd man, though he played Earp to Kirk Douglas' portrayal of Holliday in "Gunfight at the O.K. Corral." Victor Mature played the part in John Ford's "My Darling Clementine," while Cesar Romero played Doc in "Frontier Marshal," with Randolph Scott as Earp.

5. CHARLIE CHAN: Exclude J. Carrol Naish, who played Chan only in the half-hour TV series. The others played Chan several times. Representative films would be: (Oland) "Charlie Chan in Monte Carlo"; (Toler) "Charlie Chan in Panama"; and (Winters) "The Shanghai Chest."

6. BULLDOG DRUMMOND: Michael Rennie is the odd man. Ronald Colman played the title role in "Bulldog Drummond" (1929); Walter Pidgeon played the sleuth in "Calling Bulldog Drummond" (1951); while John Howard played Drummond a number of times, including "Bulldog Drummond Comes Back."

7. SHERLOCK HOLMES: William Powell doesn't belong. Barrymore did a version in 1922 with Roland Young as Watson. Clive Brook was the sound screen's first Holmes in "Return of Sherlock Holmes," and Basil Rathbone was probably the best-known Holmes, having played the sleuth a number of times, commencing with "The Hound of the Baskervilles."

8. JOHN DILLINGER: Harold Huber doesn't belong in the Dillinger line-up. Lawrence Tierney had the title role in "Dillinger," as did Nick

Adams in "Young Dillinger." Leo Gordon portrayed Dillinger as a secondary role in "Baby Face Nelson."

9. PHILIP MARLOWE: Richard Conte is the odd man here. Dick Powell played the private eye in "Murder, My Sweet"; Robert Montgomery in "Lady in the Lake"; and Humphrey Bogart in "The Big Sleep."

10. TARZAN: Chuck Connors was never a screen Tarzan. The first was Elmo K. Lincoln, in "Tarzan and the Apes." Johnny Weissmuller was the most popular Tarzan, making his debut in "Tarzan, the Ape Man." Glenn Morris was one of several successors, appearing in "Tarzan's Revenge."

NAMES IN COMMON—BUFFS AND DUFFERS

	Related	Unrelated
1. Bruce and Ruth Gordon		X
2. Etienne and Annie Girardot		X
3. Robert and Elizabeth Montgomery	Father and daughter	
4. James and Lucille Gleason	Husband and wife	
5. Ben and Celia Johnson		X
6. Gene and June Lockhart	Father and daughter	
7. Marlon and Jocelyn Brando	Brother and sister	
8. Donald and Dolores Gray		X
9. John and Hayley Milles	Father and daughter	
10. Mervyn and Glynis Johns	Father and daughter	
11. Rick and Sybil Jason		X
12. Frank and Nancy Sinatra	Father and daughter	

328

13. Michael and Joan Crawford		X
14. Edgar and Candice Bergen	Father and daughter	
15. Edmond and Margaret O'Brien		X
16. Donald and Una O'Connor		X
17. Conrad and Elsie Janis		X
18. Hoot and Virginia Gibson		X
19. Cary and Kathryn Grant		X
20. Dennis and Hedda Hopper		X

THE VIOLENT END—BUFFS AND DUFFERS

1. James Cagney   h. Killed by explosion of gasoline tank on which he was standing.

2. Kenneth Spencer   i. Beheaded by Japanese soldier.

3. Orson Welles   f. Impaled by sword on mechanical clock.

4. Van Heflin   m. Blown out of jetliner by a bomb he triggered.

5. Spencer Tracy   n. Maimed and drowned by accident at sea.

6. Jane Darwell   k. Killed by bomb thrown into house.

7. Susan Hayward   l. Drowned in a shipwreck.

8. Robert Wilke   o. Killed by thrown knife.

9. James Coburn   d. Suffocated by plastic bag.

10. Louis Calhern   c. Killed by self-inflicted gunshot.

11. Charles McGraw   b. Drowned in a pot of hot soup.

12. Edmund Gwenn   j. Fell from high building.

13. Norman Lloyd   g. Fell from Statue of Liberty.

14. Ernest Borgnine   a. Jumped into a pit of wild animals.

15. Tyrone Power   e. Gored by bull in the bull ring.

MORE QUOTABLES—BUFFS AND DUFFERS

1. "Of all the gin joints in all the towns . . ."

   m. "Casablanca"

2. "Well, nobody's perfect."

   g. "Some Like It Hot"

3. "I'll be ever'where—wherever you look . . ."

   n. "The Grapes of Wrath"

4. "Let's give 'em the gunsel . . ."

   i. "The Maltese Falcon"

5. "I don't pray. Kneeling bags my nylons."

   d. "Ace in the Hole"[1]

6. "That's what it's all about."

   l. "None But the Lonely Heart"

7. "Ach—so-o-o-o . . ."

   k. "Stalag 17"

8. "I picked you for the job . . ."

   b. "Double Indemnity"

9. "The Monte Carlo Ballet steenks!"

   j. "You Can't Take It with You"

10. "It's a problem, isn't it? . . ."

   c. "The Lost Weekend"

11. "Hi ya, Father—whaddya hear, whaddya say?"

   e. "Angels with Dirty Faces"

12. "I'd just like to keep that particular piece of paper myself . . ."

   o. "Citizen Kane"

13. "Live fast, die young—and have a good-looking corpse."

   f. "Knock on Any Door"

14. "Will I go? What a question! . . ."

   h. "The Treasure of the Sierra Madre"

15. "Paramount? Ha! Let 'em wait . . ."

   a. "Sunset Boulevard"

LA RONDE ET LA RONDE— BUFFS AND DUFFERS

A. Cary Grant and Sophia Loren

   8. "Houseboat"[2]

B. Sophia Loren and Clark Gable

   10. "It Started in Naples"

1. Or the alternate title, "The Big Carnival," in the Buffs' version.
2. In the Buffs' version, the answer "The Pride and the Passion" would be acceptable.

C. Clark Gable and Deborah Kerr

D. Deborah Kerr and Spencer Tracy

E. Spencer Tracy and Lana Turner

F. Lana Turner and Gary Cooper

G. Gary Cooper and Jean Arthur

H. Jean Arthur and James Stewart

I. James Stewart and Grace Kelly

J. Grace Kelly and Bing Crosby

K. Bing Crosby and Ingrid Bergman

L. Ingrid Bergman and Cary Grant

3. "The Hucksters"

5. "Edward, My Son"

2. "Cass Timberlane"[1]

6. "The Adventures of Marco Polo"

4. "The Plainsman"[2]

7. "You Can't Take It with You"[3]

1. "Rear Window"

11. "The Country Girl"[4]

12. "The Bells of St. Mary's"

9. "Notorious"[5]

MORE WILD CARDS—BUFFS AND DUFFERS

1. Howard Da Silva

2. Don, the hero; Nat, the bartender.

3. Six, including yourself. Though the ten names all have appeared in motion picture casting lists, they represent only five people. In most cases, the player began in films with one name, and then changed to another. In one case, one of the players, John Shepperd, briefly reverted to the name he started with. The five you have invited are:

> John Shepperd — Shepperd Strudwick
> Dorothy McNulty — Penny Singleton
> Byron Barr — Gig Young
> Herman Brix — Bruce Bennett
> Jacqueline Wells — Julie Bishop

4. The Blue Water.

5. He was injured in a college football game.

6. The Sarah Siddons Award—Anne Baxter. Parenthetically, years after the film, a group of theater devotees formed the Sarah Siddons

1. In the Buffs' version, the answer "Dr. Jekyll and Mr. Hyde" would be acceptable.
2. In the Buffs' version, the films "Mr. Deeds Goes to Town" and "Paramount on Parade" would also be acceptable.
3. In the Buffs' version, the answer "Mr. Smith Goes to Washington" would also be acceptable.
4. In the Buffs' version, "High Society" would also be acceptable.
5. In the Buffs' version, the answer "Indiscreet" would also be acceptable.

Society, in Chicago. Each year, this group presents a best actress award to an actress who appeared in the city during the preceding year. The award is known as the Sarah Siddons Award.

7. "News on the March."

8. All of the characters were portrayed by Groucho Marx:

a. "Love Happy"   d. "Room Service"   g. "Go West"
b. "At the   e. "A Night in   h. "A Day at the
   Circus"   Casablanca"   Races"
c. "A Night at   f. "Duck Soup"   i. "Horse Feathers"
   the Opera"

9. Mrs. Gulch.

10. (c) Blue Boy.

AND EVEN MORE DOUBLE DUTY—
BUFFS AND DUFFERS

1. "I Wake Up Screaming"   g. "Vicki"
2. "When Tomorrow Comes"   j. "Interlude"
3. "The Glass Slipper"   e. "Cinderfella"
4. "The Asphalt Jungle"   k. "Cairo"
5. "Brother Rat"   o. "About Face"
6. "The Champ"   f. "The Clown"
7. "If I Were King"   m. "The Vagabond King"
8. "Noting Sacred"   a. "Living It Up"
9. "Mother Carey's
   Chickens"   l. "Summer Magic"
10. "Topaze"   n. "I Like Money"
11. "Mystery of the Wax
    Museum"   c. "House of Wax"
12. "Marked Men"   i. "Three Godfathers"
13. "This Gun for Hire"   d. "Short Cut to Hell"
14. "Murders in the Rue
    Morgue"   h. "Phantom of the Rue Morgue"
15. "The Male Animal"   b. "She's Working Her Way
                                     Through College"

AND EVEN MORE DOUBLE DUTY:
CASTING—BUFFS AND DUFFERS

1. "I Wake Up Screaming"   Laird Cregar   d. Richard Boone
2. "When Tomorrow Comes"   Charles Boyer   l. Rossano Brazzi
3. "The Glass Slipper"   Leslie Caron   a. Jerry Lewis (obviously)
4. "The Asphalt Jungle"   Sam Jaffe   i. George Sanders
5. "Brother Rat"   Eddie Albert   m. Eddie Bracken
6. "The Champ"   Wallace Beery   h. Red Skelton
7. "If I Were King"   Ronald Colman   k. Oreste
8. "Nothing Sacred"   Carole Lombard   g. Jerry Lewis (that's right!)
9. "Mother Carey's Chickens" Walter Brennan   f. Burl Ives
10. "Topaze"   John Barrymore   e. Peter Sellers
11. "Mystery of the Wax Museum" Lionel Atwill   o. Vincent Price
12. "Marked Men"   Harry Carey, Sr.   n. Harry Carey, Jr.
13. "This Gun for Hire"   Laird Cregar   c. Jacques Aubuchon
14. "Murders in the Rue Morgue" Lionel Atwill   j. Karl Malden
15. "The Male Animal"   Henry Fonda   b. Ronald Reagan

FROM SHUBERT ALLEY TO THE SUNSET STRIP #2—BUFFS AND DUFFERS

1. "What a Life"	Ezra Stone	a. Jackie Cooper
2. "The Philadelphia Story"	Van Heflin	b. James Stewart
3. "Watch on the Rhine"	Mady Christians	b. Bette Davis
4. "Arsenic and Old Lace"	Boris Karloff	c. Raymond Massey
5. "Best Foot Forward"	Rosemary Lane	a. Lucille Ball
6. "The Petrified Forest"	Peggy Conklin	c. Bette Davis
7. "Death of a Salesman"	Lee J. Cobb	b. Fredric March
8. "Tomorrow the World"	Ralph Bellamy	a. Fredric March
9. "The Odd Couple"	Art Carney	c. Jack Lemmon
10. "The King and I"	Gertrude Lawrence	b. Deborah Kerr

YES, MY DARLING DAUGHTER— BUFFS AND DUFFERS

1. "Sabrina"	b. Audrey Hepburn
2. "To Catch a Thief"	c. Grace Kelly
3. "Butterfield 8"	a. Elizabeth Taylor
4. "Some Came Running"	c. Martha Hyer
5. "State Fair"	b. Jeanne Crain
6. "The Desperate Hours"	c. Mary Murphy
7. "A Place in the Sun"	c. Elizabeth Taylor
8. "Bye Bye Birdie"	c. Ann-Margret
9. "Watch on the Rhine"	a. Bette Davis
10. "A Christmas Carol"	a. June Lockhart

THE WRONG SIDE OF THE LAW—
BUFFS AND DUFFERS

1. Clyde Barrow	c. Warren Beatty	"Bonnie and Clyde"
2. Machine Gun Kelly	l. Charles Bronson	"Machine Gun Kelly"
3. Legs Diamond	j. Ray Danton	"The Rise and Fall of Legs Diamond"
4. Pretty Boy Floyd	g. John Ericson	"Pretty Boy Floyd"
5. Roger Touhy	d. Preston Foster	"Roger Touhy, Gangster"
6. Owl Banghart	i. Victor McLaglen	"Roger Touhy, Gangster"
7. Bugs Moran	b. Ralph Meeker	"The St. Valentine's Day Massacre"
8. Barbara Graham	k. Susan Hayward	"I Want to Live!"
9. Abe Reles	m. Peter Falk	"Murder Inc."
10. Caryl Chessman	a. William Campbell	"Cell 2455, Death Row"
11. Ma Barker	o. Shelley Winters	"Bloody Mama"
12. Dutch Schultz	n. Vic Morrow	"Portrait of a Mobster"
13. Baby Face Nelson	f. Mickey Rooney	"Baby Face Nelson"
14. Lucky Luciano	e. Cesar Romero	"A House Is Not a Home"
15. Bonnie Parker	h. Faye Dunaway	"Bonnie and Clyde"

OSCAR SHUFFLE #3—WILD CARD

1. N M E J A Y M N A
   (J) (A) (N) (E) W (Y) M (A) (N)
2. G R A S E N O R E R G
   G R E E (R) (G) A R S (O) N
3. V A B E T I T E D S
   B E (T) T E D A V I S

Hidden name: J A N E T G A Y N O R

TELL US WHO #3—BUFFS AND DUFFERS

1. _ d. Sam Jaffe   "Lost Horizon"
                         "The Asphalt Jungle"

2. _ h. James Stewart   "The Man Who Knew Too Much"
                         "Vertigo"

3. _ g. Frank Sinatra   "From Here to Eternity"
                         "Von Ryan's Express"

4. _ a. Robert Walker   "The Clock"
                         "Strangers on a Train"

5. _ c. Ingrid Bergman   "Saratoga Trunk"
                         "The Inn of the Sixth Happiness"

6. _ i. Richard Burton   "The Longest Day"
                         "Becket"

7. _ b. Sidney Poitier   "Guess Who's Coming to Dinner"
                         "In the Heat of the Night"

8. _ j. Elizabeth Taylor   "A Place in the Sun"
                         "The V.I.P.s"

9. _ f. Robert Blake   "The Treasure of the Sierra Madre"
                         "In Cold Blood"

10. _ e. Gloria Grahame   "The Greatest Show on Earth"
                         "The Big Heat"

MY HOME TOWN—BUFFS AND DUFFERS

1. _ p. "Mission to MOSCOW"
2. _ u. "TOKYO Joe"
3. _ g. "The SHANGHAI Gesture"
4. _ o. "DENVER and Rio Grande"
5. _ k. "Meet Me in ST. LOUIS"
6. _ v. "Five Graves to CAIRO"
7. _ e. "MANHATTAN Melodrama"
8. _ j. "HONG KONG Confidential"
9. _ a. "Two Guys from MILWAUKEE"
10. _ i. "The Flame of NEW ORLEANS"
11. _ r. "Stella DALLAS"
12. _ t. "The BOSTON Strangler"
13. _ s. "CHICAGO Deadline"

14. __ w. "PARIS Holiday"

15. __ n. "Hotel BERLIN"

16. __ b. "The CINCINNATI Kid"

17. __ x. "ROME Adventure"

18. __ d. "SPRINGFIELD Rifle"

19. __ m. "The Werewolf of LONDON"

20. __ c. "A Night in CASABLANCA"

21. __ l. "It Started in NAPLES"

22. __ f. "The PHILADELPHIA Story"

23. __ y. "Flying Down to RIO"

24. __ h. "Miss Grant Takes RICHMOND"

25. __ q. "Our Man in HAVANA"

MORE THREE OF A KIND—BUFFS AND DUFFERS

1. In "The High and the Mighty," there were three other male flight personnel in the cockpit of the airliner along with John Wayne. They were:

   b. Robert Stack; c. William Campbell; e. Wally Brown.

2. Name the three films—to date—in which Doris Day has sung "Que Será Será":

   b. "Please Don't Eat the Daisies"; d. "The Man Who Knew Too Much"; e. "The Glass Bottom Boat."

3. Name the three actresses who portrayed "Three Smart Girls":

   a. Nan Grey; c. Barbara Read; d. Deanna Durbin.

4. Name the three actors who portrayed the original "Three Mesqui-teers":

   a. Ray Corrigan; b. Robert Livingston; e. Max Terhune.

5. Name the three actors who portrayed the title roles in "Three Guys Named Mike":

   a. Van Johnson; c. Barry Sullivan; e. Howard Keel.

6. Frank Miller and three of his buddies came gunning for Gary Cooper at "High Noon." Name three of the four actors who made up this menacing quartet:

   a. Lee Van Cleef; b. Sheb Wooley; c. Ian MacDonald—and also, Robert Wilke.

7. Give us the titles of three films in which Greer Garson and Walter Pidgeon co-starred:

b. "Madame Curie"; c. "Julia Misbehaves"; e. "Blossoms in the Dust"—and for the Buffs—"Mrs. Miniver"; "The Miniver Story"; and "Mrs. Parkington."

8. Four Hollywood old-timers appeared as "the waxworks" in the bridge table scene from "Sunset Boulevard." Name three of them:

   a. Anna Q. Nilsson; b. Hedda Hopper; e. Buster Keaton—and, for the Buffs, also H. B. Warner.

9. Name three biographical roles played by Spencer Tracy:

   a. Henry M. Stanley ("Stanley and Livingstone"); d. Thomas Edison ("Edison, the Man"); e. Maj. Jimmy Doolittle ("Thirty Seconds over Tokyo"). And also—for the Buffs—Father Flanagan ("Boys Town," "Men of Boys Town"); and Maj. Robert Rogers ("Northwest Passage").

10. Give us the character names of the three farm hands in the non-dream portions of "The Wizard of Oz":

    a. Zeke; c. Hunk; e. Hickory.

AND STILL EVEN MORE "NAME THE STAR"— BUFFS ONLY

1.	Richard Burton	"Boom!"	"The V.I.P.s"
2.	Marlon Brando	"Bedtime Story"	"The Ugly American"
3.	Walter Matthau	"Fail Safe"	"The Fortune Cookie"
4.	Errol Flynn	"Virginia City"	"The Charge of the Light Brigade"
5.	Mickey Rooney	"Captains Courageous"	"The Human Comedy"
6.	Fred MacMurray	"The Apartment"	"The Absent-Minded Professor"
7.	Alice Faye	"Hello, Frisco, Hello!"	"Alexander's Ragtime Band"
8.	Kim Novak	"Vertigo"	"Kiss Me, Stupid"
9.	Bing Crosby	"The Emperor Waltz"	"If I Had My Way"
10.	Barbara Stanwyck	"These Wilder Years"	"Executive Suite"

AND STILL EVEN MORE "NAME THE STAR"—
DUFFERS' TEE

1. Richard Burton "Night of the Iguana" "Becket"
2. Marlon Brando "On the Waterfront" "A Streetcar Named Desire"
3. Walter Matthau "The Odd Couple" "Hello, Dolly!"
4. Errol Flynn "The Adventures of Robin Hood" "Captain Blood"
5. Mickey Rooney "Boys Town" "Love Finds Andy Hardy"
6. Fred MacMurray "Double Indemnity" "The Happiest Millionaire"
7. Alice Faye "In Old Chicago" "Lillian Russell"
8. Kim Novak "The Legend of Lylah Clare" "The Amorous Adventures of Moll Flanders"
9. Bing Crosby "The Country Girl" "High Society"
10. Barbara Stanwyck "Double Indemnity" "The Strange Love of Martha Ivers"

AND MORE CAREERS IN COMMON—
BUFFS AND DUFFERS

1.—c. Slim Pickens "Stagecoach" Stagecoach driver.
2.—b. Olivia de Havilland "Not As a Stranger" Nurse.
3.—a. Jack Webb "Pete Kelly's Blues" Trumpet player.
4.—c. Rock Hudson "Giant" Rancher.
5.—b. Arthur Kennedy "City for Conquest" Composer.
6.—a. Tyrone Power "Mississippi Gambler" Professional gambler.
7.—a. William Powell "The Senator Was Indiscreet" U.S. senator.
8.—b. Walter Matthau "Cactus Flower" Dentist.
9.—a. Jean Hagen "Singin' in the Rain" Motion picture actress.
10.—a. Tony Curtis "Trapeze" Trapeze performer.

THE TEENY-TINY MARQUEE
✕4—BUFFS AND DUFFERS

1.—d; l.   "Love Finds *Andy* (Devine) *Hardy* (Kruger)"

2.—a; n.   "*Anna* (Magnani) and the (Andrea) *King* of Siam"

3.—w; i.   "The Adventures of *Tom* (Neal) (Joe) *Sawyer*"

4.—x; q; z.   "The *Eve* (Arden) of (Eva Marie) *Saint Mark* (Stevens)"

5.—r; aa.   "The Guilt of *Janet* (Gaynor) (Leon) *Ames*"

6.—j; e.   "The (Frances) *Farmer* in the (Gabriel) *Dell*"

7.—u; y; c.   "The Story of (Wally) *Vernon* and *Irene* (Ryan) (Peggie) *Castle*"

8.—f; s.   "*Joe* (Penner) and *Ethel* (Merman) Turp Call on the President"

9.—v; t.   "Mighty *Joe* (Pevney) (Robert) *Young*"

10.—h; b.   "The Badge of (E. G.) *Marshall* (Walter) *Brennan*"

11.—o; k.   "*David* (McCallum) and *Lisa* (Gaye)"

12.—g; m; p.   "The (Ruth) *Roman Spring* (Byington) of Mrs. (Lewis) *Stone*"

MY SON, MY SON—BUFFS AND DUFFERS

1. "To Each His Own"   b. John Lund

2. "Friendly Persuasion"   a. Tony Perkins[1]

3. "David Copperfield"   a. Freddie Bartholomew

4. "North by Northwest"   b. Cary Grant

5. "Rebel Without a Cause"   c. James Dean

6. "None But the Lonely Heart"   c. Cary Grant

7. "Treasure Island"   a. Jackie Cooper

8. "Sergeant York"   c. Gary Cooper[2]

9. "Marty"   a. Ernest Borgnine

10. "You Can't Take It with You"   a. James Stewart

1. For the Buffs' version, Richard Eyer would also be acceptable.
2. For the Buffs' version, Dickie Moore would also be acceptable.

340

NUMBER, PLEASE—BUFFS AND DUFFERS

1. _ n.	"TWO for the Road"		2
2. _ p.	"Shack Out on 101"		101
3. _ s.	"Anne of the THOUSAND Days"		1,000
4. _ j.	"FOUR Daughters"		4
5. _ f.	"FIVE Fingers"		5
6. _ c.	"NINE Hours to Rama"		9
7. _ i.	"FOURTEEN Hours"		14
8. _ m.	"20,000 Leagues Under the Sea"		20,000
9. _ l.	"Over 21"		21
10. _ b.	"EIGHT Iron Men"		8
11. _ t.	"ONE Life to Live"		1
12. _ d.	"THIRTY Seconds over Tokyo"		30
13. _ r.	"1,001 Nights"		1,001
14. _ h.	"13 Rue Madeleine"		13
15. _ g.	"THREE Little Words"		3
16. _ o.	"ONE HUNDRED Men and a Girl"		100
17. _ a.	"The Magnificent SEVEN"		7
18. _ k.	"Pilot Number FIVE"		5
19. _ q.	"1,000,000 B.C."		1,000,000
20. _ e.	"FORTY Little Mothers"		40

Total: 1,022,364!!

AND AGAIN, MORE DOUBLE DUTY— BUFFS AND DUFFERS

1. "The Ghost Breakers"

2. "Five Came Back"

3. "Dark Victory"

4. "Craig's Wife"

5. "Ball of Fire"

6. "Bachelor Mother"

7. "Algiers"

8. "And Then There Were None"

9. "Anna and the King of Siam"

d. "Scared Stiff"

j. "Back from Eternity"

g. "Stolen Hours"

l. "Harriet Craig"

c. "A Song Is Born"

i. "Bundle of Joy"

n. "Casbah"

f. "Ten Little Indians"

m. "The King and I"

10. "The Shop Around the Corner"		a. "In the Good Old Summertime"
11. "A Lady to Love"		k. "They Knew What They Wanted"
12. "Lady for a Day"		e. "Pocketful of Miracles"
13. "The Lady Eve"		o. "The Birds and the Bees"
14. "High Sierra"		h. "I Died a Thousand Times"
15. "Grand Hotel"		b. "Weekend at the Waldorf"

AND AGAIN, MORE DOUBLE DUTY: CASTING—BUFFS AND DUFFERS

1. "The Ghost Breakers"	Paulette Goddard	c. Lizabeth Scott
2. "Five Came Back"	Lucille Ball	j. Anita Ekberg
3. "Dark Victory"	Bette Davis	h. Susan Hayward
4. "Craig's Wife"	Rosalind Russell	l. Joan Crawford
5. "Ball of Fire"	Barbara Stanwyck	i. Virginia Mayo
6. "Bachelor Mother"	Ginger Rogers	m. Debbie Reynolds
7. "Algiers"	Hedy Lamarr	d. Marta Toren
8. "And Then There Were None"	June Duprez	k. Shirley Eaton
9. "Anna and the King of Siam"	Linda Darnell	g. Rita Moreno
10. "The Shop Around the Corner"	Margaret Sullavan	o. Judy Garland
11. "Lady for a Day"	May Robson	b. Bette Davis
12. "A Lady to Love"	Vilma Banky	n. Carole Lombard
13. "The Lady Eve"	Barbara Stanwyck	a. Mitzi Gaynor
14. "High Sierra"	Ida Lupino	e. Shelley Winters
15. "Grand Hotel"	Greta Garbo	f. Ginger Rogers

342

AND EVEN MORE LINK-UPS—BUFFS AND DUFFERS

1. Benita	HUME	Cronyn
2. James	GREGORY	Peck
3. Jan	STERLING	Holloway
4. Bob	HOPE	Lange
5. Norman	LLOYD	Nolan
6. Robert	MONTGOMERY	Clift
7. Eddie	ALBERT	Basserman
8. Anne	SHIRLEY	MacLaine
9. George C.	SCOTT	Brady
10. Lee	MARVIN	Kaplan

SPOT THE BIO: SPORTS—BUFFS AND DUFFERS

1. Tony Perkins	F. Jimmy Piersall	n. "Fear Strikes Out"
2. Ronald Reagan	A. George Gipp	o. "Knute Rockne— All-American"
3. Dan Dailey	J. Dizzy Dean	c. "The Pride of St. Louis"
4. William Bendix	M. Babe Ruth	j. "The Babe Ruth Story"
5. Ronald Reagan	H. Grover Cleveland Alexander	g. "The Winning Team"
6. James Stewart	N. Monty Stratton	m. "The Stratton Story"
7. Glenn Ford	K. Ben Hogan	i. "Follow the Sun"
8. Thomas Gomez	O. Abe Saperstein	f. "The Harlem Globetrotters"
9. Coley Wallace	C. Joe Louis	l. "The Joe Louis Story"
10. Errol Flynn	L. Jim Corbett	d. "Gentleman Jim"
11. Ward Bond	B. John L. Sullivan	e. "Gentleman Jim"

12. Gary Cooper	G. Lou Gehrig	a. "Pride of the Yankees"
13. Frank Lovejoy	D. Rogers Hornsby	k. "The Winning Team"
14. Richard Crenna	I. Daffy Dean	h. "The Pride of St. Louis"
15. Paul Newman	E. Rocky Graziano	b. "Somebody Up There Likes Me"

TRUE OR FALSE, WILD CARD—
BUFFS AND DUFFERS

1. False: Abbott and Costello made their film debut in "One Night in the Tropics" in 1940. "Buck Privates" was their *second* film.

2. False: The sound elements in "The Jazz Singer" consisted only of some songs and incidental dialogue. The first *all*-talking film was Warner Brothers' "The Lights of New York."

3. False: The first Hardy film was "A Family Affair," with Lionel Barrymore and Spring Byington as the Judge and Mrs. Hardy.

4. False: The film's official release title was "All That Money Can Buy." It played *later* in some theaters as "The Devil and Daniel Webster." It was also issued briefly under the titles "Here Is a Man" and "A Certain Mr. Scratch."

5. False: What about, for example, James Cagney and his sister Jeanne playing brother and sister in "Yankee Doodle Dandy"?

6. False: Geraldine Page played in at least one film before appearing in "Hondo." She had a brief supporting role in the 20th Century-Fox film "Taxi," starring Dan Dailey and Constance Smith, which predated "Hondo."

7. False: The first expedition to Africa by a film company was for the film "Trader Horn."

8. False: He made "Mr. and Mrs. Smith," with Carole Lombard, Robert Montgomery, and Gene Raymond, which was pure comedy.

9. False: "In Old Arizona" was filmed on location, but *not* in Arizona. It was filmed in Utah and California.

10. False: He was starred in Raoul Walsh's "The Big Trail," nine years before "Stagecoach."

GREAT SUPPORT CRISSCROSS—BUFFS ONLY

Four-Letter Names
Arnt, Charles
Cook, Elisha (Jr.)
Fong, Benson
Luke, Keye
Meek, Donald
Neal, Tom

Five-Letter Names
Acuff, Eddie
Allen, Barbara Jo
Bondi, Beulah
Clark, Fred
Dalio, Marcel
Doran, Ann
Evans, Rex
Lorre, Peter
Nolan, Lloyd
Vuolo, Tito
Wolfe, Ian

Six-Letter Names
Bevans, Clem
Hobbes, Halliwell
Merkel, Una
Qualen, John
Shayne, Konstantin

Seven-Letter Names
Armetta, Henry
Darwell, Jane
Flowers, Bess
Freeman, Howard
Karloff, Boris
O'Connor, Una
Quillan, Eddie

Eight-Letter Names
Bancroft, George
De Corsia, Ted
Ferguson, Frank
Kellaway, Cecil
McIntire, John
Sokoloff, Vladimir

Nine-Letter Names
Armstrong, Robert
Dumbrille, Douglas

Eleven-Letter Names
Greenstreet, Sydney
Ouspenskaya, Maria

GREAT SUPPORT CRISSCROSS—
BUFFS AND DUFFERS

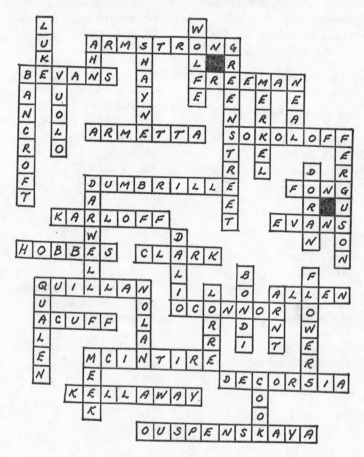

HISTORY IS MADE IN THE MOVIES—
BUFFS AND DUFFERS

1. Basil Rathbone   Pontius Pilate   "The Last Days of
                                                            Pompeii"

   Jeffrey Hunter   c. Jesus Christ   "King of Kings"
2. Elizabeth Taylor   Cleopatra   "Cleopatra"
                                                            (Mankiewicz')

Warren William	b. Caesar	"Cleopatra" (DeMille's)
3. Victor Mature	Crazy Horse	"Chief Crazy Horse"
Errol Flynn	a. Genl. Custer	"They Died with Their Boots On"
4. Ingrid Bergman	Joan	"Joan of Arc"
Richard Widmark	a. The Dauphin	"St. Joan"
5. Charles Laughton	Henry VIII	"Young Bess"[1]
Paul Scofield	a. Thomas More	"A Man for All Seasons"
6. Henry Fonda	Abe Lincoln	"Young Mr. Lincoln"
John Derek	c. John Wilkes Booth	"Prince of Players"
7. Karl Malden	Omar Bradley	"Patton"
Ralph Bellamy	c. Franklin Roosevelt	"Sunrise at Campobello"
8. Betty Hutton	Annie Oakley	"Annie Get Your Gun"
Joel McCrea	b. Buffalo Bill Cody	"Buffalo Bill"
9. Irene Dunne	Queen Victoria	"The Mudlark"
George Arliss	a. Disraeli	"Disraeli"
10. Richard Burton	Henry VIII	"Anne of the Thousand Days"
Orson Welles	a. Cardinal Wolsey	"A Man for All Seasons"

HISTORY IS MADE IN THE MOVIES
PART II—BUFFS AND DUFFERS

1. Wallace Beery	Pancho Villa	"Viva Villa!"
John Garfield	c. Porfirio Díaz	"Juarez"
2. Richard Basehart	Adolf Hitler	"Hitler"
Erich Von Stroheim	c. Erwin Rommel	"Five Graves to Cairo"
3. Jason Robards, Jr.	George Kaufman	"Act One"
Monty Woolley	a. Monty Woolley	"Night and Day"

1. Or, for the Buffs, "The Private Life of Henry VIII."

4.	George Arliss		Alexander Hamilton	"Alexander Hamilton"
	David Niven	c.	Aaron Burr	"Magnificent Doll"
5.	Larry Parks		Al Jolson	"The Jolson Story"[1]
	Deborah Kerr	c.	Sheilah Graham	"Beloved Infidel"
6.	Genevieve Bujold		Anne Boleyn	"Anne of the Thousand Days"
	Robert Donat	b.	Thomas Culpepper	"The Private Life of Henry VIII"
7.	George C. Scott		Genl. George Patton	"Patton"
	Harry Carey, Jr.	b.	Dwight Eisenhower	"The Long Gray Line"
8.	Michael Jayston		Czar Nicholas	"Nicholas and Alexandra"
	Lionel Barrymore	b.	Rasputin	"Rasputin and the Empress"
9.	Julie Andrews		Gertrude Lawrence	"Star!" ("Those Were the Days")
	George Hamilton	a.	Moss Hart	"Act One"
10.	Katharine Hepburn		Mary Stuart	"Mary of Scotland"
	Glenda Jackson	a.	Queen Elizabeth I	"Mary, Queen of Scots"

SOME DIRECTION, PLEASE—BUFFS ONLY

1. "Song of the SOUTH"
2. "Walk EAST on Beacon"
3. "SOUTH of St. Louis"
4. "SOUTHside 1-1000"
5. "NORTHWEST Passage"
6. "EAST Side of Heaven"
7. "Call NORTHside 777"
8. "Spawn of the NORTH"
9. "Mr. and Mrs. NORTH"
10. "The Ghost Goes WEST"

1. Or, for the Buffs, "Jolson Sings Again."

SOME DIRECTION, PLEASE—DUFFERS' TEE

1. "How the WEST Was Won"
2. "NORTHWEST Mounted Police"
3. "NORTH to Alaska"
4. "SOUTH Sea Sinner"
5. "EAST of Eden"
6. "SOUTH of the Border"
7. "The WEST Point Story"
8. "WESTward the Women"
9. "Four Flags WEST"
10. "NORTH by Northwest"

MORE OF "THE VIOLENT END"— BUFFS AND DUFFERS

1. C. Henry Gordon	h.	Impaled on the lances of the charging British soldiers.
2. Edna May Oliver	d.	By an Indian arrow.
3. Judith Anderson	i.	Trapped in a burning mansion.
4. Brian Aherne	b.	By firing squad.
5. Robert Taylor	l.	Frozen to death.
6. Slim Pickens	k.	Rode to his death on a falling A-bomb.
7. Margo	o.	By sudden aging on leaving Shangri-La.
8. Addison Richards	a.	Ran amok and plunged off a cliff.
9. Ronald Colman	n.	By guillotining.
10. Kirk Douglas	f.	By crucifixion.
11. Eduardo Ciannelli	m.	Jumped into a pit of poisonous snakes.
12. Luther Adler	c.	Slow strangulation by garroting.
13. Robert Walker	j.	Crushed by a runaway merry-go-round.
14. Stephen Boyd	e.	Dragged to his death behind his chariot.
15. Marlon Brando	g.	By gunfire in an ambush.

AND YET STILL MORE "NAME THE STAR"—
BUFFS ONLY

1. Jean Arthur	"The More the Merrier"	"Mr. Smith Goes to Washington"
2. Walter Brennan	"The One and Only Genuine Original Family Band"	"Stanley and Livingstone"
3. Shirley MacLaine	"Some Came Running"	"The Apartment"
4. Robert Taylor	"Many Rivers to Cross"	"Waterloo Bridge"
5. Robert Redford	"The Way We Were"	"Jeremiah Johnson"
6. Paul Newman	"Harper"	"The Outrage"
7. Julie Andrews	"The Americanization of Emily"	"Torn Curtain"
8. Lionel Barrymore	"A Guy Named Joe"	"On Borrowed Time"
9. Hedy Lamarr	"I Take This Woman"	"Tortilla Flat"
10. Lana Turner	"Dancing Coed"	"Cass Timberlane"

AND YET STILL MORE "NAME THE STAR"—
DUFFERS' TEE

1. Jean Arthur	"A Foreign Affair"	"You Can't Take It with You"
2. Walter Brennan	"Bad Day at Black Rock"	"Northwest Passage"
3. Shirley MacLaine	"Around the World in 80 Days"	"Irma La Douce"
4. Robert Taylor	"Quo Vadis"	"Camille"
5. Robert Redford	"The Great Gatsby"	"Butch Cassidy and the Sundance Kid"
6. Paul Newman	"Sweet Bird of Youth"	"The Hustler"
7. Julie Andrews	"Hawaii"	"Mary Poppins"
8. Lionel Barrymore	"You Can't Take It with You"	"The Secret of Dr. Kildare"
9. Hedy Lamarr	"Boom Town"	"The Story of Mankind"
10. Lana Turner	"Dr. Jekyll and Mr. Hyde"	"The Bad and the Beautiful"

OSCAR SHUFFLE #4—WILD CARD

1. M E G A S J C Y N E A
   (J) A (M) E (S) C A (G) (N) E Y

2. D A R N Y L I L A M
   R (A) Y M (I) L (L) A (N) D

3. T R I E S D I N Y I O P E
   S (I) D (N) E Y P O I T I (E) R

And the hidden Oscar winner is:
E M I L J A N N I N G S

THE ETERNAL TRIANGLE—BUFFS AND DUFFERS

1. Dick Powell
   Gloria
   Grahame

2. Deborah Kerr
   Philip Ober

3. Joan
   Bennett
   Robert
   Preston

4. Doris Day
   James Cagney

5. Carole
   Lombard
   Charles
   Laughton

6. Olivia de
   Havilland
   Patric
   Knowles

7. Shirley
   MacLaine
   George C.
   Scott

8. Orson Welles
   Ruth Warrick

9. Judy Holliday
   Broderick
   Crawford

G. "The Bad and the
   Beautiful"

I. "From Here to
   Eternity"

K. "The Macomber
   Affair"

O. "Love Me or Leave
   Me"

M. "They Knew What They
   Wanted"

J. "The Charge of the
   Light Brigade"

A. "The Yellow Rolls-
   Royce"

D. "Citizen Kane"

N. "Born Yesterday"

c. Gilbert Roland

f. Burt Lancaster

e. Gregory Peck

i. Cameron Mitchell

n. William Gargan

l. Errol Flynn

h. Alain Delon

g. Dorothy
   Comingore

k. William Holden

10. Rita Hayward Everett Sloane	L. "The Lady from Shanghai"	b. Orson Welles
11. Dana Andrews Virginia Mayo	B. "The Best Years of Our Lives"	m. Steve Cochran
12. Carroll Baker Karl Malden	H. "Baby Doll"	d. Eli Wallach
13. Joseph Cotten Bette Davis	E. "Beyond the Forest"	o. David Brian
14. Joan Crawford Bruce Bennett	C. "Mildred Pierce"	a. Lee Patrick
15. Gary Cooper Geraldine Fitzgerald	F. "Ten North Frederick"	j. Suzy Parker

OH, JOHNNY!—BUFFS AND DUFFERS

1. "Johnny Come Lately"	f. James Cagney
2. "Johnny Allegro"	g. George Raft
3. "Johnny Concho"	j. Frank Sinatra
4. "Johnny Cool"	b. Henry Silva
5. "Johnny Apollo"	h. Tyrone Power
6. "Johnny Eager"	i. Robert Taylor
7. "Johnny Dark"	c. Tony Curtis
8. "Johnny Rocco"	a. Stephen McNally
9. "Johnny O'Clock"	e. Dick Powell
10. "Johnny Yuma"	d. Mark Damon

OUT OF THE LIMELIGHT—BUFFS ONLY

1. Walter Pidgeon	Florenz Ziegfeld	"Funny Girl"
2. Richard Whorf	Sam Harris	"Yankee Doodle Dandy"

3.	Robert Evans	Irving Thalberg	"Man of a Thousand Faces"
4.	Leo Carrillo	Tony Pastor	"Lillian Russell"
5.	Jason Robards, Jr.	George Kaufman	"Act One"
6.	Walter Pidgeon	J. J. Shubert	"Deep in My Heart"
7.	Wallace Beery	P. T. Barnum	"The Mighty Barnum"
8.	George Hamilton	Moss Hart	"Act One"
9.	Ernest Borgnine	Boris Morros	"Man on a String"
10.	David Wayne	Sol Hurok	"Tonight We Sing"

OUT OF THE LIMELIGHT—DUFFERS' TEE

1.	Walter Pidgeon	Florenz Ziegfeld	g. "Funny Girl"
2.	Richard Whorf	Sam Harris	j. "Yankee Doodle Dandy"
3.	Wallace Beery	P. T. Barnum	d. "The Mighty Barnum"
4.	Robert Evans	Irving Thalberg	h. "Man of a Thousand Faces"
5.	Leo Carrillo	Tony Pastor	b. "Lillian Russell"
6.	Jason Robards, Jr.	George Kaufman	i. "Act One"
7.	Walter Pidgeon	J. J. Shubert	e. "Deep in My Heart"
8.	Burl Ives	P. T. Barnum	a. "Rocket to the Moon"
9.	Ernest Borgnine	Boris Morros	f. "Man on a String"
10.	David Wayne	Sol Hurok	c. "Tonight We Sing"

PROTOCOL—BUFFS AND DUFFERS

1.	Yul Brynner	o. "The KING and I"
2.	Paul Robeson	l. "The EMPEROR Jones"
3.	Robert Wagner	g. "PRINCE Valiant"
4.	Olivia de Havilland	c. "PRINCESS O'Rourke"
5.	Louis Hayward	j. "The DUKE of West Point"

6.	Vincent Price	d.	"The BARON of Arizona"
7.	Bette Davis	a.	"The Virgin QUEEN"
8.	Ethel Barrymore	m.	"Rasputin and the EMPRESS"
9.	Akim Tamiroff	e.	"The GENERAL Died at Dawn"
10.	Robert Montgomery	k.	"The EARL of Chicago"
11.	Robert Donat	n.	"The COUNT of Monte Cristo"
12.	Hedy Lamarr	h.	"HER HIGHNESS and the Bellboy"
13.	Ava Gardner	b.	"The Barefoot CONTESSA"
14.	George Arliss	f.	"CARDINAL Richelieu"
15.	Edmund Purdom	l.	"The Student PRINCE"

HISTORY IS MADE IN THE MOVIES
PART III—BUFFS AND DUFFERS

1.	Grant Mitchell		Georges Clemenceau	"The Life of Emile Zola"
	Alexander Knox	c.	Woodrow Wilson	"Wilson"
2.	Donald Crisp		Sir Francis Bacon	"The Private Lives of Elizabeth and Essex"
	Jean Simmons	a.	Queen Elizabeth	"Young Bess"
3.	Curt Jurgens		Wernher von Braun	"I Aim at the Stars"
	Luther Adler	a.	Adolf Hitler	"The Desert Fox"
4.	William Marshall		Edward Brooke	"The Boston Strangler"
	Cliff Robertson	a.	John F. Kennedy	"PT 109"
5.	Arthur Hunnicutt		Davy Crockett	"The Last Command"
	Alan Ladd	c.	Jim Bowie	"The Iron Mistress"
6.	Robert Evans		Irving Thalberg	"Man of a Thousand Faces"
	Donald O'Connor	a.	Buster Keaton	"The Buster Keaton Story"
7.	Kenneth Tobey		Bat Masterson	"Gunfight at the O.K. Corral"
	James Stewart	c.	Wyatt Earp	"Cheyenne Autumn"

8.	Spring Byington	Dolly Madison	"The Buccaneer"
	Burgess Meredith	b. James Madison	"Magnificent Doll"
9.	Porter Hall	Jack McCall	"The Plainsman"
	Howard Keel	b. Wild Bill Hickok	"Calamity Jane"
10.	Vladimir Sokoloff	Paul Cezanne	"The Life of Emile Zola"
	Kirk Douglas	a. Vincent van Gogh	"Lust for Life"

HISTORY IS MADE IN THE MOVIES
PART IV—BUFFS AND DUFFERS

1.	Edwin Maxwell	Secretary Stanton	"The Plainsman"
	Van Heflin	b. Andrew Johnson	"Tennessee Johnson"
2.	Dayton Lummis	Douglas MacArthur	"The Court-Martial of Billy Mitchell"
	James Cagney	a. Adm. William Halsey	"The Gallant Hours"
3.	Richard Gaines	George Washington	"Unconquered"
	Robert Stack	c. John Paul Jones	"John Paul Jones"
4.	Thomas Mitchell	Ned Buntline	"Buffalo Bill"
	Moroni Olsen	c. William Cody	"Annie Oakley"
5.	Joseph Crehan	U. S. Grant	"Geronimo"
	Raymond Massey	b. Abe Lincoln	"Abe Lincoln in Illinois"
6.	Alan Reed	Pancho Villa	"Viva Zapata!"
	Milburn Stone	c. John J. Pershing	"The Long Gray Line"
7.	Phil Arnold	Fiorello La Guardia	"The Court-Martial of Billy Mitchell"
	Peter Falk	a. Abe Reles	"Murder Inc."
8.	Brigid Bazlen	Salome	"King of Kings"
	Charles Laughton	c. King Herod	"Salome"
9.	Ernie Adams	Miller Huggins	"Pride of the Yankees"
	William Bendix	b. Babe Ruth	"The Babe Ruth Story"
10.	Ian Hunter	Richard the Lion-Hearted	"The Adventures of Robin Hood"
	Cornel Wilde	c. Robin Hood	"Bandit of Sherwood Forest"

THE FINAL FADE-OUT—BUFFS AND DUFFERS

1. Clark Gable		g.	"The Misfits"
2. Spencer Tracy		l.	"Guess Who's Coming to Dinner"
3. Humphrey Bogart		o.	"The Harder They Fall"
4. Gary Cooper		f.	"The Naked Edge"
5. Errol Flynn		m.	"Cuban Rebel Girls"
6. Alan Ladd		q.	"The Carpetbaggers"
7. Tyrone Power		j.	"Witness for the Prosecution"
8. Judy Garland		n.	"I Could Go On Singing"
9. Jean Harlow		a.	"Saratoga"
10. Carole Lombard		t.	"To Be or Not to Be"
11. Charles Laughton		p.	"Advise and Consent"
12. Robert Walker		r.	"My Son John"
13. John Garfield		e.	"He Ran All the Way"
14. Harold Lloyd		i.	"Mad Wednesday"
15. Wallace Beery		b.	"Big Jack"
16. Lon Chaney, Sr.		k.	"The Unholy Three"
17. Constance Bennett		s.	"Madame X"
18. Montgomery Clift		d.	"The Defector"
19. ZaSu Pitts		h.	"It's a Mad, Mad, Mad, Mad World"
20. Ethel Barrymore		c.	"Johnny Trouble"

HOMESTRETCH—BUFFS AND DUFFERS

1. Louis Calhern.
2. a. "War of the Worlds," Sir Cedric Hardwicke.
   b. "The Red Badge of Courage," James Whitmore.
   c. "Mother Wore Tights," Anne Baxter.
3. Joseph Crehan.
4. The film was "The Great Ziegfeld"
   Will Rogers—A. A. Trimble.
   Eddie Cantor—Buddy Doyle.
5. William Green.

356